The Complete Book of Cheese

THE WINE COOK BOOK

AMERICA COOKS

10,000 SNACKS

SALADS AND HERBS

THE SOUTH AMERICAN COOK BOOK

SOUPS, SAUCES AND GRAVIES

THE VEGETABLE COOK BOOK

LOOK BEFORE YOU COOK!

THE EUROPEAN COOK BOOK

THE WINING AND DINING QUIZ

MOST FOR YOUR MONEY

OUTDOOR COOKING

FISH AND SEAFOOD COOK BOOK

THE COUNTRY COOK BOOK

Co-author of Food and Drink Books by The Browns

LET THERE BE BEER!

HOMEMADE HILARITY

BOB BROWN

The Complete Book of Cheese

Introduction by Clifton Fadiman

Illustrations by Eric Blegvad

Gramercy Publishing Company
New York

Library of Congress Catalog Card Number: 55-11956

Manufactured in the United States of America

This edition published by Gramercy Publishing Company, a division of Crown Publishers, Inc., by arrangement with Random House, Inc.

H

TO

PHIL
ALPERT

Turophile Extraordinary

Contents

Introduction

In Praise of Cheese

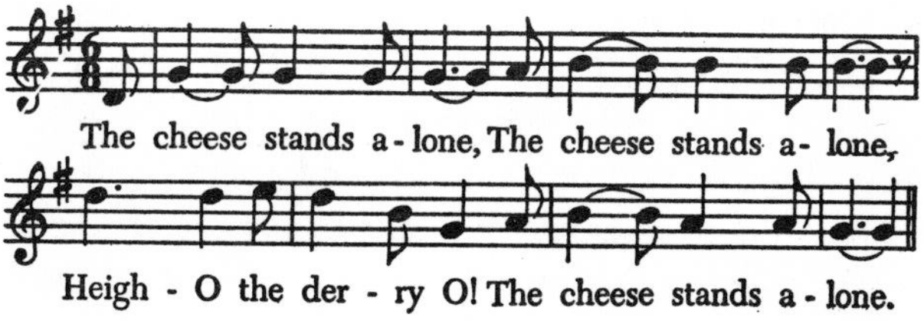
The cheese stands a - lone, The cheese stands a - lone,
Heigh - O the der - ry O! The cheese stands a - lone.

Some fifteen years ago, having resolved to write a book about cheese, I collected data on upwards of 500 varieties and accumulated specimens, often quite lively, from many of the countries of the world—literally from China to Peru. (China's soybean yields a courtesy cheese, *hoi poi;* Peru's cheeses I cannot recall.) The specimens have long since gone the way of all flesh—and dairy products. The data, however—so vast is the field—I have never been able to digest. Hence the book remains an unfulfilled dream of my youth.

For all that, I think a man should from time to time, in whatever poor phrases he may command, laud those gifts of God which have filled him with most joy. Let these rough notes, therefore, so ill-matched to the altitude of my theme, serve as a kind of thank offering.

Let them serve too as a preliminary to the main event—the book you hold in your hand. I have known the exhilarating Bob Brown for about a quarter of a century. During that period, in which the larger world has devoted itself conscientiously to the serious business of self-destruction, Bob Brown has steadily pursued his hobby—private nourishment—and his profession of writing books about food and drink. This *omnium gatherum* of information and instruction will prove one of his most inspiring manuals. No one who loves cheese can fail to enjoy it and find it useful.

Universal hungers are few: who dreams hotly of soufflé? But wine, once loved, remains a passion; so too with bread, salt, perhaps meat. As for cheese, I am on the side of the great connoisseur P. Morton Shand who deemed a love of it inherent in humanity. The Chinese, it is true, like it little, linking all milk products with their herdsmen-conquerors, the Tartars and Mongols. It is also true that man's best friend abhors it, though some dogs—house dogs, perhaps—will take to cottage cheese. But Ben Gunn, marooned on Treasure Island, with his pitiful "Many's the long night I've dreamed of cheese—toasted mostly," emblems much of mankind; and I have heard that our men on besieged Corregidor, reduced to mule meat, split into two groups—those who dreamed of chocolate, those who dreamed of cheese.

Like its great brethren, bread and wine, cheese is born of a miracle. At the very instant when the milk is on the road to ruin, mysterious lactic acid or that more mysterious ferment, rennet (extracted—who knows first by whom?—from the fourth stomach of the suckling calf), works like grace upon it and raises it to the higher life of curd. Curd, pressed and treated, is touched again by grace, this time in the guise of bacteria or mold. Time passes. Now the curd, Odysseus before Penelope, throws off its grossness, growing godlike in form and feature. It has become

Cheese. It has voyaged in one superb celestial arc to the very end of the Milky Way.

Cheese is not the gift of the cow alone, but of the ewe, the goat, the reindeer, the zebu, the buffalo, the camel, the llama, the mare, the ass, the zebra, the yak. It may even be, if we are to trust Maurice des Ombiaux's droll anecdote in his *Les Fromages,* the gift of the human female. In color it shades from the delicate rose of a virgin's blush to the grand severity of Pentelic marble. In form it is protean: the ball and the brick, the cube and the cucumber, the disc and the dumbbell, the melon and the millstone, the bologna and the ostrich egg, the pineapple and the parallelepiped. On New York's First Avenue, near East 116th Street, there used to be and perhaps still is a veritable Cellini of cheesemongers who would sculpt your cheese to your fancy.

The eye of the turophile may consider the eighteen basic varities of cheese or the thousand variations on those varieties. In either case he tries to classify. He may arrange them according to the quality of their resistance to life's onslaught: yielding, such as the chaste cream, the mold-matured Camembert, the bacteria-ripened Roquefort; firm, such as Gorgonzola or Münster; obdurate, such as Parmesan. Or, with André Simon, he may grade them by the degree of their aggressiveness: the gentle Petit Suisse, the strong Roquefort, the brutal Limburger or Marolles. Or he may borrow the late Edward Bunyard's division, based on their poetical style: the romantic cheese, like Brie, given to excess, even to tears; the classic cheese, such as Stilton, growing like Nestor nobler as it ages.

Ancient is the lineage of cheese. A legend, deeply unreliable, has it that some thousands of years ago an Arab merchant named Kanana, wandering over the desert, stopped for lunch, poured out the milk that he had kept in a skin bottle made from the lining of a calf's stomach, and found an odd but attractive-tasting mess, now known as curd. As a child, Queen Semiramis was fed cheese by the birds. Zoroaster, who flourished about 1000 B.C., lived, says Pliny, exclusively on a cheese for twenty years. (It has been deduced that this could only have been a Gibraltar of a Parmesan weighing about one ton, twelve and a half hundred-weight.)

The Greeks attributed the invention of cheese to the demigod Aristaeus, son of Apollo. In Book 9 of the *Odyssey* Homer describes the dairy techniques of the one-eyed Polyphemus who seems to have gone in for something like our domestic Ricotta, a rather insipid by-product of Asiago or Parmesan whey. Hippocrates mentions it as being made of both goat's and mare's milk. The Old Testament (see I Samuel 17:18) speaks well of cheese.

The poet Martial tells us the ancient Romans were fond of the cheeses of Toulouse. The Emperor Augustus favored them, especially Salonite cheese, which he ate with small fish, brown bread and figs. The learned Palladius, the more learned elder Pliny, mention cheese. When British soil first shook under the tread of Caesar's legions, Cheshire cheese was already being made there. His affection for Roquefort, first mentioned in a monkish chronicle of 1070, ennobles the character of Charlemagne.

The genealogy of the literature of cheese is also venerable. The first important publication, Pantaleo de Confluentia's *De Laticiniis,* was issued at Turin as long ago as 1477. Since then earnest students of the subject have not been lacking.

Enfeebled as we are by the processed horrors of our century (what dolt said good things come in small packages?), we have forgotten that cheese is what Hilaire Belloc said it is; a profound matter. Only countrymen, leading quieter, wiser lives than ours, still know this. In England's remoter countryside, when a birth is expected, a vast cartwheel of cheese is piously set aside. Day by day it is cut out at the center so that at last there remains a large ring through which on his christening day the fortunate babe is ritually passed. Switzerland's Saanen, an Emmentaler cheese, takes six years to ripen and will keep till the blast of Gabriel. In our culture, a privileged child is at birth put down for Groton and Harvard. In Switzerland, when a baby is born, a wheel of Saanen is marked with his name. On all the holiest occasions of his mortality—christening, betrothal, marriage—his private cheese is served; and when he dies the mourners consume the last of this ceremonial Wheel of Life.

Provided it be well and truly made there is really, for the confirmed turophile, no such thing as a *bad* cheese. A cheese may disappoint. It may be dull, it may be naïve, it may be oversophisticated. Yet it remains cheese, milk's leap toward immortality.

Edam's crimson cannon balls, for example, may seem a bit plodding. But a thick round of Edam or Gouda on the blackest of bread, companioned by the blackest of coffee, makes a muscular breakfast that puts to shame epicene toast-and-orange-juice. Nor does the more reflective palate disdain that rarity, Edam, that is sharp, dry and two years of age.

Let us remember also that Balzac, no inconsiderable gastronome, pays tribute to Dutch cheeses as the cheap but sound nourisher of needy genius in its attic.

"Swiss" cheese, Emmentaler or Gruyère, would seem to have too obvious an appeal. But there is virtue in simple candor. (Try simple candor with beer.) Look to it, however, that your Gruyère betrays around its eyes that trace of lachrymose moisture which announces its ripeness, its readiness to be yours. Hardest of all to come by is the supreme Gruyère, long past its salad days when it was green in judgment—Gruyère that is rich, salty, nutlike and virtually holeless.

I will confess Bel Paese a neutral affair at best, but Taleggio shows to what it may aspire, and Pont l'Evêque seems to me the highest avatar of the type. Pont l'Evêque now appears rarely, but it has an attractive cousin in Mont Doré, a Rhone Valley whole-milk cheese I have found in many New York shops. Soft, yellow, delicate without effeminacy, Mont Doré was the favorite cheese of Pascal, whose *Pensées* must owe some of their powerful grace to its ingestion.

Parmesan, the carborundum of cheeses, is humble fare. Marry

it to onion soup and it becomes royal. One recalls Willa Cather's Bishop Latour in *Death Comes for the Archbishop,* savoring such a parmesanctified soup, rich in its "nearly a thousand years of history." One bows the head in gratitude to Louis XV's father-in-law, the exiled Polish king Stanislaus Leszczynski, who made it famous. Mark well, however, that God did not make it in canisters. It was not born grated; it does not achieve gratedness; it must virtually at table have gratedness thrust upon it.

Gentlemen, let us raise our sights. Let us praise the immortal French triad, the Three Musketeers: Roquefort, Camembert, Brie.

Ewe-born, cave-educated, perfected by moldy bread, greenish-blue-veined Roquefort was called by Grimod de la Reynière "the toper's biscuit." So joyfully does it mate with wine that wine buyers will not use it as a palate cleanser lest it mask the wine's poorer qualities. The poet Baudelaire, liking perhaps its faint tantalizing hint of decay, was an amateur of Roquefort, pairing it with that Burgundy of beautiful balance, Corton. We receive great Roquefort rarely, for it is often oversalted for export purposes. Though it lacks the true Roquefort texture, our native Langlois Blue from Oregon is no bad substitute.

Esteeming Roquefort, I view it without passion. Yet I can conceive why Emile Zola, describing a cheese market, speaks of "majestic Roqueforts looking down with princely contempt upon the others, through the glass of their crystal covers."

For full persuasion Camembert, like a good orator, should stop short just this side of fluency. Before this stage it speaks of chalk; past it, of ammonia. For perfect Camembert the recipe is simple: go to Normandy. Our present law demands pasteurization of the milk before the cheese may be exported to us: the equivalent of assassination.

Perhaps this law is being slyly evaded, for I have recently eaten good Brie. (Domestic Brie, pleasant enough, is not Brie at all.) When you speak of Brie, uncover: Talleyrand called it the King of Cheeses; the only king, it has been noted, to whom he remained faithful. In its subtlety, its delicacy, its beauty and its appeal to the intellect, Brie might quite as aptly be called the Poet of Cheeses. Like many fine poets, it is hard to get at. The ordinary cheese knife, an abomination, is powerless; a razor blade has been suggested; I have found a small demitasse spoon the very thing for those cryptic corners. A perfect Brie cannot be produced by standardized methods; it is the end product of a series of miracles. Essays are writ by fools like me, but only God can make a Brie.

As for English cheeses, only one (but that the lordliest, Stilton) seems to reach our shores today. Cheddar, Cheshire, Gloucester, Double Gloucester—all could after patient research once be found. Now, I hear, supreme examples of these cheeses are even on their native heath hard to come by. Pity; for, while England may well survive the falling away of her colonies, a falling off in her cheese whispers of some deep and stanchless inner wound.

Great Cheddar, I hope, Englishmen still enjoy. As for ourselves, domestic Cheddar lies around us in its infancy, and some in its maturity. I have found few domestic Cheddars more honest than the sharp variety sold by Jack and Marion Ayres of Sugarbush Farm, Woodstock, Vermont. But even at its shelf-cured, three-year-old Vermont best, our Cheddar cannot equal a fine English Farmhouse Cheddar. (Farmhouse Cheddar is satisfactory; the other kind merely Factory.) A good Cheddar, like a human being, needs at least nine months to round into decent enough shape to make a public appearance. I prefer a more elephantine period of gestation. A knowledgeable Englishman, John Houghton, once suggested two to five years. But his counsel was offered two and a half centuries ago when both men and cheese were allowed time to live. To Cheddar—as to all cheeses of character—Edgar's wise words in *King Lear* must apply: "Ripeness is all."

Of Stilton it is hard to speak without emotion. Its azure veins avouching noble lineage, it thrones itself as the world's most regal

Blue, exerting, like any true aristocrat, authority without aggressiveness. A Stilton's self-confidence springs from its past (the richest milk and cream) and its future, which can only be one of glory. John Galsworthy in *The Forsyte Saga* refers to "grand years-old Stilton." Charles Lamb speaks of some Stilton as "the delicatest, rainbow-hued melting piece I ever tasted." John Jay Chapman recalls a morsel "that was like Agincourt. It was sonorous, undying." Here Chapman strikes the right note. There's such divinity doth hedge a Stilton as aureoles no other cheese. It is magisterial.

See, however, that your Stilton be of a healthy cream color, not anemic, with a hint of greenish-yellow, its edges brownish, its veins wide-branching, its texture not overflaky, its vast interior uncrevassed. If you can, buy a whole Stilton or at least a half. The grandiose gesture will repay you; properly kept at room temperature a well-bought, well-bred Stilton will for many months share with you its nobility. With careful stroke remove the crown. Then cut out a wedge perhaps one and a half inches high, and further wedges as required of exactly the same height, until a new smooth top is exposed. Replace the crown so that it fits tightly; keep truncating your Stilton in this manner till you have disposed of the last bit. Then buy another Stilton.

Stilton, as I say, does reach us, as do many other fine cheeses: the unctuous Stracchino, the subtle, feminine Hablé Crème Chantilly, the devourable Provolone, the mild Gruyèrish Banquet from Iceland. Phil Alpert, the master cheesemonger of East 10th Street, New York, offers hundreds of "cheeses of all nations," but most of them are made here in excellent imitation of their originals. To secure, however, a wide and deep understanding of cheese one must and should travel. The pleasures of a cheese tour are subtler than those of a châteaux tour, for there is always the chance that you will make a great discovery. Besides, cheeses taste better on the home grounds.

We come now to our own land, with which from the cheese-lover's viewpoint we may merge our good neighbor Canada. A Rembrandtesque picture presents itself, a dramatic mingling of light and shade.

The blackest shadow, of course, is cast by processed "cheese." The word should always, like Soviet "democracy," be framed in quotes, for no matter what the law may say, I refuse to call this cheese. For me (though it is only fair to state that millions of us seem to like the stuff) processed "cheese" belongs to the same Kallikak family as ordinary commercial white bread, powdered coffee, cellophaned cake and our more popular carbonated beverages. The best I can say for it is that it is nonpoisonous; the worst, that it represents the triumph of technology over conscience.

In the preparation of this solidified floor wax—often the product of emulsification with sodium citrate, sodium phosphate or rochelle salts; of steaming and frequently blending odd lots of cheese; of paralyzing whatever germs might result either in loss of profit or gain of flavor—every problem but one is solved: packaging, keeping, distribution, slicing, cost. One problem alone is not solved: that of making cheese.

Bernard Shaw once warned us (he was speaking of mass entertainment) to be sure to get what we liked; otherwise we might begin to like what we got. There is the point—not that processed "cheese" is so bad in itself (though it is) but that its convenience, neatness and cheapness give it so many advantages that it may elbow real cheese aside and in the end compass the death of our cheese-palates. Let us not be fooled. My guinea-pig son, aged one year and seven months, was not: fed a "cheese spread," he spat it out; fed a tiny bit of Stilton he took to it like an angel. Give our American children the processed corpse of milk and they will grow (I dare not say mature) into processed men, all package and no character.

I can call to mind one exception to these strictures. But even that is not a native product. It is a Danish import called, horribly enough, Littlefellow, a processed cheese spread, mild, creamy, with an interesting tang. As for other processed plastics, remember only that the wrappings of foil are the cerements of death.

But enough of bitterness. It is sad work and I take little pleasure in it. Processed "cheese," "cheese spreads" and "cheese foods" (often hypoed with onions, garlic and similar horrors in order to mask the taste of the corpse) represent only the baser element in what is on the whole an honorable and progressive industry. Let us joyfully aver that we have a God's plenty of sound, decent domestic cheeses, most of it Cheddarish in nature, some of it an excellent aping of greater European originals, such as Gruyère or Roquefort.

Our basic trouble is that we are in a hurry and cheese is not. Honest, edible Cheddar is easily found, but really mature, shelf-cured Cheddar, dry and on the point of the crumble, is rare. Still, I have eaten good Cheddar from Canada, Vermont, New York and Wisconsin; and I once tasted an Oregon Tillamook filled with both the goodness and the severity of God. Sage Cheddar, Vermont's pride, can be a wondrous thing. It eats supremely well on a hot summer afternoon in the country (circumstances alter cheeses), especially if you mate it incestuously with its mother, milk, and support it on cracker-barrel crackers—even though for the most part crackers are the enemy of cheese, just as bread is its friend. I mean real bread—pumpernickel, dark rye, stone-ground whole-grain bread, or crusty French loaf, not the pre-sliced leprous "bread" of large-scale commerce.

The great war, as in other areas, is between the urge to standardize and the urge to create. More often than one would think, the creator wins. One of our finest native cheeses is the work of a creative artist, Emil Frey of Monroe, New York. This cheese offers a good example of serendipity. Frey was experimenting with a formula for a German-type cheese (probably Limburger, which is originally Belgian) and accidentally came up with something new. But it takes greatness to recognize greatness, and Frey, being great, knew he had something. He called it Liederkranz—one of the most beautiful and odorous soft cheeses in the world, and named after a famous New York singing society.

The roll of individualistic, ruggedly independent American cheeses is a long one. Let me mention only a few. There is, for carefree nibbling, the plain, honest Jack from California. From the Colorado Rockies comes a little flattened sphere of black-rinded whole-milk Cheddar, Mountain Blackie—an utterly delicious, subtly acid, eating cheese, imperfect for wine but otherwise a fresh and lovely thing. Poona, a Pont l'Evêque-like cheese made in New York State, has extraordinary breeding. Canada's Oka, lineally descended from Port-Salut, can be superior, though I fear it is cured too quickly. The secretary of the Cistercian Abby of la Trappe d'Oka (where the cheese is made) writes me that its unique flavor is due "partly to the special bacteria of our cellars, and partly to the rich pasture ground of our hilly country." Its brother-abbey of Gethsemani in Kentucky makes a similar cheese I have found supremely good of its kind.

Yes, the mind that refuses to be processed still lives and flourishes, in our dairies as well as in our politics and arts and sciences. Certain strange and wonderful cheeses of Europe I may never taste—Sweden's Prestost or Saaland Pfarr, whose curd is washed in whiskey; Rumania's Brânja de Cosulet, a creamy sheep's-milk cheese, resinous from its pine-bark casing; Septmoncel from the Jura, ranked by some experts above Roquefort; England's esoteric Blue Vinny and Wensleydale . . . But no matter: there is enough fine cheese in my own country to last my time and give it edge, savor and unctuousness. And there is always the hope that, like a new planet, a truly supreme American cheese will swim into my ken and that I too shall at last look

> ". . . with a wild surmise,
> Silent, upon a peak in dairyin'."

Clifton Fadiman

The Complete Book of Cheese

Chapter One

I Remember Cheese

Cheese market day in a town in the north of Holland. All the cheese-fanciers are out, thumping the cannon-ball Edams and the millstone Goudas with their bare red knuckles, plugging in with a hollow steel tool for samples. In Holland the business of judging a crumb of cheese has been taken with great seriousness for centuries. The abracadabra is comparable to that of the wine-taster or tea-taster. These Edamers have the trained ear of music-masters and, merely by knuckle-rapping, can tell down to an air pocket left by a gas bubble just how mature the interior is.

The connoisseurs use gingerbread as a mouth-freshener; and I, too, that sunny day among the Edams, kept my gingerbread handy and made my way from one fine cheese to another, trying out generous plugs from the heaped cannon balls that looked like the ammunition dump at Antietam.

I remember another market day, this time in Lucerne. All morning I stocked up on good Schweizerkäse and better Gruyère. For lunch I had cheese salad. All around me the farmers were rolling two-hundred-pound Emmentalers, bigger than oxcart wheels. I sat in a little café, absorbing cheese and cheese lore in equal quantities. I learned that a prize cheese must be chock-full of equal-sized eyes, the gas holes produced during fermentation. They must glisten like polished bar glass. The cheese itself must be of a light, lemonish yellow. Its flavor must be nutlike. (Nuts and Swiss cheese complement each other as subtly as Gorgonzola and a ripe banana.) There are, I learned, "blind" Swiss cheeses as well, but the million-eyed ones are better.

But I don't have to hark back to Switzerland and Holland for cheese memories. Here at home we have increasingly taken over the cheeses of all nations, first importing them, then imitating them, from Swiss Engadine to what we call Genuine Sprinz. We've naturalized Scandinavian Blues and smoked browns and baptized our own Saaland Pfarr in native whiskey. Of fifty popular Italian types we duplicate more than half, some fairly well, others badly.

We have our own legitimate offspring too, beginning with the Pineapple, supposed to have been first made about 1845 in Litchfield County, Connecticut. We have our own creamy Neufchâtel, New York Coon, Vermont Sage, the delicious Liederkranz, California Jack, Nuworld, and dozens of others, not all quite so original.

And, true to the American way, we've organized cheese-eating. There's an annual cheese week, and a cheese month (October). We even boast a mail-order Cheese-of-the-Month Club. We haven't yet reached the point of sophistication, however, attained by a Paris cheese club that meets regularly. To qualify for membership you have to identify two hundred basic cheeses, and you have to do it blindfolded.

This is a test I'd prefer not to submit to, but in my amateur way I have during the past year or two been sharpening my cheese perception with whatever varieties I could encounter around New York. I've run into briny Caucasian Cossack, Corsican Gricotta, and exotics like Rarush Durmer, Travnik, and Karaghi La-la. Cheese-hunting is one of the greatest—and least competitively crowded—of sports. I hope this book may lead others to give it a try.

Chapter Two

The Big Cheese

One of the world's first outsize cheeses officially weighed in at four tons in a fair at Toronto, Canada, seventy years ago. Another monstrous Cheddar tipped the scales at six tons in the New York State Fair at Syracuse in 1937.

Before this, a one-thousand-pounder was fetched all the way from New Zealand to London to star in the Wembley Exposition of 1924. But, compared to the outsize Syracusan, it looked like a Baby Gouda. As a matter of fact, neither England nor any of her great dairying colonies have gone in for mammoth jobs, except Canada, with that four-tonner shown at Toronto.

We should mention two historic king-size Chesters. You can find out all about them in *Cheddar Gorge,* edited by Sir John Squire. The first of them weighed 149 pounds, and was the largest made, up to the year 1825. It was proudly presented to H.R.H. the Duke of York. (Its heft almost tied the 147-pound Green

County wheel of Wisconsin Swiss presented by the makers to President Coolidge in 1928 in appreciation of his raising the protective tariff against genuine Swiss to 50 percent.) While the cheese itself weighed a mite under 150, His Royal Highness, ruff, belly, knee breeches, doffed high hat and all, was a hundredweight heavier, and thus almost dwarfed it.

It was almost a century later that the second record-breaking Chester weighed in, at only 200 pounds. Yet it won a Gold Medal and a Challenge Cup and was presented to the King, who graciously accepted it. This was more than Queen Victoria had done with a bridal gift cheese that tipped the scales at 1,100 pounds. It took a whole day's yield from 780 contented cows, and stood a foot and eight inches high, measuring nine feet, four inches around the middle. The assembled donors of the cheese were so proud of it that they asked royal permission to exhibit it on a round of country fairs. The Queen assented to this ambitious request, perhaps prompted by the exhibition-minded Albert. The publicity-seeking cheesemongers assured Her Majesty that the gift would be returned to her just as soon as it had been exhibited. But the Queen didn't want it back after it was show-worn. The donors began to quarrel among themselves about what to do with the remains, until finally it got into Chancery where so many lost causes end their days. The cheese was never heard of again.

While it is generally true that the bigger the cheese the better (much the same as a magnum bottle of champagne is better than a pint), there is a limit to the obesity of a block, ball or brick of almost any kinds of cheese. When they pass a certain limit, they lack homogeneity and are not nearly so good as the smaller ones. Today a good magnum size for an exhibition Cheddar is 560 pounds; for a prize Provolone, 280 pounds; while a Swiss wheel of only 210 will draw crowds to any food-shop window.

Yet by and large it's the monsters that get into the Cheese Hall of Fame and come down to us in song and story. For example, that four-ton Toronto affair inspired a cheese poet, James McIntyre, who doubled as the local undertaker.

We have thee, mammoth cheese,
Lying quietly at your ease;
Gently fanned by evening breeze,
Thy fair form no flies dare seize.

All gaily dressed soon you'll go
To the greatest provincial show,
To be admired by many a beau
In the city of Toronto.

May you not receive a scar as
We have heard that Mr. Harris
Intends to send you off as far as
The great world's show at Paris.

Of the youth beware of these,
For some of them might rudely squeeze
And bite your cheek; then song or glees
We could not sing, oh, Queen of Cheese.

An ode to a one hundred percent American mammoth was inspired by "The Ultra-Democratic, Anti-Federalist Cheese of Cheshire." This was in the summer of 1801 when the patriotic people of Cheshire, Massachusetts, turned out en masse to concoct a mammoth cheese on the village green for presentation to their beloved President Jefferson. The unique demonstration occurred spontaneously in jubilant commemoration of the greatest political triumph of a new country in a new century—the victory of the Democrats over the Federalists. Its collective making was heralded in Boston's *Mercury and New England Palladium*, September 8, 1801:

The Mammoth Cheese

AN EPICO-LYRICO BALLAD

From meadows rich, with clover red,
  A thousand heifers come;

The tinkling bells the tidings spread,
The milkmaid muffles up her head,
  And wakes the village hum.

In shining pans the snowy flood
  Through whitened canvas pours;
The dyeing pots of otter good
And rennet tinged with madder blood
  Are sought among their stores.

The quivering curd, in panniers stowed,
  Is loaded on the jade,
The stumbling beast supports the load,
While trickling whey bedews the road
  Along the dusty glade.

As Cairo's slaves, to bondage bred,
  The arid deserts roam,
Through trackless sands undaunted tread,
With skins of water on their head
  To cheer their masters home,

So here full many a sturdy swain
  His precious baggage bore;
Old misers e'en forgot their gain,
And bed-rid cripples, free from pain,
  Now took the road before.

The widow, with her dripping mite
  Upon her saddle horn,
Rode up in haste to see the sight
And aid a charity so right,
  A pauper so forlorn.

The circling throng an opening drew
  Upon the verdant grass
To let the vast procession through

To spread their rich repast in view,
  And Elder J. L. pass.

Then Elder J. with lifted eyes
  In musing posture stood,
Invoked a blessing from the skies
To save from vermin, mites and flies,
  And keep the bounty good.

Now mellow strokes the yielding pile
  From polished steel receives,
And shining nymphs stand still a while,
Or mix the mass with salt and oil,
  With sage and savory leaves.

Then sextonlike, the patriot troop,
  With naked arms and crown,
Embraced, with hardy hands, the scoop,
And filled the vast expanded hoop,
  While beetles smacked it down.

Next girding screws the ponderous beam,
  With heft immense, drew down;
The gushing whey from every seam
Flowed through the streets a rapid stream,
  And shad came up to town.

This spirited achievement of early democracy is commemorated today by a sign set up at the ancient and honorable town of Cheshire, located between Pittsfield and North Adams, on Route 8.

Jefferson's speech of thanks to the democratic people of Cheshire rings out in history: "I look upon this cheese as a token of fidelity from the very heart of the people of this land to the great cause of equal rights to all men."

This popular presentation started a tradition. When Van Buren succeeded to the Presidency, he received a similar mammoth cheese in token of the high esteem in which he was held. A monstrous one, bigger than the Jeffersonian, was made by New Englanders to show their loyalty to President Jackson. For weeks this stood in state in the hall of the White House. At last the floor was a foot deep in the fragments remaining after the enthusiastic Democrats had eaten their fill.

Chapter Three

Foreign Greats

Ode to Cheese

God of the country, bless today Thy cheese,
For which we give Thee thanks on bended knees.
Let them be fat or light, with onions blent,
Shallots, brine, pepper, honey; whether scent
Of sheep or fields is in them, in the yard
Let them, good Lord, at dawn be beaten hard.
And let their edges take on silvery shades
Under the moist red hands of dairymaids;
And, round and greenish, let them go to town
Weighing the shepherd's folding mantle down;
Whether from Parma or from Jura heights,
Kneaded by august hands of Carmelites,
Stamped with the mitre of a proud abbess.
Flowered with the perfumes of the grass of Bresse,
From hollow Holland, from the Vosges, from Brie,
From Roquefort, Gorgonzola, Italy!

Bless them, good Lord! Bless Stilton's royal fare,
Red Cheshire, and the tearful cream Gruyère.

FROM JETHRO BITHELL'S TRANSLATION
OF A POEM BY M. Thomas Braun

Symphonie des Fromages

A giant Cantal, seeming to have been chopped open with an ax, stood aside of a golden-hued Chester and a Swiss Gruyère resembling the wheel of a Roman chariot. There were Dutch Edams, round and blood-red, and Port-Saluts lined up like soldiers on parade. Three Bries, side by side, suggested phases of the moon; two of them, very dry, were amber-colored and "full," and the third, in its second quarter, was runny and creamy, with a "milky way" which no human barrier seemed able to restrain. And all the while majestic Roqueforts looked down with princely contempt upon the other, through the glass of their crystal covers.

Emile Zola

In 1953 the United States Department of Agriculture published Handbook No. 54, entitled *Cheese Varieties and Descriptions,* with this comment: "There probably are only about eighteen distinct types or kinds of natural cheese." All the rest (more than 400 names) are of local origin, usually named after towns or communities. A list of the best-known names applied to each of these distinct varieties or groups is given:

Brick	Gouda	Romano
Camembert	Hand	Roquefort
Cheddar	Limburger	Sapsago
Cottage	Neufchâtel	Swiss
Cream	Parmesan	Trappist
Edam	Provolone	Whey cheeses (Mysost and Ricotta)

May we nominate another dozen to form our own Cheese Hall of Fame? We begin our list with a partial roll call of the big Blues family and end it with members of the monastic order of Port-Salut Trappist that includes Canadian Oka and our own Kentucky thoroughbred.

The Blues that Are Green

Stilton, Roquefort and Gorgonzola form the triumvirate that rules a world of lesser Blues. They are actually green, as green as the mythical cheese the moon is made of.

In almost every land where cheese is made you can sample a handful of lesser Blues and imitations of the invincible three and try to classify them, until you're blue in the face. The best we can do in this slight summary is to mention a few of the most notable, aside from our own Blues of Minnesota, Wisconsin, Oregon and other states that major in cheese.

Danish Blues are popular and splendidly made, such as "Flower of Denmark." The Argentine competes with a pampas-grass Blue all its own. But France and England are the leaders in this line, France first with a sort of triple triumvirate within a triumvirate—Septmoncel, Gex, and Sassenage, all three made with three milks mixed together: cow, goat and sheep. Septmoncel is the leader of these, made in the Jura mountains and considered by many French caseophiles to outrank Roquefort.

This class of Blue or marbled cheese is called fromage persillé, as well as fromage bleu and pâte bleue. Similar mountain cheeses are made in Auvergne and Aubrac and have distinct qualities that have brought them fame, such as Cantal, bleu d'Auvergne Guiole or Laguiole, bleu de Salers, and St. Flour. Olivet and Queville come within the color scheme, and sundry others such as Champoléon, Journiac, Queyras and Sarraz.

Of English Blues there are several celebrities beside Stilton and Cheshire Stilton. Wensleydale was one in the early days, and still is, together with Blue Dorset, the deepest green of them all, and esoteric Blue Vinny, a choosey cheese not liked by everybody, the favorite of Thomas Hardy.

Brie

Sheila Hibben once wrote in *The New Yorker:*

> I can't imagine any difference of opinion about Brie's being the queen of all cheeses, and if there is any such difference, I shall certainly ignore it. The very shape of Brie—so uncheese-like and so charmingly fragile—is exciting. Nine times out of ten a Brie will let you down—will be all caked into layers, which shows it is too young, or at the over-runny stage, which means it is too old—but when you come on the tenth Brie, *coulant* to just the right delicate creaminess, and the color of fresh, sweet butter, no other cheese can compare with it.

The season of Brie, like that of oysters, is simple to remember: only months with an "R," beginning with September, which is the best, bar none.

Caciocavallo

From Bulgaria to Turkey the Italian "horse cheese," as Caciocavallo translates, is as universally popular as it is at home and in all the Little Italies throughout the rest of the world. Flattering imitations are made and named after it, as follows:

BULGARIA:	**Kascaval**
GREECE:	**Kashcavallo** and **Caskcaval**
HUNGARY:	**Parencia**
RUMANIA:	**Pentele** and **Kascaval**
SERBIA:	**Katschkawalj**
SYRIA:	**Cashkavallo**

TRANSYLVANIA: **Kascaval** (as in Rumania)
TURKEY: **Cascaval Penir**
YUGOSLAVIA: **Kackavalj**

A horse's head printed on the cheese gave rise to its popular name and to the myth that it is made of mare's milk. It is, however, curded from cow's milk, whole or partly skimmed, and sometimes from water buffalo; hard, yellow and so buttery that the best of it, which comes from Sorrento, is called *Cacio burro,* butter cheese. Slightly salty, with a spicy tang, it is eaten sliced when young and mild and used for grating and seasoning when old, not only on the usual Italian pastes but on sweets.

Different from the many grating cheeses made from little balls of curd called *grana,* Caciocavallo is a *pasta fileta,* or drawn-curd product. Because of this it is sometimes drawn out in long thick threads and braided. It is a cheese for skilled artists to make sculptures with, sometimes horses' heads, again bunches of grapes and other fruits, even as Provolone is shaped like apples and pears and often worked into elaborate bas-relief designs. But ordinarily the horse's head is a plain tenpin in shape or a squat bottle with a knob on the side by which it has been tied up, two cheeses at a time, on opposite sides of a rafter, while being smoked lightly golden and rubbed with olive oil and butter to make it all the more buttery.

In Calabria and Sicily it is very popular, and although the best comes from Sorrento, there is keen competition from Abruzzi, Apulian Province and Molise. It keeps well and doesn't spoil when shipped overseas.

In his *Little Book of Cheese* Osbert Burdett recommends the high, horsy strength of this smoked Cacio over tobacco smoke after dinner:

> Only monsters smoke at meals, but a monster assured me that Gorgonzola best survives this malpractice. Clearly, some pungency is necessary, and confidence suggests rather Cacio which would survive anything, the monster said.

Camembert

Camembert is called "mold-matured" and all that is genuine is labeled *Syndicat du Vrai Camembert.* The name in full is *Syndicat des Fabricants du Véritable Camembert de Normandie* and we agree that this is "a most useful association for the defense of one of the best cheeses of France." Its extremely delicate piquance cannot be matched, except perhaps by Brie.

Napoleon is said to have named it and to have kissed the waitress who first served it to him in the tiny town of Camembert. And there a statue stands today in the market place to honor Marie Harel who made the first Camembert.

Camembert is equally good on thin slices of apple, pineapple, pear, French "flute" or pumpernickel. As with Brie and with oysters, Camembert should be eaten only in the "R" months, and of these September is the best.

Since Camembert rhymes with beware, if you can't get the *véritable* don't fall for a domestic imitation or any West German abomination such as one dressed like a valentine in a heart-shaped box and labeled "Camembert—Cheese Exquisite." They are equally tasteless, chalky with youth, or choking with ammoniacal gas when old and decrepit.

Cheddar

The English *Encyclopedia of Practical Cookery* says:

> Cheddar cheese is one of the kings of cheese; it is pale coloured, mellow, salvy, and, when good, resembling a hazelnut in flavour. The Cheddar principle pervades the whole cheesemaking districts of America, Canada and New Zealand, but no cheese imported into England can equal the Cheddars of Somerset and the West of Scotland.

Named for a village near Bristol where farmer Joseph Harding first manufactured it, the best is still called Farmhouse Cheddar, but in America we have practically none of this. Farmhouse Cheddar must be ripened at least nine months to a mellowness, and little of our American cheese gets as much as that. Back in 1695 John Houghton wrote that it "contended in goodness (if kept from two to five years, according to magnitude) with any cheese in England."

Today it is called "England's second-best cheese," second after Stilton, of course.

In early days a large cheese sufficed for a year or two of family feeding, according to this old note: "A big Cheddar can be kept for two years in excellent condition if kept in a cool room and turned over every other day."

But in old England some were harder to preserve: "In Bath . . . I asked one lady of the larder how she kept Cheddar cheese. Her eyes twinkled: 'We don't keep cheese; we eats it.' "

Cheshire

A Cheshireman sailed into Spain
  To trade for merchandise;
When he arrived from the main
  A Spaniard him espies.
Who said, "You English rogue, look here!
  What fruits and spices fine
Our land produces twice a year.
  Thou has not such in thine."

The Cheshireman ran to his hold
  And fetched a Cheshire cheese,
And said, "Look here, you dog, behold!
  We have such fruits as these.
Your fruits are ripe but twice a year,
  As you yourself do say,
But such as I present you here
  Our land brings twice a day."

Anonymous

> Let us pass on to cheese. We have some glorious cheeses, and far too few people glorying in them. The Cheddar of the inn, of the chophouse, of the average English home, is a libel on a thing which, when authentic, is worthy of great honor. Cheshire, divinely commanded into existence as to three parts to precede and as to one part to accompany certain Tawny Ports and some Late-Bottled Ports, can be a thing for which the British Navy ought to fire a salute on the principle on which Colonel Brisson made his regiment salute when passing the great Burgundian vineyard.
>
> T. Earle Welby,
> IN "THE DINNER KNELL"

Cheshire is not only the most literary cheese in England, but the oldest. It was already manufactured when Caesar conquered Britain, and tradition is that the Romans built the walled city of Chester to control the district where the precious cheese was made. Chester on the River Dee was a stronghold against the Roman invasion.

It came to fame with The Old Cheshire Cheese in Elizabethan times and waxed great with Samuel Johnson presiding at the Fleet Street Inn where White Cheshire was served "with radishes or watercress or celery when in season," and Red Cheshire was served toasted or stewed in a sort of Welsh Rabbit. (*See* Chapter 5.)

The Blue variety is called Cheshire-Stilton, and Vyvyan Holland in *Cheddar Gorge* suggests that "it was no doubt a cheese of this sort, discovered and filched from the larder of the Queen of Hearts, that accounted for the contented grin on the face of the Cheshire Cat in Alice in Wonderland."

All very English, as recorded in Victor Meusy's couplet:

Dans le Chester sec et rose
A longues dents, l'Anglais mord.

In the Chester dry and pink
The long teeth of the English sink.

Edam and Gouda

Edam in Peace and War

There also coming into the river two Dutchmen, we sent a couple of men on board and brought three Holland cheeses, cost 4d. a piece, excellent cheeses.

Pepys' *Diary*, March 2, 1663

Commodore Coe, of the Montevidian Navy, defeated Admiral Brown of the Buenos Ayrean Navy, in a naval battle, when he used Holland cheese for cannon balls.

The Harbinger (Vermont), December 11, 1847

The crimson cannon balls of Holland have been heard around the world. Known as "red balls" in England and *katzenkopf*, "cat's head," in Germany, they differ from Gouda chiefly in the shape, Gouda being round but flattish and now chiefly imported as one-pound Baby Goudas.

Edam when it is good is very, very good, but when it is bad it is horrid. Sophisticated ones are sent over already scalloped for the ultimate consumer to add port, and there are crocks of Holland cheese potted with sauterne. Both Edam and Gouda should be well aged to develop full-bodied quality, two years being the accepted standard for Edam.

The best Edams result from a perfect combination of Breed (black-and-white Dutch Friesian) and Feed (the rich pasturage of Friesland and Noord Holland).

The Goudas, shaped like English Derby and Belgian Delft and Leyden, come from South Holland. Some are specially made for the Jewish trade and called Kosher Gouda. Both Edam and Gouda are eaten at mealtimes thrice daily in Holland. A Dutch breakfast without one or the other on black bread with butter and black coffee would be unthinkable. They're also boon companions to plum bread and Dutch cocoa.

"Eclair Edams" are those with soft insides.

Emmentaler, Gruyère and Swiss

When the working woman
Takes her midday lunch,
It is a piece of Gruyère
Which for her takes the place of roast.
Victor Meusy

Whether an Emmentaler is eminently Schweizerkäse, grand Gruyère from France, or lesser Swiss of the United States, the shape, size and glisten of the eyes indicate the stage of ripeness, skill of making and quality of flavor. They must be uniform, roundish, about the size of a big cherry and, most important of all, must glisten like the eye of a lass in love, dry but with the suggestion of a tear.

Gruyère does not see eye to eye with the big-holed Swiss Saanen cartwheel or American imitation. It has tiny holes, and many of them; let us say it is freckled with pinholes, rather than pockmarked. This variety is technically called a *niszler,* while one without any holes at all is "blind." Eyes or holes are also called vesicles.

Gruyère Trauben (Grape Gruyère) is aged in Neuchâtel wine in Switzerland, although most Gruyère has been made in France since its introduction there in 1722. The most famous is made in the Jura, and another is called Comté from its origin in Franche-Comté.

A blind Emmentaler was made in Switzerland for export to Italy where it was hardened in caves to become a grating cheese called Raper, and now it is largely imitated there. Emmentaler, in fact, because of its piquant pecan-nut flavor and inimitable quality, is simulated everywhere, even in Switzerland.

Besides phonies from Argentina and countries as far off as Finland, we get a flood of imported and domestic Swisses of all sad sorts, with all possible faults—from too many holes, that make a flabby, wobbly cheese, to too few—cracked, dried-up, collapsed or utterly ruined by molding inside. So it will pay you to buy only the kind already marked genuine in Switzerland. For there cheese such as Saanen takes six years to ripen, improves with age, and keeps forever.

Cartwheels well over a hundred years old are still kept in cheese cellars (as common in Switzerland as wine cellars are in France), and it is said that the rank of a family is determined by the age and quality of the cheese in its larder.

Feta and Casere

The Greeks have a name for it—Feta. Their neighbors call it Greek cheese. Feta is to cheese what Hymettus is to honey. The two together make ambrosial manna. Feta is soft and as blinding white as a plate of fresh Ricotta smothered with sour cream. The whiteness is preserved by shipping the cheese all the way from Greece in kegs sloshing full of milk, the milk being renewed from time to time. Having been cured in brine, this great sheep-milk curd is slightly salty and somewhat sharp, but superbly spicy.

When first we tasted it fresh from the keg with salty milk dripping through our fingers, we gave it full marks. This was at the Staikos Brothers Greek-import store on West 23rd Street in Manhattan. We then compared Feta with thin wisps of its grown-up brother, Casere. This gray and greasy, hard and brittle palate-tickler of sheep's milk made us bleat for more Feta.

Gorgonzola

Gorgonzola, least pretentious of the Blues triumvirate (including Roquefort and Stilton) is nonetheless by common consent monarch of all other Blues from Argentina to Denmark. In England, indeed, many epicures consider Gorgonzola greater than Stilton, which is the highest praise any cheese can get there.

Like all great cheeses it has been widely imitated, but never equaled. Imported Gorgonzola, when fruity ripe, is still firm but creamy and golden inside with rich green veins running through. Very pungent and highly flavored, it is eaten sliced or crumbled to flavor salad dressings, like Roquefort.

Hablé Crème Chantilly

The name Hablé Crème Chantilly sounds French, but the cheese is Swedish and actually lives up to the blurb in the imported package: "The overall characteristic is indescribable and delightful freshness."

This exclusive product of the Walla Gärd Creamery was hailed by Sheila Hibben in *The New Yorker* of May 6, 1950, as enthusiastically as Brillat-Savarin would have greeted a new dish, or the Planetarium a new star:

> Endeavoring to be as restrained as I can, I shall merely suggest that the arrival of Crème Chantilly is a historic event and that in reporting on it I feel something of the responsibility that the contemporaries of Madame Harel, the famous cheese-making lady of Normandy, must have felt when they were passing judgment on the first Camembert.

Miss Hibben goes on to say that only a fromage à la crème made in Quebec had come anywhere near her impression of the new Swedish triumph. She quotes the last word from the makers themselves: "This is a very special product that has never been made on this earth before," and speaks of "the elusive flavor of mushrooms" before summing up, "the exquisitely textured curd and the unexpectedly fresh flavor combine to make it one of the most subtly enjoyable foods that have come my way in a long time."

And so say we—all of us.

Hand Cheese

Hand cheese has this niche in our Cheese Hall of Fame not because we consider it great, but because it is usually included among the eighteen varieties on which the hundreds of others are based. It is named from having been molded into its final shape by hand. Universally popular with Germanic races, it is too strong for the others. To our mind, Hand cheese never had anything that Allgäuer or Limburger hasn't improved upon.

It is the only cheese that is commonly melted into steins of beer and drunk instead of eaten. It is usually studded with caraway seeds, the most natural spice for curds.

Limburger

Limburger has always been popular in America, ever since it was brought over by German-American immigrants; but England never took to it. This is eloquently expressed in the following entry in the English *Encyclopedia of Practical Cookery:*

> Limburger cheese is chiefly famous for its pungently offensive odor. It is made from skimmed milk, and allowed to partially decompose before pressing. It is very little known in this country, and might be less so with advantage to consumers.

But this is libel. Butter-soft and sapid, Limburger has brought gustatory pleasure to millions of hardy gastronomes since it came to light in the province of Lüttich in Belgium. It has been Americanized for almost a century and is by now one of the very few cheeses successfully imitated here, chiefly in New York and Wisconsin.

Early Wisconsiners will never forget the Limburger Rebellion in Green County, when the people rose in protest against the Limburger caravan that was accustomed to park in the little town of Monroe where it was marketed. They threatened to stage a modern Boston Tea Party and dump the odoriferous bricks in the river, when five or six wagonloads were left ripening in the sun in front of the town bank. The Limburger was finally stored safely underground.

Livarot

Livarot has been described as decadent, "The very Verlaine of them all," and Victor Meusy personifies it in a poem dedicated to all the great French cheeses, of which we give a free translation:

In the dog days
In its overflowing dish
Livarot gesticulates
Or weeps like a child.

Münster

At the diplomatic banquet
One must choose his piece.
All is politics,
A cheese and a flag.

You annoy the Russians
If you take Chester;
You irritate the Prussians
In choosing Münster.
Victor Meusy

Like Limburger, this male cheese, often caraway-flavored, does not fare well in England. Although over here we consider Münster far milder than Limburger, the English writer Eric Weir in *When Madame Cooks* will have none of it:

I cannot think why this cheese was not thrown from the aeroplanes during the war to spread panic amongst enemy troops. It would have proved far more efficacious than those nasty deadly gases that kill people permanently.

Neufchâtel

If the cream cheese be white
Far fairer the hands that made them.
Arthur Hugh Clough

Although originally from Normandy, Neufchâtel, like Limburger, was so long ago welcomed to America and made so splendidly at home here that we may consider it our very own. All we have against it is that it has served as the model for too many processed abominations.

Parmesan, Romano, Pecorino, Pecorino Romano

Parmesan when young, soft and slightly crumbly is eaten on bread. But when well aged, let us say up to a century, it becomes Rock of Gibraltar of cheeses and really suited for grating. It is easy to believe that the so-called "Spanish cheese" used as a barricade by Americans in Nicaragua almost a century ago was none other than the almost indestructible Grana, as Parmesan is called in Italy.

The association between cheese and battling began in B.C. days with the Jews and Romans, who fed cheese to their soldiers not only for its energy value but as a convenient form of rations, since every army travels on its stomach and can't go faster than its impedimenta. The last notable mention of cheese in war was the name of the *Monitor:* "A cheese box on a raft."

Romano is not as expensive as Parmesan, although it is as friable, sharp and tangy for flavoring, especially for soups such as onion and minestrone. It is brittle and just off-white when well aged.

Although made of sheep's milk, Pecorino is classed with both Parmesan and Romano. All three are excellently imitated in Argentina. Romano and Pecorino Romano are interchangeable names for the strong, medium-sharp and piquant Parmesan types that sell for considerably less. Most of it is now shipped from Sardinia. There are several different kinds: Pecorino Dolce (sweet), Sardo Tuscano, and Pecorino Romano Cacio, which relates it to Caciocavallo.

Kibitzers complain that some of the cheaper types of Pecorino are soapy. but fans give it high praise. Gillian F., in her "Letter from Italy" in Osbert Burdett's delectable *Little Book of Cheese,* writes:

> Out in the orchard, my companion, I don't remember how, had provided the miracle: a flask of wine, a loaf of bread and a slab of fresh Pecorino cheese (there wasn't any "thou" for either) . . . But that cheese was Paradise; and the flask was emptied, and a wood dove cooing made you think that the flask's contents were in a crystal goblet instead of an enamel cup . . . one only . . . and the cheese broken with the fingers . . . a cheese of cheeses.

Pont L'Evêque

This semisoft, medium-strong, golden-tinted French classic made since the thirteenth century, is definitely a dessert cheese whose excellence is brought out best by a sound claret or tawny port.

Port-Salut (*See* **Trappist**)

Provolone

Within recent years Provolone has taken America by storm, as Camembert, Roquefort, Swiss, Limburger, Neufchâtel and such great ones did long before. But it has not been successfully imitated here because the original is made of rich water-buffalo milk unattainable in the Americas.

With Caciocavallo, this mellow, smoky flavorsome delight is put up in all sorts of artistic forms, red-cellophaned apples, pears, bells, a regular zoo of animals, and in all sorts of sizes, up to a monumental hundred-pound bas-relief imported for exhibition purposes by Phil Alpert.

Roquefort

Homage to this *fromage!* Long hailed as *le roi* Roquefort, it has filled books and booklets beyond count. By the miracle of *Penicillium Roqueforti* a new cheese was made. It is placed historically back around the eighth century when Charlemagne was found picking out the green spots of Persillé with the point of his knife, thinking them decay. But the monks of Saint-Gall, who were his hosts, recorded in their annals that when they regaled him with Roquefort (because it was Friday and they had no fish) they also made bold to tell him he was wasting the best part of the cheese. So he tasted again, found the advice excellent and liked it so well he ordered two *caisses* of it sent every year to his palace at Aix-la-Chapelle. He also suggested that it be cut in half first, to make sure it was well veined with blue, and then bound up with a wooden fastening.

Perhaps he hoped the wood would protect the cheeses from mice and rats, for the good monks of Saint-Gall couldn't be expected to send an escort of cats from their chalky caves to guard them—even for Charlemagne. There is no telling how many cats were mustered out in the caves, in those early days, but a recent census put the number at five hundred. We can readily imagine the head handler in the caves leading a night inspection with a candle, followed by his chief taster and a regiment of cats. While the Dutch and other makers of cheese also employ cats to patrol their storage caves, Roquefort holds the record for number. An interesting point in this connection is that as rats and mice pick only the prime cheeses, a gnawed one is not thrown away but greatly prized.

Sapsago, Schabziger or Swiss Green Cheese

The name Sapsago is a corruption of Schabziger, German for whey cheese. It's a hay cheese, flavored heavily with melilot, a kind of clover that's also grown for hay. It comes from Switzerland in a hard, truncated cone wrapped in a piece of paper that says:

> To be used grated only
> Genuine Swiss Green Cheese
> Made of skimmed milk and herbs

> To the housewives! Do you want a change in your meals? Try the contents of this wrapper! Delicious as spreading mixed with butter, excellent for flavoring eggs, macaroni, spaghetti, potatoes, soup, etc. Can be used in place of any other cheese. *Do not take too much, you might spoil the flavor.*

We put this wrapper among our papers, sealed it tight in an envelope, and to this day, six months later, the scent of Sapsago clings 'round it still.

Stilton

Honor for Cheeses

> Literary and munching circles in London are putting quite a lot of thought into a proposed memorial to Stilton cheese. There is a Stilton Memorial Committee, with Sir John Squire at the head, and already the boys are fighting.

One side, led by Sir John, is all for a monument.

This, presumably, would not be a replica of Stilton itself, although Mr. Epstein could probably hack out a pretty effective cheese-shaped figure and call it "Dolorosa."

The monument-boosters plan a figure of Mrs. Paulet, who first introduced Stilton to England. (Possibly a group showing Mrs. Paulet holding a young Stilton by the hand and introducing it, while the Stilton curtsies.)

T. S. Eliot does not think that anyone would look at a monument, but wants to establish a Foundation for the Preservation of Ancient Cheeses. The practicability of this plan would depend largely on the site selected for the treasure house and the cost of obtaining a curator who could, or would, give his whole time to the work.

Mr. J. A. Symonds, who is secretary of the committee, agrees with Mr. Eliot that a simple statue is not the best form.

"I should like," he says, "something irrelevant—gargoyles, perhaps."

I think that Mr. Symonds has hit on something there.

I would suggest, if we Americans can pitch into this great movement, some gargoyles designed by Mr. Rube Goldberg.

If the memorial could be devised so as to take on an international scope, an exchange fellowship might be established between England and America, although the exchange, in the case of Stilton, would have to be all on England's side.

We might be allowed to furnish the money, however, while England furnishes the cheese.

There is a very good precedent for such a bargain between the two countries.

Robert Benchley, in
After 1903—What?

When all seems lost in England there is still Stilton, an endless after-dinner conversation piece to which England points with pride. For a sound appreciation of this cheese see Clifton Fadiman's introduction to this book.

Taleggio and Bel Paese

When the great Italian cheese-maker, Galbini, first exported Bel Paese some years ago, it was an eloquent ambassador to America. But as the years went on and imitations were made in many lands, Galbini deemed it wise to set up his own factory in *our* beautiful country. However, the domestic Bel Paese and a minute one-pounder called Bel Paesino just didn't have that old Alpine zest. They were no better than the German copy called Schönland, after the original, or the French Fleur des Alpes.

Mel Fino was a blend of Bel Paese and Gorgonzola. It perked up the market for a full, fruity cheese with snap. Then Galbini hit the jackpot with his Taleggio that fills the need for the sharpest, most sophisticated pungence of them all.

Trappist, Port-Salut, or Port du Salut, and Oka

In spite of its name Trappist is no rat-trap commoner. Always of the elect, and better known as Port-Salut or Port du Salut from the original home of the Trappist monks in their chief French abbey, it is also set apart from the ordinary Canadians under the name of Oka, from the Trappist monastery there. It is made by Trappist monks all over the world, according to the original secret formula, and by Trappist Cistercian monks at the Abbey of Gethsemani Trappist in Kentucky.

This is a soft cheese, creamy and of superb flavor. You can't go wrong if you look for the monastery name stamped on, such as Harzé in Belgium, Mont-des-Chats in Flanders, Sainte Anne d'Auray in Brittany, and so forth.

Last but not least, a commercial Port-Salut entirely without benefit of clergy or monastery is made in Milwaukee under the Lion Brand. It is one of the finest American cheeses in which we have ever sunk a fang.

Chapter Four

Native Americans

American Cheddars

The first American Cheddar was made soon after 1620 around Plymouth by Pilgrim fathers who brought along not only cheese from the homeland but a live cow to continue the supply. Proof of our ability to manufacture Cheddar of our own lies in the fact that by 1790 we were exporting it back to England.

It was called Cheddar after the English original named for the village of Cheddar near Bristol. More than a century ago it made a new name for itself, Herkimer County cheese, from the section of New York State where it was first made best. Herkimer still equals its several distinguished competitors, Coon, Colorado Blackie, California Jack, Pineapple, Sage, Vermont Colby and Wisconsin Longhorn.

The English called our imitation Yankee, or American, Cheddar, while here at home it was popularly known as yellow or store cheese from its prominent position in every country store; also apple-pie cheese because of its affinity for the all-American dessert.

The first Cheddar factory was founded by Jesse Williams in Rome, New York, just over a century ago and, with Herkimer County Cheddar already widely known, this established "New York" as the preferred "store-boughten" cheese.

An account of New York's cheese business in the pioneer Wooden Nutmeg Era is found in Ernest Elmo Calkins' interesting book, *They Broke the Prairies.* A Yankee named Silvanus Ferris, "the most successful dairyman of Herkimer County," in the first decades of the 1800's teamed up with Robert Nesbit, "the old Quaker Cheese Buyer." They bought from farmers in the region and sold in New York City. And "according to the business ethics of the times," Nesbit went ahead to cheapen the cheese offered by deprecating its quality, hinting at a bad market and departing without buying. Later when Ferris arrived in a more optimistic mood, offering a slightly better price, the seller, unaware they were partners, and ignorant of the market price, snapped up the offer.

Similar sharp-trade tactics put too much green cheese on the market, so those honestly aged from a minimum of eight months up to two years fetched higher prices. They were called "old," such as Old Herkimer, Old Wisconsin Longhorn, and Old California Jack.

Although the established Cheddar ages are three, fresh, medium-cured, and cured or aged, commercially they are divided into two and described as mild and sharp. The most popular are named for their states: Colorado, Illinois, Kentucky, New York, Ohio, Vermont and Wisconsin. Two New York Staters are called and named separately, Coon and Herkimer County. Tillamook goes by its own name with no mention of Oregon. Pineapple, Monterey Jack and Sage are seldom listed as Cheddars at all, although they are basically that.

Brick

Brick is the one and only cheese for which the whole world gives America credit. Runners-up are Liederkranz, which rivals say is too close to Limburger, and Pineapple, which is only a Cheddar under its crisscrossed, painted and flavored rind. Yet Brick is no more distinguished than either of the hundred percent Americans, and in our opinion is less worth bragging about.

It is a medium-firm, mild-to-strong slicing cheese for sandwiches and melting in hot dishes. Its texture is elastic but not rubbery, its taste sweetish, and it is full of little round holes or eyes. All this has inspired enthusiasts to liken it to Emmentaler. The most appropriate name for it has long been "married man's Limburger." To make up for the mildness caraway seed is sometimes added.

About Civil War time, John Jossi, a dairyman of Dodge County, Wisconsin, came up with this novelty, a rennet cheese made of whole cow's milk. The curd is cut like Cheddar, heated, stirred and cooked firm to put in a brick-shaped box without a bottom and with slits in the sides to drain. When this is set on the draining table a couple of bricks are also laid on the cooked curd for pressure. It is this double use of bricks, for shaping and for pressing, that has led to the confusion about which came first in originating the name.

The formed "bricks" of cheese are rubbed with salt for three days and they ripen slowly, taking up to two months.

We eat several million pounds a year and 95 percent of that comes from Wisconsin, with a trickle from New York.

Colorado Blackie Cheese

A subtly different American Cheddar is putting Colorado on our cheese map. It is called Blackie from the black-waxed rind and it resembles Vermont State cheese, although it is flatter. This is a proud new American product, proving that although Papa Cheddar was born in England his American kinfolk have developed independent and valuable characters all on their own.

Coon Cheese

Coon cheese is full of flavor from being aged on shelves at a higher temperature than cold storage. Its rind is darker from the growth of mold and this shade is sometimes painted on more ordinary Cheddars to make them look like Coon, which always brings a 10 percent premium above the general run.

Made at Lowville, New York, it has received high praise from a host of admirers, among them the French cook, Clementine, in Phineas Beck's *Kitchen,* who raised it to the par of French immortals by calling it Fromage de Coon. Clementine used it "with scintillating success in countless French recipes which ended with the words *gratiner au four et servir très chaud.* She made *baguettes* of it by soaking sticks three-eights-inch square and one and a half inches long in lukewarm milk, rolling them in flour, beaten egg and bread crumbs and browning them instantaneously in boiling oil.

Herkimer County Cheese

The standard method for making American Cheddar was established in Herkimer County, New York, in 1841 and has been rigidly maintained down to this day. Made with rennet and a bacterial "starter," the curd is cut and pressed to squeeze out all of the whey and then aged in cylindrical forms for a year or more.

Herkimer leads the whole breed by being flaky, brittle, sharp and nutty, with a crumb that will crumble, and a soft, mouthwatering pale orange color when it is properly aged.

Isigny

Isigny is a native American cheese that came a cropper. It seems to be extinct now, and perhaps that is all to the good, for it never meant to be anything more than another Camembert, of which we have plenty of imitation.

Not long after the Civil War the attempt was made to perfect Isigny. The curd was carefully prepared according to an original formula, washed and rubbed and set aside to come of age. But when it did, alas, it was more like Limburger than Camembert, and since good domestic Limburger was then a dime a pound, obviously it wouldn't pay off. Yet in shape the newborn resembled Camembert, although it was much larger. So they cut it down and named it after the delicate French Crème d'Isigny.

Jack, California Jack and Monterey Jack

Jack was first known as Monterey cheese from the California county where it originated. Then it was called Jack for short, and only now takes its full name after sixty years of popularity on the West Coast. Because it is little known in the East and has to be shipped so far, it commands the top Cheddar price.

Monterey Jack is a stirred curd Cheddar without any annatto coloring. It is sweeter than most and milder when young, but it gets sharper with age and more expensive because of storage costs.

Liederkranz

No native American cheese has been so widely ballyhooed, and so deservedly, as Liederkranz, which translates "Wreath of Song."

Back in the gay, inventive nineties, Emil Frey, a young delicatessen keeper in New York, tried to please some bereft customers by making an imitation of Bismarck Schlosskäse. This was imperative because the imported German cheese didn't stand up during the long sea trip and Emil's customers, mostly members of the famous Liederkranz singing society, didn't feel like singing without it. But Emil's attempts at imitation only added indigestion to their dejection, until one day—*fabelhaft!* One of those cheese dream castles in Spain came true. He turned out a tawny, altogether golden, tangy and mellow little marvel that actually was an improvement on Bismarck's old Schlosskäse. Better than Brick, it was a deodorized Limburger, both a man's cheese and one that cheese-conscious women adored.

Emil named it "Wreath of Song" for the Liederkranz customers. It soon became as internationally known as tabasco from Texas or Parisian Camembert which it slightly resembles. Borden's bought out Frey in 1929 and they enjoy telling the story of a G.I. who, to celebrate V-E Day in Paris, sent to his family in Indiana, only a few miles from the factory at Van Wert, Ohio, a whole case of what he had learned was "the finest cheese France could make." And when the family opened it, there was Liederkranz.

Another deserved distinction is that of being sandwiched in between two foreign immortals in the following recipe:

☛ Schnitzelbank Pot

1 ripe Camembert cheese	1 tablespoon flour
1 Liederkranz	1 cup cream
⅛ pound imported Roquefort	½ cup finely chopped olives
¼ pound butter	¼ cup canned pimiento

A sprinkling of cayenne

Depending on whether or not you like the edible rind of Camembert and Liederkranz, you can leave it on, scrape any thick part off, or remove it all. Mash the soft creams together with the Roquefort, butter and flour, using a silver fork. Put the mix into an enameled pan, for anything with a metal surface will turn the cheese black in cooking.

Stir in the cream and keep stirring until you have a smooth, creamy sauce. Strain through sieve or cheesecloth, and mix in the olives and pimiento thoroughly. Sprinkle well with cayenne and put into a pot to mellow for a few days, or much longer.

The name *Schnitzelbank* comes from "school bench," a game. This snappy-sweet pot is specially suited to a beer party and stein songs. It is also the affinity-spread with rye and pumpernickel, and may be served in small sandwiches or on crackers, celery and such, to make appetizing tidbits for cocktails, tea, or cider.

Like the trinity of cheeses that make it, the mixture is eaten best at room temperature, when its flavor is fullest. If kept in the refrigerator, it should be taken out a couple of hours before serving. Since it is a natural cheese mixture, which has gone through no process or doping with preservative, it will not keep more than two weeks. This mellow-sharp mix is the sort of ideal the factory processors shoot at with their olive-pimiento abominations. Once you've potted your own, you'll find it gives the same thrill as garnishing your own Liptauer.

Minnesota Blue

The discovery of sandstone caves in the bluffs along the Mississippi, in and near the Twin Cities of Minnesota, has established a distinctive type of Blue cheese named for the state. Although the Roquefort process of France is followed and the cheese is inoculated in the same way by mold from bread, it can never equal the genuine imported, marked with its red-sheep brand, because the milk used in Minnesota Blue is cow's milk, and the caves are sandstone instead of limestone. Yet this is an excellent Blue cheese in its own right.

Pineapple

Pineapple cheese is named after its shape rather than its flavor, although there are rumors that some pineapple flavor is noticeable near the oiled rind. This flavor does not penetrate through to the Cheddar center. Many makers of processed cheese have tampered with the original, so today you can't be sure of anything except getting a smaller size every year or two, at a higher price. Originally six pounds, the Pineapple has shrunk to nearly six ounces. The proper bright-orange, oiled and shellacked surface is more apt to be a sickly lemon.

Always an ornamental cheese, it once stood in state on the sideboard under a silver bell also made to represent a pineapple. You cut a top slice off the cheese, just as you would off the fruit, and there was a rose-colored, fine-tasting, mellow-hard cheese to spoon out with a special silver cheese spoon or scoop. Between meals the silver top was put on the silver holder and the oiled and shellacked rind kept the cheese moist. Even when the Pineapple was eaten down to the rind the shell served as a dunking bowl to fill with some salubrious cold Fondue or salad.

Made in the same manner as Cheddar with the curd cooked harder, Pineapple's distinction lies in being hung in a net that makes diamond-shaped corrugations on the surface, simulating the sections of the fruit. It is a pioneer American product with almost a century and a half of service since Lewis M. Norton conceived it in 1808 in Litchfield County, Connecticut. There in 1845 he built a factory and made a deserved fortune out of his decorative ingenuity with what before had been plain, unromantic yellow or store cheese.

Perhaps his inspiration came from cone-shaped Cheshire in old England, also called Pineapple cheese, combined with the hanging up of Provolones in Italy that leaves the looser pattern of the four sustaining strings.

Sage, Vermont Sage and Vermont State

The story of Sage cheese, or green cheese as it was called originally, shows the several phases most cheeses have gone through, from their simple, honest beginnings to commercialization, and sometimes back to the real thing.

The English *Encyclopedia of Practical Cookery* has an early Sage recipe:

> This is a species of cream cheese made by adding sage leaves and greening to the milk. A very good receipt for it is given thus: Bruise the tops of fresh young red sage leaves with an equal quantity of spinach leaves and squeeze out the juice. Add this to the extract of rennet and stir into the milk as much as your taste may deem sufficient. Break the curd when it comes, salt it, fill the vat high with it, press for a few hours, and then turn the cheese every day.

Fancy Cheese in America, by Charles A. Publow, records the commercialization of the cheese mentioned above, a century or two later, in 1910:

> Sage cheese is another modified form of the Cheddar variety. Its distinguishing features are a mottled green color and a sage flavor. The usual method of manufacture is as follows: One-third of the total amount of milk is placed in a vat by itself and colored green by the addition of eight to twelve ounces of commercial sage color to each 1,000 pounds of milk. If green corn leaves (unavailable in England) or other substances are used for coloring, the amounts will vary accordingly. The milk is then made up by the regular Cheddar method, as is also the remaining two-thirds, in a separate vat. At the time of removing the whey the green and white curds are mixed. Some prefer, however, to mix the curds at the time of milling, as a more distinct color is secured. After milling, the sage extract flavoring is sprayed over the curd with an atomizer. The curd is then

salted and pressed into the regular Cheddar shapes and sizes.

A very satisfactory Sage cheese is made at the New York State College of Agriculture by simply dropping green coloring, made from the leaves of corn and spinach, upon the curd, after milling. An even green mottling is thus easily secured without additional labor. Sage flavoring extract is sprayed over the curd by an atomizer. One-half ounce of flavoring is usually sufficient for a hundred pounds of curd and can be secured from dairy supply houses.

A modern cheese authority reported on the current (1953) method:

Instead of sage leaves, or tea prepared from them, at present the cheese is flavored with oil of Dalmatian wild sage because it has the sharpest flavor. This piny oil, thujone, is diluted with water, 250 parts to one, and either added to the milk or sprayed over the curds, one-eighth ounce for 500 quarts of milk.

In scouting around for a possible maker of the real thing today, we wrote to Vrest Orton of Vermont, and got this reply:

Sage cheese is one of the really indigenous and best native Vermont products. So far as I know, there is only one factory making it and that is my friend, George Crowley's. He makes a limited amount for my Vermont Country Store. It is the fine old-time full cream cheese, flavored with real sage.

On this hangs a tale. Some years ago I couldn't get enough sage cheese (we never can) so I asked a Wisconsin cheese-maker if he would make some. Said he would but couldn't at that time—because the alfalfa wasn't ripe. I said, "What in hell has alfalfa got to do with sage cheese?" He said, "Well, we flavor the sage cheese with a synthetic sage flavor and then throw in some pieces of chopped-up alfalfa to make it look green."

So I said to hell with that and the next time I saw George Crowley I told him the story and George said, "We don't use synthetic flavor, alfalfa or anything like that."

"Then what do you use, George?" I inquired.

"We use real sage."

"Why?"

"Well, because it's cheaper than that synthetic stuff."

The genuine Vermont Sage arrived. Here are our notes on it:

> Oh, wilderness were Paradise enow! My taste buds come to full flower with the Sage. There's a slight burned savor recalling smoked cheese, although not related in any way. Mildly resinous like that Near East one packed in pine, suggesting the well-saged dressing of a turkey. A round mouthful of luscious mellowness, with a bouquet—a snapping reminder to the nose. And there's just a soupçon of new-mown hay above the green freckles of herb to delight the eye and set the fancy free. So this is the *véritable vert,* green cheese—the moon is made of it! *Vert véritable.* A general favorite with everybody who ever tasted it, for generations of lusty crumblers.

Old-Fashioned Vermont State Store Cheese

We received from savant Vrest Orton another letter, together with some Vermont store cheese and some crackers.

> This cheese is our regular old-fashioned store cheese—it's been in old country stores for generations and we have been pioneers in spreading the word about it. It is, of course, a natural aged cheese, no processing, no fussing, no fooling with it. It's made the same way it was back in 1870, by the old-time Colby method which makes a cheese which is not so dry as Cheddar and also has holes in it, something like Swiss. Also, it ages faster.
>
> Did you know that during the last part of the nineteenth century and part of the twentieth, Vermont was the leading cheese-making state in the Union? When I was a lad, every town in Vermont had one or more cheese factories. Now there are only two left—not counting any that make process. Process isn't cheese!

> The crackers are the old-time store cracker—every Vermonter used to buy a big barrel once a year to set in the buttery and eat. A classic dish is crackers, broken up in a bowl of cold milk, with a hunk of Vermont cheese like this on the side. Grand snack, grand midnight supper, grand anything. These crackers are not sweet, not salt, and as such make a good base for anything—swell with clam chowder, also with toasted cheese. . . .

Tillamook

It takes two pocket-sized, but thick, yellow volumes to record the story of Oregon's great Tillamook. *The Cheddar Box,* by Dean Collins, comes neatly boxed and bound in golden cloth stamped with a purple title, like the rind of a real Tillamook. Volume I is entitled *Cheese Cheddar,* and Volume II is a two-pound Cheddar cheese labeled Tillamook and molded to fit inside its book jacket. We borrowed Volume I from a noted *littérateur,* and never could get him to come across with Volume II. We guessed its fate, however, from a note on the flyleaf of the only tome available: "This is an excellent cheese, full cream and medium sharp, and a unique set of books in which Volume II suggests Bacon's: 'Some books are to be tasted, others to be swallowed, and some few to be chewed and digested.' "

Wisconsin Longhorn

Since we began this chapter with all-American Cheddars, it is only fitting to end with Wisconsin Longhorn, a sort of national standard, even though it's not nearly so fancy or high-priced as some of the regional natives that can't approach its enormous output. It's one of those all-purpose round cheeses that even taste round in your mouth. We are specially partial to it.

Most Cheddars are named after their states. Yet, putting all of these thirty-seven states together, they produce only about half as much as Wisconsin alone.

Besides Longhorn, in Wisconsin there are a dozen regional competitors ranging from White Twin Cheddar, to which no annatto coloring has been added, through Green Bay cheese to Wisconsin Redskin and Martha Washington Aged, proudly set forth by P. H. Kasper of Bear Creek, who is said to have "won more prizes in forty years than any ten cheesemakers put together."

To help guarantee a market for all this excellent apple-pie cheese, the Wisconsin State Legislature made a law about it, recognizing the truth of Eugene Field's jingle:

> Apple pie without cheese
> Is like a kiss without a squeeze.

Small matter in the Badger State when the affinity is made legal and the couple lawfully wedded in Statute No. 160,065. It's still in force:

> *Butter and cheese to be served.* Every person, firm or corporation duly licensed to operate a hotel or restaurant shall serve with each meal for which a charge of twenty-five cents or more is made, at least two-thirds of an ounce of Wisconsin butter and two-thirds of an ounce of Wisconsin cheese.

Besides Longhorn, Wisconsin leads in Limburger. It produces so much Swiss that the state is sometimes called Swissconsin.

Chapter Five

Sixty-five Sizzling Rabbits

That nice little smoky room at the "Salutation," which is even now continually presenting itself to my recollection, with all its associated train of pipes, egg-hot, welsh-rabbits, metaphysics and poetry.

Charles Lamb,
IN A LETTER TO COLERIDGE

Unlike the beginning of the classical Jugged Hare recipe: "First catch your hare!" we modern Rabbit-hunters start off with "First catch your Cheddar!" And some of us go so far as to smuggle in formerly forbidden *fromages* such as Gruyère, Neufchâtel, Parmesan, and mixtures thereof. We run the gamut of personal preferences in selecting the Rabbit cheese itself, from old-time American, yellow or store cheese, to Coon and Canadian-smoked, though all of it is still Cheddar, no matter how you slice it.

Then, too, guests are made to run the gauntlet of all-American trimmings from pin-money pickles to peanut butter, succotash and maybe marshmallows; we add mustard, chili, curry, tabasco and sundry bottled red devils from the grocery store, to add pep and piquance to the traditional cayenne and black pepper. This results in Rabbits that are out of focus, out of order and out of this world.

Among modern sins of omission, the Worcestershire sauce is left out by braggarts who aver that they can take it or leave it. And, in these degenerate days, when it comes to substitutions for the original beer or stale pale ale, we find the gratings of great Cheddars wet down with mere California sherry or even ginger ale—yet so far, thank goodness, no Cokes. And there's tomato juice out of a can into the Rum Tum Tiddy, and sometimes celery soup in place of milk or cream.

In view of all this, we can only look to the standard cookbooks for salvation. These are mostly compiled by women, our thoughtful mothers, wives and sweethearts who have saved the twin Basic Rabbits for us. If it weren't for these Fanny Farmers, the making of a real aboriginal Welsh Rabbit would be a lost art—lost in sporting male attempts to improve upon the original.

The girls are still polite about the whole thing and protectively pervert the original spelling of "Rabbit" to "Rarebit" in their culinary guides. We have heard that once a club of ladies in high society tried to high-pressure the publishers of Mr. Webster's dictionary to change the old spelling in their favor. Yet there is a lot to be said for this more genteel and appetizing rendering of the word, for the Welsh masterpiece is, after all, a very rare bit of cheesemongery, male or female.

Yet in dealing with "Rarebits" the distaff side seldom sets down more than the basic Adam and Eve in a whole Paradise of Rabbits: No. 1, the wild male type made with beer, and No. 2, the mild female made with milk. Yet now that the chafing dish has come back to stay, there's a flurry in the Rabbit warren and the new cooking encyclopedias give up to a dozen variants. Actually there are easily half a gross of valid ones in current esteem.

The two basic recipes are differentiated by the liquid ingredient, but both the beer and the milk are used only one way—warm, or anyway at room temperature. And again for the two, there is but one traditional cheese—Cheddar, ripe, old or merely aged from six months onward. This is also called American, store, sharp, Rabbit, yellow, beer, Wisconsin Longhorn, mouse, and even rat.

The seasoned, sapid Cheddar-type, so indispensable, includes dozens of varieties under different names, regional or commercial. These are easily identified as sisters-under-the-rinds by all five senses:

sight: Golden yellow and mellow to the eye. It's one of those round cheeses that also tastes round in the mouth.

hearing: By thumping, a cheese-fancier, like a melon-picker, can tell if a Cheddar is rich, ripe and ready for the Rabbit. When you hear your dealer say, "It's six months old or more," enough said.

smell: A scent as fresh as that of the daisies and herbs the mother milk cow munched "will hang round it still." Also a slight beery savor.

touch: Crumbly—a caress to the fingers.

taste: The quintessence of this fivefold test. Just cuddle a crumb with your tongue and if it tickles the taste buds it's prime. When it melts in your mouth, that's proof it will melt in the pan.

Beyond all this (and in spite of the school that plumps for the No. 2 temperance alternative) we must point out that beer has a special affinity for Cheddar. The French have clearly established this in their names for Welsh Rabbit, *Fromage Fondue à la Bière* and *Fondue à l'Anglaise.*

To prepare such a cheese for the pan, each Rabbit hound may have a preference all his own, for here the question comes up of how it melts best. Do you shave, slice, dice, shred, mince, chop, cut, scrape or crumble it in the fingers? This will vary according to one's temperament and the condition of the cheese. Generally, for best results it is coarsely grated. When it comes to making all this into a rare bit of Rabbit there is:

The One and Only Method

Use a double boiler, or preferably a chafing dish, avoiding aluminum and other soft metals. Heat the upper pan by simmering water in the lower one, but don't let the water boil up or touch the top pan.

Most, but not all, Rabbits are begun by heating a bit of butter or margarine in the pan in which one cup of roughly grated cheese, usually sharp Cheddar, is melted and mixed with one-half cup of liquid, added gradually. (The butter isn't necessary for a cheese that should melt by itself.)

The two principal ingredients are melted smoothly together and kept from curdling by stirring steadily in one direction only, over an even heat. The spoon used should be of hard wood, sterling silver or porcelain. Never use tin, aluminum or soft metal—the taste may come off to taint the job.

Be sure the liquid is at room temperature, or warmer, and add it gradually, without interrupting the stirring. Do not let it come to the bubbling point, and never let it boil.

Add seasonings only when the cheese is melted, which will take two or three minutes. Then continue to stir in the same direction without an instant's letup, for maybe ten minutes or more, until the Rabbit is smooth. The consistency and velvety smoothness depend a good deal on whether or not an egg, or a beaten yolk, is added.

The hotter the Rabbit is served, the better. You can sizzle the top with a salamander or other branding iron, but in any case set it forth as nearly sizzling as possible, on toast hellishly hot, whether it's browned or buttered on one side or both.

Give a thought to the sad case of the "little dog whose name was Rover, and when he was dead he was dead all over." Something very similar happens with a Rabbit that's allowed to cool down—when it's cold it's cold all over, and you can't resuscitate it by heating.

BASIC WELSH RABBIT

No. 1 (with beer)

2 tablespoons butter
3 cups grated old Cheddar
½ teaspoon English dry mustard
½ teaspoon salt
A dash of cayenne
1 teaspoon Worcestershire sauce
2 egg yolks, lightly beaten with
½ cup light beer or ale
4 slices hot buttered toast

Over boiling water melt butter and cheese together, stirring steadily with a wooden (or other tasteless) spoon in one direction only. Add seasonings and do not interrupt your rhythmic stirring, as you pour in a bit at a time of the beer-and-egg mixture until it's all used up.

It may take many minutes of constant stirring to achieve the essential creamy thickness and then some more to slick it out as smooth as velvet.

Keep it piping hot but don't let it bubble, for a boiled Rabbit is a spoiled Rabbit. Only unremitting stirring (and the best of cheese) will keep it from curdling, getting stringy or rubbery.

Pour the Rabbit generously over crisp, freshly buttered toast and serve instantly on hot plates.

Usually crusts are cut off the bread before toasting, and some aesthetes toast one side only, spreading the toasted side with cold butter for taste contrast. Lay the toast on the hot plate, buttered side down, and pour the Rabbit over the porous untoasted side so it can soak in. (This is recommended in Lady Llanover's recipe, which appears on page 52 of this book.)

Although the original bread for Rabbit toast was white, there is now no limit in choice among whole wheat, graham, rolls, muffins, buns, croutons and crackers, to infinity.

☛ No. 2 (with milk)

For a rich milk Rabbit use ½ cup thin cream, evaporated milk, whole milk or buttermilk, instead of beer as in No. 1. Then, to keep everything bland, cut down the mustard by half or leave it out, and use paprika in place of cayenne. As in No. 1, the use of Worcestershire sauce is optional, although our feeling is that any spirited Rabbit would resent its being left out.

Either of these basic recipes can be made without eggs, and more cheaply, although the beaten egg is a guarantee against stringiness. When the egg is missing, we are sad to record that a teaspoon or so of cornstarch generally takes its place.

Rabbiteers are of two minds about fast and slow heating and stirring, so you'll have to adjust that to your own experience and rhythm. As a rule, the heat is reduced when the cheese is almost melted, and speed of stirring slows when the eggs and last ingredients go in.

Many moderns who have found that monosodium glutamate steps up the flavor of natural cheese, put it in at the start, using one-half teaspoon for each cup of grated Cheddar. When it comes to pepper you are fancy-free. As both black and white pepper are now held in almost equal esteem, you might equip your hutch with twin hand-mills to do the grinding fresh, for this is always worth the trouble. Tabasco sauce is little used and needs a cautious hand, but some addicts can't leave it out any more than they can swear off the Worcestershire.

The school that plumps for malty Rabbits and the other that goes for milky ones are equally emphatic in their choice. So let us consider the compromise of our old friend Frederick Philip Stieff, the Baltimore *homme de bouche,* as he set it forth for us years ago in *10,000 Snacks:* "The idea of cooking a Rabbit with beer is an exploded and dangerous theory. Tap your keg or open your case of ale or beer and serve *with,* not in your Rabbit."

☛ **The Stieff Recipe** BASIC MILK RABBIT

(*completely surrounded by a lake of malt beverages*)

2 cups grated sharp cheese
3 heaping tablespoons butter
1½ cups milk
4 eggs
1 heaping tablespoon mustard
2 teaspoons Worcestershire sauce
Pepper, salt and paprika to taste—then add more of each.

Grease well with butter the interior of your double boiler so that no hard particles of cheese will form in the mixture later and contribute undesirable lumps.

Put cheese, well-grated, into the double boiler and add butter and milk. From this point vigorous stirring should be indulged in until Rabbit is ready for serving.

Prepare a mixture of Worcestershire sauce, mustard, pepper, salt and paprika. These should be beaten until light and then slowly poured into the double boiler. Nothing now remains to be done except to stir and cook down to proper consistency over a fairly slow flame. The finale has not arrived until you can drip the rabbit from the spoon and spell the word *finis* on the surface.

Pour over two pieces of toast per plate and send anyone home who does not attack it at once.

This is sufficient for six gourmets or four gourmands.

Nota bene: A Welsh Rabbit, to be a success, should never be of the consistency whereby it may be used to tie up bundles, nor yet should it bounce if inadvertently dropped on the kitchen floor.

☛ Lady Llanover's Toasted Welsh Rabbit

Cut a slice of the real Welsh cheese made of sheep's and cow's milk; toast it at the fire on both sides, but not so much as to drop (melt). Toast on one side a piece of bread less than ¼ inch thick, to be quite crisp, and spread it very thinly with fresh, cold butter on the toasted side. (It must not be saturated.) Lay the toasted cheese upon the untoasted bread side and serve immediately on a very hot plate. The butter on the toast can, of course, be omitted. (It is more frequently eaten without butter.)

From this original toasting of the cheese many Englishmen still call Welsh Rabbit "Toasted Cheese," but Lady Llanover goes on to point out that the Toasted Rabbit of her Wales and the Melted or Stewed Buck Rabbit of England (which has become our American standard) are as different in the making as the regional cheeses used in them, and she says that while doctors prescribed the toasted Welsh as salubrious for invalids, the stewed cheese of Olde England was "only adapted to strong digestions."

English literature rings with praise for the toasted cheese of Wales and England. There is Christopher North's eloquent "threads of unbeaten gold, shining like gossamer filaments (that may be pulled from its tough and tenacious substance)."

Yet not all of the references are complimentary.

Thus Shakespeare in *King Lear:*

> Look, look a mouse!
> Peace, peace;—this piece of toasted cheese will do it.

And Sydney Smith's:

> Old friendships are destroyed by toasted cheese, and hard salted meat has led to suicide.

But Rhys Davis in *My Wales* makes up for such rudenesses:

> *The Welsh Enter Heaven*
>
> The Lord had been complaining to St. Peter of the dearth of good singers in Heaven. "Yet," He said testily, "I hear excellent singing outside the walls. Why are not those singers here with me?"
>
> St. Peter said, "They are the Welsh. They refuse to come in; they say they are happy enough outside, playing with a ball and boxing and singing such songs as '*Suspan Fach.*' "
>
> The Lord said, "I wish them to come in here to sing Bach and Mendelssohn. See that they are in before sundown."
>
> St. Peter went to the Welsh and gave them the commands of the Lord. But still they shook their heads. Harassed, St. Peter went to consult with St. David, who, with a smile, was reading the works of Caradoc Evans.
>
> St. David said, "Try toasted cheese. Build a fire just inside the gates and get a few angels to toast cheese in front of it." This St. Peter did. The heavenly aroma of the sizzling, browning cheese was wafted over the walls and, with loud shouts, a great concourse of the Welsh came sprinting in. When sufficient were inside to make up a male voice choir of a hundred, St. Peter slammed the gates. However, it is said that these are the only Welsh in Heaven.

And, lest we forget, the wonderful drink that made Alice grow and grow to the ceiling of Wonderland contained not only strawberry jam but toasted cheese.

Then there's the frightening nursery rhyme:

> The Irishman loved usquebaugh,
> The Scot loved ale called Bluecap.
> The Welshman, he loved toasted cheese,
> And made his mouth like a mousetrap.
>
> The Irishman was drowned in usquebaugh,
> The Scot was drowned in ale,
> The Welshman he near swallowed a mouse
> But he pulled it out by the tail.

And, perhaps worst of all, Shakespeare, no cheese-lover, this time in *Merry Wives of Windsor:*

> 'Tis time I were choked by a bit of toasted cheese.

An elaboration of the simple Welsh original went English with Dr. William Maginn, the London journalist whose facile pen enlivened the *Blackwood's Magazine* era with *Ten Tales:*

☛ Dr. Maginn's Rabbit

> Much is to be said in favor of toasted cheese for supper. It is the cant to say that Welsh rabbit is heavy eating. I like it best in the genuine Welsh way, however—that is, the toasted bread buttered on both sides profusely, then a layer of cold roast beef with mustard and horseradish, and then, on the top of all, the superstratum of Cheshire *thoroughly* saturated, while in the process of toasting, with genuine porter, black pepper, and shallot vinegar. I peril myself upon the assertion that this is not a heavy supper for a man who has been busy all day till dinner in reading, writing, walking or riding—who has occupied himself between dinner and supper in the discussion of a bottle or two of sound wine, or any equivalent—and who proposes to swallow at least three tumblers of something hot ere he resigns himself to the embrace of Somnus. With these provisos, I recommend toasted cheese for supper.

The popularity of this has come down to us in the succinct summing-up, "Toasted cheese hath no master."

The Welsh original became simple after Dr. Maginn's supper sandwich was served, a century and a half ago; for it was served as a savory to sum up and help digest a dinner, in this form:

☛ **After-Dinner Rabbit**

> Remove all crusts from bread slices, toast on both sides and soak to saturation in hot beer. Melt thin slices of sharp old cheese in butter in an iron skillet, with an added spot of beer and dry English mustard. Stir steadily with a wooden spoon and, when velvety, serve a-sizzle on piping hot beer-soaked toast.

While toasted cheese undoubtedly was the Number One dairy dish of Anglo-Saxons, stewed cheese came along to rival it in Elizabethan London. This sophisticated, big-city dish, also called a Buck Rabbit, was the making of Ye Olde Cheshire Cheese on Fleet Street, where Dr. Johnson later presided. And it must have been the pick of the town back in the days when barrooms still had sawdust on the floor, for the learned Doctor endorsed old Omar Khayyam's love of the pub with: "There is nothing which has been contrived by man by which so much happiness is produced as by a good tavern." Yet he was no gourmet, as may be judged by his likening of a succulent, golden-fried oyster to "a baby's ear dropped in sawdust."

Perhaps it is just as well that no description of the world's first Golden Buck has come down from him. But we don't have to look far for on-the-spot pen pictures by other men of letters at "The Cheese," as it was affectionately called. To a man they sang praises for that piping hot dish of preserved and beatified milk.

Inspired by stewed cheese, Mark Lemon, the leading rhymester of *Punch,* wrote the following poem and dedicated it to the memory of Lovelace:

Champagne will not a dinner make,
Nor caviar a meal.
Men gluttonous and rich may take
Those till they make them ill.
If I've potatoes to my chop,
And after chop have cheese,
Angels in Pond and Spiers's shop
Know no such luxuries.

All that's necessary is an old-time "cheese stewer" or a reasonable substitute. The base of this is what was once quaintly called a "hot-water bath." This was a sort of miniature wash boiler just big enough to fit in snugly half a dozen individual tins, made squarish and standing high enough above the bath water to keep any of it from getting into the stew. In these tins the cheese is melted. But since such a tinsmith's contraption is hard to come by in these days of fireproof cooking glass, we suggest muffin tins, ramekins or even small cups to crowd into the bottom of your double boiler or chafing dish. But beyond this we plump for a revival of the "cheese stewer" in stainless steel, silver or glass.

In the ritual at "The Cheese," these dishes, brimming over, "bubbling and blistering with the stew," followed a pudding that's still famous. Although down the centuries the recipe has been kept secret, the identifiable ingredients have been itemized as follows: "Tender steak, savory oyster, seductive kidney, fascinating lark, rich gravy, ardent pepper and delicate paste"—not to mention mushrooms. And after the second or third helping of pudding, with a pint of stout, bitter, or the mildest and mellowest brown October Ale in a dented pewter pot, "the stewed Cheshire cheese."

Cheese was the one and only other course prescribed by tradition and appetite from the time when Charles II aled and regaled Nell Gwyn at "The Cheese," where Shakespeare is said to have sampled this "kind of a glorified Welsh Rarebit, served piping hot in the square shallow tins in which it is cooked and garnished with sippets of delicately colored toast."

Among early records is this report of Addison's in *The Spectator* of September 25, 1711:

> They yawn for a Cheshire cheese, and begin about midnight, when the whole company is disposed to be drowsy. He that yawns widest, and at the same time so naturally as to produce the most yawns amongst his spectators, carries home the cheese.

Only a short time later, in 1725, the proprietor of Simpson's in the Strand inaugurated a daily guessing contest that drew crowds to his fashionable eating and drinking place. He would set forth a huge portion of cheese and wager champagne and cigars for the house that no one present could correctly estimate the weight, height and girth of it.

As late as 1795, when Boswell was accompanying Dr. Johnson to "The Cheese," records of St. Dunstan's Club, which also met there, showed that the current price of a Buck Rabbit was tuppence, and that this was also the amount of the usual tip.

Ye Original Recipe

1½ ounces butter
1 cup cream
1½ cups grated Cheshire cheese (more pungent, snappier, richer, and more brightly colored than its first cousin, Cheddar)

Heat butter and cream together, then stir in the cheese and let it stew.

You dunk fingers of toast directly into your individual tin, or pour the Stewed Rabbit over toast and brown the top under a blistering salamander.

The salamander is worth modernizing, too, so you can brand your own Rabbits with your monogram or the design of your own Rabbitry. Such a branding iron might be square, like the stew tin, and about the size of a piece of toast.

It is notable that there is no beer or ale in this recipe, but not lamentable, since all aboriginal cheese toasts were washed down in tossing seas of ale, beer, porter, stout, and 'arf and 'arf.

This creamy Stewed Buck, on which the literary greats of Johnson's time supped while they smoked their church wardens, received its highest praise from an American newspaper woman who rhapsodized in 1891: "Then came stewed cheese, on the thin shaving of crisp, golden toast in hot silver saucers—so hot that the cheese was the substance of thick cream, the flavor of purple pansies and red raspberries commingled."

This may seem a bit flowery, but in truth many fine cheeses hold a trace of the bouquet of the flowers that have enriched the milk. Alpine blooms and herbs haunt the Gruyère, Parmesan wafts the scent of Parma violets, the Flower Cheese of England is perfumed with the petals of rose, violet, marigold and jasmine.

☛ **Oven Rabbit** (FROM AN OLD RECIPE)

Chop small ½ pound of cooking cheese. Put it, with a piece of butter the size of a walnut, in a little saucepan, and as the butter melts and the cheese gets warm, mash them together.

When softened add 2 yolks of eggs, ½ teacupful of ale, a little cayenne pepper and salt. Stir with a wooden spoon one way only, until it is creamy, but do not let it boil, for that would spoil it. Place some slices of buttered toast on a dish, pour the Rarebit upon them, and set inside the oven about 2 minutes before serving.

☛ **Yorkshire Rabbit**

(*originally called Gherkin Buck, from a pioneer recipe*)

Put into a saucepan ½ pound of cheese, sprinkle with pepper (black, of course) to taste, pour over ½ teacup of ale, and convert the whole into a smooth, creamy mass, over the fire, stirring continually, for about 10 minutes.

In 2 more minutes it should be done. (10 minutes altogether is the minimum.) Pour it over slices of hot toast, place a piece of broiled bacon on the top of each and serve as hot as possible.

☛ Golden Buck

A Golden Buck is simply the Basic Welsh Rabbit with beer (No. 1) plus a poached egg on top. The egg, sunny side up, gave it its shining name a couple of centuries ago. Nowadays some chafing dish show-offs try to gild the Golden Buck with dashes of ginger and spice.

☛ Golden Buck II

This is only a Golden Buck with the addition of bacon strips.

☛ The Venerable Yorkshire Buck

Spread ½-inch slices of bread with mustard and brown in hot oven. Then moisten each slice with ½ glass of ale, lay on top a slice of cheese ¼-inch thick, and 2 slices of bacon on top of that. Put back in oven, cook till cheese is melted and the bacon crisp, and serve piping hot, with tankards of cold ale.

Bacon is the thing that identifies any Yorkshire Rabbit.

☛ Yale College Welsh Rabbit (MORIARTY'S)

- 1 jigger of beer
- ¼ teaspoon salt
- ¼ teaspoon black pepper
- ¼ teaspoon mustard
- 1½ cups grated or shaved cheese
- More beer

Pour the jigger of beer into "a low saucepan," dash on the seasonings, add the cheese and stir unremittingly, moistening from time to time with more beer, a pony or two at a time.

When creamy, pour over buttered toast (2 slices for this amount) and serve with still more beer.

There are two schools of postgraduate Rabbit-hunters: Yale, as above, with beer both in the Rabbit and with it; and the other featured in the Stieff Recipe, which prefers leaving it out of the Rabbit, but taps a keg to drink with it.

The ancient age of Moriarty's campus classic is registered by the use of pioneer black pepper in place of white, which is often used today and is thought more sophisticated by some than the red cayenne of Rector's Naughty Nineties Chafing Dish Rabbit, which is precisely the same as our Basic Recipe No. 1.

☛ **Border-hopping Bunny, or Frijole Rabbit**

1½ tablespoons butter
1½ tablespoons chopped onion
2 tablespoons chopped pepper, green or red, or both
1½ teaspoon chili powder
1 small can kidney beans, drained
1½ tablespoons catsup
½ teaspoon Worcestershire
Salt
2 cups grated cheese

Cook onion and pepper lightly in butter with chili powder; add kidney beans and seasonings and stir in the cheese until melted.

Serve this beany Bunny peppery hot on tortillas or crackers, toasted and buttered.

In the whole hutch of kitchen Rabbitry the most popular modern ones are made with tomato, a little or lots. They hop in from everywhere, from Mexico to South Africa, and call for all kinds of quirks, down to mixing in some dried beef, and there is even a skimpy Tomato Rabbit for reducers, made with farmer cheese and skimmed milk.

Although the quaintly named Rum Tum Tiddy was doubtless the great-grandpappy of all Tomato Rabbits, a richer, more buttery and more eggy one has taken its place as the standard today. The following is a typical recipe for this, tried and true, since it has had a successful run through a score of the best modern cookbooks, with only slight personal changes to keep its juice a-flowing blood-red.

☛ Tomato Rabbit

- 2 tablespoons butter
- 2 tablespoons flour
- ¾ cup thin cream or evaporated milk
- ¾ cup canned tomato pulp, rubbed through a sieve to remove seeds
- A pinch of soda
- 3 cups grated cheese
- Pinches of dry mustard, salt and cayenne
- 2 eggs, lightly beaten

Blend flour in melted butter, add cream slowly, and when this white sauce is a little thick, stir in tomato sprinkled with soda. Keep stirring steadily while adding cheese and seasonings, and when cooked enough, stir in the eggs to make a creamy texture, smooth as silk. Serve on buttered whole wheat or graham bread for a change.

Instead of soda, some antiquated recipes call for "a tablespoon of bicarbonate of potash."

☛ South African Tomato Rabbit

This is the same as above, except that ½ teaspoon of sugar is used in place of the soda and the Rabbit is poured over baked pastry cut into squares and sprinkled with parsley, chopped fine, put in the oven and served immediately.

☛ Rum Tum Tiddy, Rink Tum Ditty, etc. (OLD BOSTON STYLE)

- 1 tablespoon butter
- 1 onion, minced
- 1 teaspoon salt
- 1 big pinch of pepper
- 2 cups cooked tomatoes
- 1 tablespoon sugar
- 3 cups grated store cheese
- 1 egg, lightly beaten

Slowly fry onion bright golden in butter, season and add tomatoes with sugar. Heat just under the bubbling point. Don't let it boil, but keep adding cheese and shaking the pan until it melts. Then stir in egg gently and serve very hot.

Tomato Soup Rabbit

1 can condensed tomato soup
2 cups grated cheese
¼ teaspoon English mustard
1 egg, lightly beaten
Salt and pepper

Heat soup, stir in cheese until melted, add mustard and egg slowly, season and serve hot.

This is a quickie Rum Tum Tiddy, without any onion, a poor, housebroken version of the original. It can be called a Celery Rabbit if you use a can of celery soup in place of the tomato.

Onion Rum Tum Tiddy

Prepare as in Rum Tum Tiddy, but use only 1½ cups cooked tomatoes and add ½ cup of mashed boiled onions.

Sherry Rum Tum Tiddy

1 tablespoon butter
1 small onion, minced
1 small green pepper, minced
1 can tomato soup
¾ cup milk
3 cups grated cheese
½ teaspoon Worcestershire sauce
Salt and pepper
1 egg, lightly beaten
1 jigger sherry
Crackers

Prepare as in Rum Tum Tiddy. Stir in sherry last to retain its flavor. Crumble crackers into a hot tureen until it's about ⅓ full and pour the hot Rum Tum Tiddy over them.

☛ Blushing Bunny

This is a sister-under-the-skin to the old-fashioned Rum Tum Tiddy, except that her complexion is made a little rosier with a lot of paprika in place of plain pepper, and the paprika cooked in from the start, of course.

Blushing Bunny is one of those playful English names for dishes, like Pink Poodle, Scotch Woodcock (given below), Bubble and Squeak (*Bubblum Squeakum*), and Toad in the Hole.

☛ Scotch Woodcock

Another variant of Rum Tum Tiddy. Make your Rum Tum Tiddy, but before finishing up with the beaten egg, stir in 2 heaping tablespoons of anchovy paste and prepare the buttered toast by laying on slices of hard-cooked eggs.

☛ American Woodchuck

1½ cups tomato purée
2 cups grated cheese
1 egg, lightly beaten
Cayenne
1 tablespoon brown sugar
Salt and pepper

Heat the tomato and stir in the cheese. When partly melted stir in the egg and, when almost cooked, add seasonings without ever interrupting the stirring. Pour over hot toasted crackers or bread.

No doubt this all-American Tomato Rabbit with brown sugar was named after the native woodchuck, in playful imitation of the Scotch Woodcock above. It's the only Rabbit we know that's sweetened with brown sugar.

☛ Running Rabbit

(*as served at the Waldorf-Astoria, First Annual Cheeselers Field Day, November 12, 1937*)

Cut finest old American cheese in very small pieces and melt in saucepan with a little good beer. Season and add Worcestershire sauce. Serve instantly with freshly made toast.

This running cony can be poured over toast like any other Rabbit, or over crushed crackers in a hot tureen, as in Sherry Rum Tum Tiddy, or served like Fondue, in the original cooking bowl or pan, with the spoon kept moving in it in one direction only and the Rabbit following the spoon, like a greyhound following the stuffed rabbit at the dog races.

☛ **Mexican Chilaly**

1 tablespoon butter
3 tablespoons chopped green pepper
1½ tablespoons chopped onion
1 cup chopped and drained canned tomatoes, without seeds
2½ cups grated cheese
¾ teaspoon salt
Dash of cayenne
1 egg, lightly beaten
2 tablespoons canned tomato juice
Water cress

Cook pepper and onion lightly in butter, add tomato pulp and cook 5 minutes before putting over boiling water and stirring steadily as you add cheese and seasonings. Moisten the egg with the tomato juice and stir in until the Rabbit is thick and velvety.

Serve on toast and dress with water cress.

This popular modern Rabbit seems to be a twin to Rum Tum Tiddy in spite of the centuries' difference in age.

☛ **Fluffy, Eggy Rabbit**

Stir up a Chilaly as above, but use 2 well-beaten eggs to make it more fluffy, and leave out the watercress. Serve it hot over cold slices of hard-cooked eggs crowded flat on hot buttered toast, to make it extra eggy.

☛ Grilled Tomato Rabbit

Slice big, red, juicy tomatoes ½-inch thick, season with salt, pepper and plenty of brown sugar. Dot both sides with all the butter that won't slip off.

Heat in moderate oven, and when almost cooked, remove and broil on both sides. Put on hot plates in place of the usual toast and pour the Rabbit over them. (The Rabbit is made according to either Basic Recipe No. 1 or No. 2.)

Slices of crisp bacon on top of the tomato slices and a touch of horseradish help.

☛ Grilled Tomato and Onion Rabbit

Slice ¼-inch thick an equal number of tomato and onion rings. Season with salt, pepper, brown sugar and dots of butter. Heat in moderate oven, and when almost cooked remove and broil lightly.

On hot plates lay first the onion rings, top with the tomato ones and pour the Rabbit over, as in the plain Grilled Tomato recipe above.

For another onion-flavored Rabbit see Celery and Onion Rabbit.

☛ The Devil's Own

(*a fresh tomato variant*)

2 tablespoons butter
1 large peeled tomato in 4 thick slices
2½ cups grated cheese
¼ teaspoon English mustard
A pinch of cayenne
A dash of tabasco sauce
2 tablespoons chili sauce
½ cup ale or beer
1 egg, lightly beaten

Sauté tomato slices lightly on both sides in 1 tablespoon butter. Keep warm on hot platter while you make the toast and a Basic

Rabbit, pepped up by the extra-hot seasonings listed above. Put hot tomato slices on hot toast on hot plates; pour the hot mixture over.

☛ Dried Beef or Chipped Beef Rabbit

1 tablespoon butter
1 cup canned tomato, drained, chopped and de-seeded
¼ pound dried beef, shredded
2 eggs, lightly beaten
¼ teaspoon pepper
2 cups grated cheese

Heat tomato in butter, add beef and eggs, stir until mixed well, then sprinkle with pepper, stir in the grated cheese until smooth and creamy. Serve on toast.

No salt is needed on this jerked steer meat that is called both dried beef and chipped beef on this side of the border, *tasajo* on the other side, and *xarque* when you get all the way down to Brazil.

☛ Kansas Jack Rabbit

1 cup milk
3 tablespoons butter
3 tablespoons flour
2 cups grated cheese
1 cup cream-style corn
Salt and pepper

Make a white sauce of milk, butter and flour and stir in cheese steadily and gradually until melted. Add corn and season to taste. Serve on hot buttered toast.

Kansas has plenty of the makings for this, yet the dish must have been easier to make on Baron Münchhausen's "Island of Cheese," where the cornstalks produced loaves of bread, ready-made, instead of ears, and were no doubt crossed with long-eared jacks to produce Corn Rabbits quite as miraculous.

After tomatoes, in popularity, come onions and then green peppers or canned pimientos as vegetable ingredients in modern, Americanized Rabbits. And after that, corn, as in the following recipe which appeals to all Latin-Americans from Mexico to Chile because it has everything.

☛ Latin-American Corn Rabbit

- 2 tablespoons butter
- 1 green pepper, chopped
- 1 large onion, chopped
- ½ cup condensed tomato soup
- 3 cups grated cheese
- 1 teaspoon salt
- ¼ teaspoon black pepper
- ½ teaspoon Worcestershire sauce
- 1 cup canned corn
- 1 egg, lightly beaten

Fry pepper and onion 5 minutes in butter; add soup, cover and cook 5 minutes more. Put over boiling water; add cheese with seasonings and stir steadily, slowly adding the corn, and when thoroughly blended and creamy, moisten the egg with a little of the liquid, stir in until thickened and then pour over hot toast or crackers.

☛ Mushroom-Tomato Rabbit

In one pan commence frying in butter 1 cup of sliced fresh mushrooms, and in another make a Rabbit by melting over boiling water 2 cups of grated cheese with ½ teaspoon salt and ½ teaspoon paprika. Stir steadily and, when partially melted, stir in a can of condensed tomato soup, previously heated. Then add the fried mushrooms slowly, stir until creamy and pour over hot toast or crackers.

☛ Celery and Onion Rabbit

- ½ cup chopped hearts of celery
- 1 small onion, chopped
- 1 tablespoon butter
- 1½ cups grated sharp cheese
- Salt and pepper

In a separate pan boil celery and onion until tender. Meanwhile, melt cheese with butter and seasonings and stir steadily. When nearly done stir the celery and onion in gradually, until smooth and creamy.

Pour over buttered toast and brown with a salamander or under the grill.

☛ Asparagus Rabbit

Make as above, substituting a cupful of tender sliced asparagus tops for the celery and onion.

☛ Oyster Rabbit

2 dozen oysters and their liquor
1 teaspoon butter
1 large pinch of salt
1 small pinch of cayenne
3 cups grated cheese
2 eggs, lightly beaten

Heat oysters until edges curl and put aside to keep warm while you proceed to stir up a Rabbit. When cheese is melted add the eggs with some of the oyster liquor and keep stirring. When the Rabbit has thickened to a smooth cream, drop in the warm oysters to heat a little more, and serve on hot buttered toast.

☛ Sea-food Rabbits

(*crab, lobster, shrimp, scallops, clams, mussels, abalone, squid, octopi; anything that swims in the sea or crawls on the bottom of the ocean*)

Shred, flake or mince a cupful of any freshly cooked or canned sea food and save some of the liquor, if any. Make according to Oyster Rabbit recipe above.

Instead of using only one kind of sea food, try several, mixed according to taste. Spike this succulent Sea Rabbit with horseradish or a dollop of sherry, for a change.

☛ "Bouquet of the Sea" Rabbit

The seafaring Portuguese set the style for this lush bouquet of as many different kinds of cooked fish (tuna, cod, salmon, etc.) as can be sardined together in the whirlpool of melted cheese in the chafing dish. They also accent it with tidbits of sea food as above.

☛ Other Fish Rabbit, Fresh or Dried

Any cooked fresh fish, flaked or shredded, from the alewife to the whale, or cooked dried herring, finnan haddie, mackerel, cod, and so on, can be stirred in to make a basic Rabbit more tasty. Happy combinations are hit upon in mixing leftovers of several kinds by the cupful. So the odd old cookbook direction, "Add a cup of fish," takes on new meaning.

☛ Grilled Sardine Rabbit

Make a Basic Rabbit and pour it over sardines, skinned, boned, halved and grilled, on buttered toast.

Similarly cooked fillets of any small fish will make as succulent a grilled Rabbit.

☛ Roe Rabbits

Slice cooked roe of shad or toothsome eggs of other fish, grill on toast, butter well and pour a Basic Rabbit over. Although shad roe is esteemed the finest, there are many other sapid ones of salmon, herring, flounder, cod, etc.

☛ Plain Sardine Rabbit

Make Basic Rabbit with only 2 cups of cheese, and in place of the egg yolks and beer, stir in a large tin of sardines, skinned, boned and flaked.

☛ Anchovy Rabbit

Make Basic Rabbit, add 1 tablespoon of imported East Indian chutney with the egg yolks and beer at the finish, spread toast thickly with anchovy paste and butter, and pour the Rabbit over.

☛ Smoked sturgeon, whiting, eel, smoked salmon, and the like

Lay cold slices or flakes of any fine smoked fish (and all of them are fine) on hot buttered toast and pour a Basic Rabbit over the fish.

The best combination we ever tasted is made by laying a thin slice of smoked salmon over a thick one of smoked sturgeon.

☛ Smoked Cheddar Rabbit

With or without smoked fish, Rabbit-hunters whose palates crave the savor of a wisp of smoke go for a Basic Rabbit made with smoked Cheddar in place of the usual aged, but unsmoked, Cheddar. We use a two-year-old that Phil Alpert, Mr. Cheese himself, brings down from Canada and has specially smoked in the same savory room where sturgeon is getting the works. So his Cheddar absorbs the de luxe flavor of six-dollar-per-pound sturgeon and is sold for a fraction of that.

And just in case you are fishing around for something extra special, serve this smoky Rabbit on oven-browned Bombay ducks, those crunchy flat toasts of East Indian fish.

Or go Oriental by accompanying this with cups of smoky Lapsang Soochong China tea.

☛ Crumby Rabbit

1 tablespoon butter
2 cups grated cheese
1 cup stale bread crumbs soaked with
1 cup milk
1 egg, lightly beaten
Salt
Cayenne
Toasted crackers

Melt cheese in butter, stir in the soaked crumbs and seasonings. When cooked smooth and creamy, stir in the egg to thicken the mixture and serve on toasted crackers, dry or buttered, for contrast with the bread.

Some Rabbiteers monkey with this, lacing it with half a cup of catsup, making a sort of pink baboon out of what should be a white monkey.

There is a cult for Crumby Rabbits variations on which extend all the way to a deep casserole dish called Baked Rabbit and consisting of alternate layers of stale bread crumbs and grated-cheese crumbs. This illegitimate three-layer Rabbit is moistened with eggs beaten up with milk, and seasoned with salt and paprika.

☛ Crumby Tomato Rabbit

2 teaspoons butter
2 cups grated cheese
½ cup soft bread crumbs
1 cup tomato soup
Salt and pepper
1 egg, lightly beaten

Melt cheese in butter, moisten bread crumbs with the tomato soup and stir in; season, add egg and keep stirring until velvety. Serve on toasted crackers, as a contrast to the bread crumbs.

☛ Gherkin or Irish Rabbit

2 tablespoons butter
2 cups grated cheese
½ cup milk (or beer)
A dash of vinegar
½ teaspoon mustard
Salt and pepper
⅓ cup chopped gherkin pickles

Melt cheese in butter, steadily stir in liquid and seasonings. Keep stirring until smooth, then add the pickles and serve.

This may have been called Irish after the green of the pickle.

☛ Dutch Rabbit

Melt thin slices of any good cooking cheese in a heavy skillet with a little butter, prepared mustard, and a splash of beer.

Have ready some slices of toast soaked in hot beer or ale and pour the Rabbit over them.

The temperance version of this substitutes milk for beer and delicately soaks the toast in hot water instead.

Proof that there is no Anglo-Saxon influence here lies in the use of prepared mustard. The English, who still do a lot of things the hard way, mix their biting dry mustard fresh with water before every meal, while the Germans and French bottle theirs, as we do.

☛ Pumpernickel Rabbit

This German deviation is made exactly the same as the Dutch Rabbit above, but its ingredients are the opposite in color. Black bread (pumpernickel) slices are soaked in heated dark beer (porter or stout) and the yellow cheese melted in the skillet is also stirred up with brunette beer.

Since beer is a kind of liquid bread, it is natural for the two to commingle in Rabbits whether they are blond Dutch or black pumpernickel. And since cheese is only solid milk, and the Cheddar is noted for its beery smell, there is further affinity here. An old English proverb sums it up neatly: "Bread and cheese are the two targets against death."

By the way, the word pumpernickel is said to have been coined when Napoleon tasted his first black bread in Germany. Contemptuously he spat it out with: "This would be good for my horse, Nicole." "*Bon pour Nicole*" in French.

☛ Gruyère Welsh Rabbit *au gratin*

Cut crusts from a half-dozen slices of bread. Toast them lightly, lay in a roasting pan and top each with a matching slice of imported Gruyère ⅜-inch thick. Pepper to taste and cover with bread crumbs. Put in oven 10 minutes and rush to the ultimate consumer.

To our American ears anything *au gratin* suggests "with cheese," so this Rabbit *au gratin* may sound redundant. To a Frenchman, however, it means a dish covered with bread crumbs.

☛ Swiss Cheese Rabbit

- ½ cup white wine, preferably Neufchâtel
- ½ cup grated Gruyère
- 1 teaspoon Worcestershire sauce
- ½ saltspoon paprika
- 2 egg yolks

Stir wine and seasonings together with the cheese until it melts, then thicken with the egg yolks, stirring at least 3 more minutes until smooth.

☛ Sherry Rabbit

- 3 cups grated cheese
- ½ cup cream or evaporated milk
- ½ cup sherry
- ¼ teaspoon English mustard
- ½ teaspoon Worcestershire sauce
- A dash of paprika

Heat cheese over hot water, with or without a bit of butter, and when it begins to melt, stir in the cream. Keep stirring until almost all of the cheese is melted, then add sherry. When smooth and creamy, stir in the mustard and Worcestershire sauce, and after pouring over buttered toast dash with paprika for color.

☛ Spanish Sherry Rabbit

3 tablespoons butter
3 tablespoons flour
1 bouillon cube, mashed
½ teaspoon salt
½ teaspoon dry mustard
1½ cups milk
1½ cups grated cheese
1 jigger sherry

Make a smooth paste of butter, flour, bouillon cube and seasonings, and add milk slowly. When well-heated stir in the cheese gradually. Continue stirring at least 10 minutes, and when well-blended stir in the sherry and serve on hot, buttered toast.

☛ Pink Poodle

2 tablespoons butter
1 tablespoon chopped onion
1 tablespoon flour
1 jigger California claret
1 cup cream of tomato soup
A pinch of soda
½ teaspoon dry mustard
½ teaspoon salt
1 teaspoon paprika
A dash of powdered cloves
3 cups grated cheese
1 egg, lightly beaten

Cook onion in butter until light golden, then blend in flour, wine and soup with the soda and all seasonings. Stir in cheese slowly until melted and finish off by thickening with the egg and stirring until smooth and velvety. Serve on crisp, buttered toast with a dry red wine.

Although wine Rabbits, red or white, are as unusual as Swiss ones with Gruyère in place of Cheddar, wine is commonly drunk with anything from a Golden Buck to a Blushing Bunny. But for most of us, a deep draught of beer or ale goes best with an even deeper draught of the mellow scent of a Cheddar golden-yellow.

☛ Savory Eggy Dry Rabbit

⅛ pound butter	Salt
2 cups grated Gruyère	Pepper
4 eggs, well-beaten	Mustard

Melt butter and cheese together with the beaten eggs, stirring steadily with wooden spoon until soft and smooth. Season and pour over dry toast.

This "dry" Rabbit, in which the volume of the eggs makes up for any lacking liquid, is still served as a savory after the sweets to finish a fine meal in some old-fashioned English homes and hostelries.

☛ Cream Cheese Rabbit

This Rabbit, made with a package of cream cheese, is more scrambled hen fruit than Rabbit food, for you simply scramble a half-dozen eggs with butter, milk, salt, pepper and cayenne, and just before the finish work in the cheese until smooth and serve on crackers—water crackers for a change.

☛ Reducing Rarebit (Tomato Rarebit) *

YIELD: 2 servings. 235 calories per serving.

½ pound farmer cheese
2 eggs
1 level tablespoon powdered milk
1 level teaspoon baking powder
1 teaspoon gelatin or agar powder
4 egg tomatoes, quartered, or 2 tomatoes, quartered
1 teaspoon caraway seeds
¼ teaspoon garlic powder
1 teaspoon parsley flakes
½ head lettuce and/or 1 cucumber
¼ cup wine vinegar
Salt and pepper to taste

* (from *The Low-Calory Cookbook* by Bernard Koten, published by Random House)

Fill bottom of double boiler with water to ¾ mark. Sprinkle salt in upper part of double boiler. Boil over medium flame. When upper part is hot, put in cheese, powdered milk, baking powder, gelatin, caraway seeds and pepper and garlic powder to taste. Mix. Break eggs into this mixture, cook over low flame, continually stirring. Add tomatoes when mixture bubbles and continue cooking and stirring until tomatoes have been cooked soft. Remove to lettuce and/or cucumber (sliced thin) which has been slightly marinated in wine vinegar and sprinkle the parsley flakes over the top of the mixture.

☛ Curry Rabbit

1 tablespoon cornstarch
2 cups milk
2½ cups grated cheese
1 tablespoon minced chives
2 green onions, minced
2 shallots, minced
¼ teaspoon imported curry powder
1 tablespoon chutney sauce

Dissolve cornstarch in a little of the milk and scald the rest over hot water. Thicken with cornstarch mixture and stir in the cheese, chives, onions, shallots, curry and chutney while wooden-spooning steadily until smooth and sizzling enough to pour over buttered toast.

People who can't let well enough alone put cornstarch in Rabbits, just as they add soda to spoil the cooking of vegetables.

☛ Ginger Ale Rabbit

Simply substitute ginger ale for the real thing in the No. 1 Rabbit of all time.

☛ Buttermilk Rabbit

Substitute buttermilk for plain milk in the No. 2 Rabbit. To be consistent, use fresh-cured Buttermilk Cheese, instead of the usual Cheddar of fresh cow's milk. This is milder.

☛ Eggnog Rabbit

2 tablespoons sweet butter
2 cups grated mellow Cheddar
1½ cups eggnog
Dashes of spice to taste.

After melting the cheese in butter, stir in the eggnog and keep stirring until smooth and thickened. Season or not, depending on taste and the quality of eggnog employed.

Ever since the innovation of bottled eggnogs fresh from the milkman in holiday season, such supremely creamy and flavorful Rabbits have been multiplying as fast as guinea pigs.

☛ All-American Succotash Rabbit

1 cup milk
3 tablespoons butter
3 tablespoons flour
3 cups grated cheese
1 cup creamed succotash, strained
Salt and pepper

Make a white sauce of milk, butter and flour and stir in the cheese steadily and gradually until melted. Add the creamed succotash and season to taste.

Serve on toasted, buttered corn bread.

☛ Danish Rabbit

1 quart warm milk
2 cups grated cheese

Stir together to boiling point and pour over piping-hot toast in heated bowl. This is an esteemed breakfast dish in north Denmark.

As in all Rabbits, more or less cheese may be used, to taste.

☛ Easy English Rabbit

Soak bread slices in hot beer. Melt thin slices of cheese with butter in iron frying pan, stir in a few spoonfuls of beer and a bit of prepared mustard. When smoothly melted, pour over the piping-hot, beer-soaked toast.

Chapter Six

The Fondue

There is a conspiracy among the dictionary makers to take the heart out of the Fondue. Webster makes it seem no better than a collapsed soufflé, with his definition:

> **Fondue.** Also, erroneously, *fondu.* A dish made of melted cheese, butter, eggs, and, often, milk and bread crumbs.

Thorndike-Barnhart further demotes this dish, that for centuries has been one of the world's greatest, to "a combination of melted cheese, eggs and butter" and explains that the name comes from the French *fondre,* meaning melt. The latest snub is delivered by the up-to-date *Cook's Quiz* compiled by TV culinary experts:

> A baked dish with eggs, cheese, butter, milk and bread crumbs.

A baked dish, indeed! Yet the Fondue has added to the gaiety and inebriety of nations, if not of dictionaries. It has commanded the respect of the culinary great. Savarin, Boulestin, André Simon, all have hailed its heavenly consistency, all have been regaled with its creamy, nay velvety, smoothness.

A touch of garlic, a dash of kirsch, fresh ground black pepper, nutmeg, black pearl truffles of Bugey, red cayenne pepper, the luscious gravy of roast turkey—such little matters help to make an authentic dunking Fondue, not a baked Fondue, mind you. Jean-Anthelme Brillat-Savarin a century and a half ago brought the original "receipt" with him and spread it around with characteristic generosity during the two years of his exile in New York after the French Revolution. In his monumental *Physiologie du Goût* he records an incident that occurred in 1795:

> Whilst passing through Boston . . . I taught the restaurant-keeper Julien to make a *Fondue,* or eggs cooked with cheese. This dish, a novelty to the Americans, became so much the rage, that he (Julien) felt himself obliged, by way of thanks, to send me to New York the rump of one of those pretty little roebucks that are brought from Canada in winter, and which was declared exquisite by the chosen committee whom I convoked for the occasion.

As the great French gourmet, Savarin was born on the Swiss border (at Belley, in the fertile Province of Bugey, where Gertrude Stein later had a summer home), he no doubt ate Gruyère three times a day, as is the custom in Switzerland and adjacent parts. He sets down the recipe just as he got it from its Swiss source, the papers of Monsieur Trolliet, in the neighboring Canton of Berne:

> Take as many eggs as you wish to use, according to the number of your guests. Then take a lump of good Gruyère cheese, weighing about a third of the eggs, and a nut of butter about half the weight of the cheese. (Since today's eggs in America weigh about 1½ ounces apiece, if you start the Fondue with 8.

> your lump of good Gruyère would come to ¼ pound and your butter to ⅛ pound.)
>
> Break and beat the eggs well in a flat pan, then add the butter and the cheese, grated or cut in small pieces.
>
> Place the pan on a good fire and stir with a wooden spoon until the mixture is fairly thick and soft; put in a little or no salt, according to the age of the cheese, and a good deal of pepper, for this is one of the special attributes of this ancient dish.
>
> Let it be placed on the table in a hot dish, and if some of the best wines be produced, and the bottle passed quite freely, a marvelous effect will be beheld.

This has long been quoted as the proper way to make the national dish of Switzerland. Savarin tells of hearing oldsters in his district laugh over the Bishop of Belley eating his Fondue with a spoon instead of the traditional fork, in the first decade of the 1700's. He tells, too, of a Fondue party he threw for a couple of his septuagenarian cousins in Paris "about the year 1801."

The party was the result of much friendly taunting of the master: "By Jove, Jean, you have been bragging for such a long time about your Fondues, you have continually made our mouths water. It is high time to put a stop to all this. We will come and breakfast with you some day and see what sort of thing this dish is."

Savarin invited them for ten o'clock next day, started them off with the table laid on a "snow white cloth, and in each one's place two dozen oysters with a bright golden lemon. At each end of the table stood a bottle of sauterne, carefully wiped, excepting the cork, which showed distinctly that it had been in the cellar for a long while. . . . After the oysters, which were quite fresh, came some broiled kidneys, a *terrine* of *foie gras*, a pie with truffles, and finally the Fondue. The different ingredients had all been assembled in a stewpan, which was placed on the table over a chafing dish, heated with spirits of wine.

"Then," Savarin is quoted, "I commenced operations on the field of battle, and my cousins did not lose a single one of my movements. They were loud in the praise of this preparation, and asked me to let them have the receipt, which I promised them. . . ."

This Fondue breakfast party that gave the nineteenth century such a good start was polished off with "fruits in season and sweets, a cup of genuine mocha . . . and finally two sorts of liqueurs, one a spirit for cleansing, and the other an oil for softening."

This primitive Swiss Cheese Fondue is now prepared more elaborately in what is called:

☛ Neufchâtel Style

2½ cups grated imported Swiss	1 jigger kirsch
1½ tablespoons flour	Salt
1 clove of garlic	Pepper
1 cup dry white wine	Nutmeg

Crusty French "flute" or hard rolls cut into big mouthfuls, handy for dunking

The cheese should be shredded or grated coarsely and mixed well with the flour. Use a chafing dish for cooking and a small heated casserole for serving. Rub the bottom and sides of the blazer well with garlic, pour in the wine and heat to bubbling, just under boiling. Add cheese slowly, half a cup at a time, and stir steadily in one direction only, as in making Welsh Rabbit. Use a silver fork. Season with very little salt, always depending on how salty the cheese is, but use plenty of black pepper, freshly ground, and a touch of nutmeg. Then pour in the kirsch, stir steadily and invite guests to dunk their forked bread in the dish or in a smaller preheated casserole over a low electric or alcohol burner on the dining table. The trick is to keep the bubbling melted cheese in rhythmic motion with the fork, both up and down and around and around.

The dunkers stab the hunks of crusty French bread through the soft part to secure a firm hold in the crust, for if your bread comes off in dunking you pay a forfeit, often a bottle of wine.

The dunking is done as rhythmically as the stirring, guests taking regular turns at twirling the fork to keep the cheese swirling. When this "chafing dish cheese custard," as it has been called in England, is ready for eating, each in turn thrusts in his fork, sops up a mouthful with the bread for a sponge and gives the Fondue a final stir, to keep it always moving in the same direction. All the while the heat beneath the dish keeps it gently bubbling.

Such a Neufchâtel party was a favorite of King Edward VII, especially when he was stepping out as the Prince of Wales. He was as fond of Fondue as most of the great gourmets of his day and preferred it to Welsh Rabbit, perhaps because of the wine and kirsch that went into it.

At such a party a little heated wine is added if the Fondue gets too thick. When finally it has cooked down to a crust in the bottom of the dish, this is forked out by the host and divided among the guests as a very special dividend.

Any dry white wine will serve in a pinch, and the Switzerland Cheese Association, in broadcasting this classical recipe, points out that any dry rum, slivovitz, or brandy, including applejack, will be a valid substitute for the kirsch. To us, applejack seems specially suited, when we stop to consider our native taste that has married apple pie to cheese since pioneer times.

In culinary usage fondue means "melting to an edible consistency" and this, of course, doesn't refer to cheese alone, although we use it chiefly for that.

In France Fondue is also the common name for a simple dish of eggs scrambled with grated cheese and butter and served very hot on toasted bread, or filled into fancy paper cases, quickly browned on top and served at once. The reason for this is that all baked Fondues fall as easily and as far as Soufflés, although the latter are more noted for this failing. There is a similarity in the soft fluffiness of both, although the Fondues are always more moist. For there is a stiff, stuffed-shirt buildup around any Soufflé, suggesting a dressy dinner, while Fondue started as a self-service dunking bowl.

Our modern tendency is to try to make over the original French Fondue on the Welsh Rabbit model—to turn it into a sort of French Rabbit. Although we know that both Gruyère and Emmentaler are what we call Swiss and that it is impossible in America to duplicate the rich Alpine flavor given by the mountain herbs, we are inclined to try all sorts of domestic cheeses and mixtures thereof. But it's best to stick to Savarin's "lump of Gruyère" just as the neighboring French and Italians do. It is interesting to note that this Swiss Alpine cooking has become so international that it is credited to Italy in the following description we reprint from *When Madame Cooks,* by an Englishman, Eric Weir:

☛ **Fondue à l'Italienne**

This is one of those egg dishes that makes one feel really grateful to hens. From its name it originated probably in Italy, but it has crossed the Alps. I have often met it in France, but only once in Italy.

First of all, make a very stiff white sauce with butter, flour and milk. The sauce should be stiff enough to allow the wooden spoon to stand upright or almost.

Off the fire, add yolks of eggs and 4 ounces of grated Gruyère cheese. Mix this in well with the white sauce and season with salt, pepper and some grated nutmeg. Beat whites of egg firm. Add the whites to the preparation, stir in, and pour into a pudding basin.

Take a large saucepan and fill half full of water. Bring to a boil, and then place the pudding basin so that the top of the basin is well out of the water. Allow to boil gently for 1½ to 2 hours. Renew the boiling water from time to time, as it evaporates, and take care that the water, in boiling, does not bubble over the mixture.

Test with a knife, as for a cake, to see if it is cooked. When the knife comes out clean, take the basin out of the water and turn the Fondue out on a dish. It should be fairly firm and keep the shape of the basin.

Sprinkle with some finely chopped ham and serve hot.

The imported Swiss sometimes is cubed instead of grated, then marinated for four or five hours in dry white wine, before being melted and liquored with the schnapps. This can be pleasantly adopted here in:

☛ All-American Fondue

1 pound imported Swiss cheese, cubed
¾ cup scuppernong or other American white wine
1½ jiggers applejack

After marinating the Swiss cubes in the wine, simply melt together over hot water, stir until soft and creamy, add the applejack and dunk with fingers of toast or your own to a chorus of "All Bound Round with a Woolen String."

Of course, this can be treated as a mere vinous Welsh Rabbit and poured over toast, to be accompanied by beer. But wine is the thing, for the French Fondue is to dry wine what the Rabbit is to stale ale or fresh beer.

We say French instead of Swiss because the French took over the dish so eagerly, together with the great Gruyère that makes it distinctive. They internationalized it, sent it around the world with bouillabaisse and onion soup, that celestial *soupe à l'oignon* on which snowy showers of grated Gruyère descend.

To put the Welsh Rabbit in its place they called it Fondue à l'Anglaise, which also points up the twinlike relationship of the world's two favorite dishes of melted cheese. But to differentiate and show they are not identical twins, the No. 1 dish remained Fromage Fondue while the second was baptized Fromage Fondue à la Bière.

Beginning with Savarin the French whisked up more rapturous, rhapsodic writing about Gruyère and its offspring, the Fondue, together with the puffed Soufflé, than about any other imported cheese except Parmesan.

Parmesan and Gruyère were praised as the two greatest culinary cheeses. A variant Fondue was made of the Italian cheese.

☛ Parmesan Fondue

3 tablespoons butter
1 cup grated Parmesan cheese
4 eggs, lightly beaten
Salt
Pepper

Over boiling water melt butter and cheese slowly, stir in the eggs, season to taste and stir steadily in one direction only, until smooth.

Pour over fingers of buttered toast. Or spoon it up, as the ancients did, before there were any forks. It's beaten with a fork but eaten catch-as-catch-can, like chicken-in-the-rough.

☛ Sapsago Swiss Fondue

2 tablespoons butter
2 tablespoons flour
½ teaspoon salt
1½ cups milk
2½ cups shredded Swiss cheese
2½ tablespoons grated Sapsago
½ cup dry white wine
Pepper, black and red, freshly ground
Fingers of toast

Over boiling water stir the first four ingredients into a smooth, fairly thick cream sauce. Then stir in Swiss cheese until well melted. After that add the Sapsago, finely grated, and wine in small splashes. Stir steadily, in one direction only, until velvety. Season sharply with the contrasting peppers and serve over fingers of toast.

This is also nice when served bubbling in individual, preheated pastry shells, casseroles or ramekins, although this way most of the fun of the dunking party is left out. To make up for it, however, cooked slices of mushrooms are sometimes added.

At the Cheese Cellar in the New York World's Fair Swiss Pavilion, where a continual dunking party was in progress, thousands of amateurs learned such basic things as not to overcook the Fondue lest it become stringy, and the protocol of dunking in turn and keeping the mass in continual motion until the next on the Fondue line dips in his cube of bread. The success of the dish depends on making it quickly, keeping it gently a-bubble and never letting it stand still for a split second.

The Swiss, who consume three or four times as much cheese per capita as we, and almost twice as much as the French, are willing to share Fondue honors with the French Alpine province of Savoy, a natural cheese cellar with almost two dozen distinctive types of its very own, such as Fat cheese, also called Death's Head; La Grande Bornand, a luscious half-dried sheep's milker; Chevrotins, small, dry goat milk cheeses; and Le Vacherin. The latter, made in both Savoy and Switzerland, boasts two interesting variants:

1. *Vacherin Fondue or Spiced Fondue:* Made about the same as Emmentaler, ripened to sharp age, and then melted, spices added and the cheese re-formed. It is also called Spiced Fondue and sells for about two dollars a pound. Named Fondue from being melted, though it's really recooked.

2. *Vacherin à la Main:* This is a curiosity in cheeses, resembling a cold, uncooked Fondue. Made of cow's milk, it is round, a foot in diameter and half a foot high. It is salted and aged until the rind is hard and the inside more runny than the ripest Camembert, so it can be eaten with a spoon (like the cooked Fondue) as well as spread on bread. The local name for it is *Tome de Montagne.*

Here is a good assortment of Fondues:

☛ Vacherin-Fribourg Fondue

2 tablespoons butter
1 clove garlic, crushed
2 cups shredded Vacherin cheese
2 tablespoons hot water

This authentic quickie is started by cooking the garlic in butter until the butter is melted. Then remove garlic and reduce heat. Add the soft cheese and stir with silver fork until smooth and velvety. Add the water in little splashes, stirring constantly in one direction. Dunk! (In this melted Swiss a little water takes the place of a lot of wine.)

☛ La Fondue Comtois

This regional specialty of Franche-Comté is made with white wine. Sauterne, Chablis, Riesling or any Rhenish type will serve splendidly. Also use butter, grated Gruyère, beaten eggs and that touch of garlic.

☛ Chives Fondue

3 cups grated Swiss cheese
3 tablespoons flour
2 tablespoons butter
1 garlic clove, crushed
3 tablespoons finely chopped chives
1 cup dry white wine
Salt
Freshly ground pepper
A pinch of nutmeg
¼ cup kirsch

Mix cheese and flour. Melt butter in chafing-dish blazer rubbed with garlic. Cook chives in butter 1 minute. Add wine and heat just under boiling. Keep simmering as you add cheese-and-flour mix gradually, stirring always in one direction. Salt according to age and sharpness of cheese; add plenty of freshly ground pepper and the pinch of nutmeg.

When everything is stirred smooth and bubbling, toss in the kirsch without missing a stroke of the fork and get to dunking.

Large, crisp, hot potato chips make a pleasant change for dunking purposes. Or try assorted crackers alternating with the absorbent bread, or hard rolls.

☛ Tomato Fondue

- 2 tomatoes, skinned, seeded and chopped
- ½ teaspoon dried sweet basil
- 1 clove garlic
- 2 tablespoons butter
- ½ cup dry white wine
- 2 cups grated Cheddar cheese
- Paprika

Mix basil with chopped tomatoes. Rub chafing dish with garlic, melt butter, add tomatoes and much paprika. Cook 5 to 6 minutes, add wine, stir steadily to boiling point. Then add cheese, half a cup at a time, and keep stirring until everything is smooth.

Serve on hot toast, like Welsh Rabbit.

Here the two most popular melted-cheese dishes tangle, but they're held together with the common ingredient, tomato.

Fondue also appears as a sauce to pour over baked tomatoes. Stale bread crumbs are soaked in tomato juice to make:

☛ Tomato Baked Fondue

- 1 cup tomato juice
- 1 cup stale bread crumbs
- 1 cup grated sharp American cheese
- 1 tablespoon melted butter
- Salt
- 4 eggs, separated and well beaten

Soak crumbs in tomato juice, stir cheese in butter until melted, season with a little or no salt, depending on saltiness of the cheese. Mix in the beaten yolks, fold in the white and bake about 50 minutes in moderate oven.

BAKED FONDUES

Although Savarin's dunking Fondue was first to make a sensation on these shores and is still in highest esteem among epicures, the Fondue America took to its bosom was baked. The original recipe came from the super-caseous province of Savoy under the explicit title, *La Fondue au Fromage.*

☛ La Fondue au Fromage

Make the usual creamy mixture of butter, flour, milk, yolks of eggs and Gruyère, in thin slices for a change. Use red pepper instead of black, splash in a jigger of kirsch but no white wine. Finally fold in the egg whites and bake in a mold for 45 minutes.

We adapted this to our national taste which had already based the whole business of melted cheese on the Welsh Rabbit with stale ale or milk instead of white wine and Worcestershire, mustard and hot peppers. Today we have come up with this:

☛ 100% American Fondue

2 cups scalded milk
2 cups stale bread crumbs
½ teaspoon dry English mustard
Salt
Dash of nutmeg
Dash of pepper
2 cups American cheese (Cheddar)
2 egg yolks, well beaten
2 egg whites, beaten stiff

Soak crumbs in milk, season and stir in the cheese until melted. Add the beaten egg yolks and stir until you have a smooth mixture. Let this cool while beating the whites stiff, leaving them slightly moist. Fold the whites into the cool, custardy mix and bake in a buttered dish until firm. (About 50 minutes in a moderate oven.)

This is more of a baked cheese job than a true Fondue, to our way of thinking, and the scalded milk doesn't exactly take the place of the wine or kirsch. It is characteristic of our bland cookery.

OTHER FONDUES PLAIN AND FANCY, BAKED AND NOT

Quickie Catsup Tummy Fondiddy

¾ pound sharp cheese, diced
1 can condensed tomato soup
½ cup catsup
½ teaspoon mustard
1 egg, lightly beaten

In double boiler melt cheese in soup. Blend thoroughly by constant stirring. Remove from heat, lightly whip or fold in the catsup and mustard mixed with egg. Serve on Melba toast or rusks.

This might be suggested as a novel midnight snack, with a cup of cocoa, for a change.

Cheese and Rice Fondue

1 cup cooked rice
2 cups milk
4 eggs, separated and well beaten
½ cup grated cheese
½ teaspoon salt
Cayenne, Worcestershire sauce or tabasco sauce, or all three

Heat rice (instead of bread crumbs) in milk, stir in cheese until melted, add egg yolks beaten lemon-yellow, season, fold in stiff egg whites. Serve hot on toast.

Corn and Cheese Fondue

1 cup bread crumbs
1 large can creamed corn
1 small onion, chopped
½ green pepper, chopped
2 cups cottage cheese
½ teaspoon salt
½ cup milk
2 eggs, well beaten

Mix all ingredients together and bake in buttered casserole set in pan of hot water. Bake about 1 hour in moderate oven, or until set.

Cheese Fondue

1 cup grated Cheddar
½ cup crumbled Roquefort
1 cup pimento cheese
3 tablespoons cream
3 tablespoons butter
1 teaspoon Worcestershire

Stir everything together over hot water until smooth and creamy. Then whisk until fluffy, moistening with more cream or mayonnaise if too stiff.

Serve on Melba toast, or assorted thin toasted crackers.

Brick Fondue

⅓ cup butter
2 cups grated Brick cheese
⅓ cup warm milk
½ teaspoon salt
2 eggs

Melt butter and cheese together, use wire whisk to whip in the warm milk. Season. Take from fire and beat in the eggs, one at a time. Please note that Fondue protocol calls for each egg to be beaten separately in cases like this.

Serve over hot toast or crackers.

Cheddar Dunk Bowl

¾ pound sharp Cheddar cheese	⅔ teaspoon dry mustard
3 tablespoons cream	1½ teaspoons Worcestershire

Grate the cheese powdery fine and mash it together with the cream until fluffy. Season and serve in a beautiful bowl for dunking in the original style of Savarin, although this is a static imitation of the real thing.

All kinds of crackers and colorful dips can be used, from celery stalks and potato chips to thin paddles cut from Bombay duck.

Chapter Seven

Soufflés, Puffs and Ramekins

There isn't much difference between Cheese Soufflés, Puffs and Ramekins. The *English Encyclopedia of Practical Cookery,* the oldest, biggest and best of such works in English, lumps Cheese Puffs and Ramekins together, giving the same recipes for both, although it treats each extensively under its own name when not made with cheese.

Cheese was the basis of the original French Ramequin, cheese and bread crumbs or puff paste, baked in a mold (with puff again the principal factor in Soufflé, from the French *souffler,* puff up).

Basic Soufflé

3 tablespoons butter or margarine
4 tablespoons flour
1¼ cups hot milk, scalded
1 teaspoon salt
A dash of cayenne
½ cup grated Cheddar cheese, sharp
2 egg yolks, beaten lemon-yellow
2 egg whites, beaten stiff

Melt butter, stir in flour and milk gradually until thick and smooth. Season and add the cheese, continuing the cooking and slow stirring until velvety. Remove from heat and let cool somewhat; then stir in the egg yolks with a light hand and an upward motion. Fold in the stiff whites and when evenly mixed pour into a big, round baking dish. (Some butter it and some don't.) To make sure the top will be even when baked, run a spoon or knife around the surface, about 1 inch from the edge of the dish, before baking slowly in a moderate oven until puffed high and beautifully browned. Serve instantly for fear the Soufflé may fall. The baking takes up to an hour and the egg whites shouldn't be beaten so stiff they are hard to fold in and contain no air to expand and puff up the dish.

To perk up the seasonings, mustard, Worcestershire sauce, lemon juice, nutmeg and even garlic are often used to taste, especially in England.

While Cheddar is the preferred cheese, Parmesan runs it a close second. Then comes Swiss. You may use any two or all three of these together. Sometimes Roquefort is added, as in the Ramekin recipes below.

Parmesan Soufflé

Make the same as Basic Soufflé, with these small modifications in the ingredients:

1 full cup of grated Parmesan in place of the ½ cup of Cheddar cheese
1 extra egg
A little more butter
Black pepper, not cayenne

Swiss Soufflé

Make the same as Basic Soufflé, with these slight changes:

1¼ cups grated Swiss cheese instead of the Cheddar cheese
Nutmeg in place of the cayenne

Parmesan-Swiss Soufflé

Make the same as Basic Soufflé, with these little differences:

½ cup grated Swiss cheese, and ½ cup grated Parmesan in place of the Cheddar cheese
¼ teaspoon each of sugar and black pepper for seasoning.

Any of these makes a light, lovely luncheon or a proper climax to a grand dinner.

Cheese-Corn Soufflé

Make as Basic Soufflé, substituting for the scalded milk 1 cup of sieved and strained juice from cream-style canned corn.

Cheese-Spinach Soufflé

Sauté 1½ cups of finely chopped, drained spinach in butter with 1 teaspoon finely grated onion, and then whip it until light and fluffy. Mix well into the white sauce of the Basic Soufflé before adding the cheese and following the rest of the recipe.

Cheese-Tomato Soufflé

Substitute hot tomato juice for the scalded milk.

Cheese-Sea-food Soufflé

Add 1½ cups finely chopped or ground lobster, crab, shrimp, other sea food or mixture thereof, with any preferred seasoning added.

Cheese-Mushroom Soufflé

1½ cups grated sharp Cheddar
1 cup cream of mushroom soup
Paprika, to taste
Salt
2 egg yolks, well beaten
2 egg whites, beaten stiff
2 tablespoons chopped, cooked bacon
2 tablespoons sliced, blanched almonds

Heat cheese with soup and paprika, adding the cheese gradually and stirring until smooth. Add salt and thicken the sauce with egg yolks, still stirring steadily, and finally fold in the whites. Sprinkle with bacon and almonds and bake until golden brown and puffed high (about 1 hour).

Cheese-Potato Soufflé (Potato Puff)

6 potatoes
2 onions
1 tablespoon butter or margarine
1 cup hot milk
¾ cup grated Cheddar cheese
1 teaspoon salt
A dash of pepper
2 egg yolks, well beaten
2 egg whites, beaten stiff
¼ cup grated Cheddar cheese

Cook potatoes and onions together until tender and put through a ricer. Mix with all the other ingredients except the egg whites and the Cheddar. Fold in the egg whites, mix thoroughly and pour into a buttered baking dish. Sprinkle the ¼ cup of Cheddar on top and bake in moderate oven about ½ hour, until golden-brown and well puffed. Serve instantly.

Variations of this popular Soufflé leave out the onion and simplify matters by using 2 cups of mashed potatoes. Sometimes 1 tablespoon of catsup and another of minced parsley is added to the mixture. Or onion juice alone, to take the place of the cooked onions—about a tablespoon, full or scant.

The English, in concocting such a Potato Puff or Soufflé, are inclined to make it extra peppery, as they do most of their Cheese Soufflés, with not only "a dust of black pepper" but "as much cayenne as may be stood on the face of a sixpence."

☛ Cheese Fritter Soufflés

These combine ham with Parmesan cheese and are even more delicately handled in the making than crêpes suzette.

PUFFS

☛ Three-in-One Puffs

1 cup grated Swiss
1 cup grated Parmesan
1 cup cream cheese
5 eggs, lightly beaten
salt and pepper

Mix the cheeses into one mass moistened with the beaten eggs, splashed on at intervals. When thoroughly incorporated, put in ramekins, tiny tins, cups, or any sort of little mold of any shape. Bake in hot oven about 10 minutes, until richly browned.

Such miniature Soufflés serve as liaison officers for this entire section, since they are baked in ramekins, or ramequins, from the French word for the small baking dish that holds only one portion. These may be paper boxes, usually round, earthenware, china, Pyrex, of any attractive shape in which to bake or serve the Puffs.

More commonly, in America at least, Puffs are made without ramekin dishes, as follows:

☛ Fried Puffs

2 egg whites, beaten stiff
½ cup grated cheese
1 tablespoon flour
Salt
Paprika

Into the stiff egg whites fold the cheese, flour and seasonings. When thoroughly mixed pat into shape desired, roll in crumbs and fry.

☛ Roquefort Puffs

⅛ pound genuine French Roquefort
1 egg white, beaten stiff
8 crackers or 2-inch bread rounds

Cream the Roquefort, fold in the egg white, pile on crackers and bake 15 minutes in slow oven.

The constant repetition of "beaten stiff" in these recipes may give the impression that the whites are badly beaten up, but such is not the case. They are simply whipped to peaks and left moist and glistening as a teardrop, with a slight sad droop to them that shows there is still room for the air to expand and puff things up in cooking.

☛ Parmesan Puffs

Make a spread of mayonnaise or other salad dressing with equal parts of imported Parmesan, grated fine. Spread on a score or more of crackers in a roomy pan and broil a couple of minutes till they puff up golden-brown.

Use only the best Parmesan, imported from Italy; or, second best, from Argentina where the rich pampas grass and Italian settlers get together on excellent Parmesan and Romano. Never buy Parmesan already grated; it quickly loses its flavor.

☛ Breakfast Puffs

1 cup flour
1 cup milk
¼ cup finely grated cheese
1 egg, lightly beaten
½ teaspoon salt

Mix all together to a smooth, light batter and fill ramekins or cups half full; then bake in quick oven until they are puffing over the top and golden-brown.

☛ Danish Fondue Puffs

1 stale roll
½ cup boiling hot milk
Salt
Pepper
2 cups freshly grated Cheddar cheese
4 egg yolks, beaten lemon-yellow
4 egg whites, beaten stiff

Soak roll in boiling milk and beat to a paste. Mix with cheese and egg yolks. When smooth and thickened fold in the egg whites and fill ramekins, tins, cups or paper forms and slowly bake until puffed up and golden-brown.

☛ New England Cheese Puffs

1 cup sifted flour
1 teaspoon baking powder
½ teaspoon salt
½ teaspoon Hungarian paprika
¼ teaspoon dry mustard
2 egg yolks, beaten lemon-yellow
½ cup milk
1 cup freshly grated Cheddar cheese
2 egg whites, beaten stiff but not dry

Sift dry ingredients together, mix yolks with milk and stir in. Add cheese and when thoroughly incorporated fold in the egg whites to make a smooth batter. Drop from a big spoon into hot deep fat and cook until well browned.

Caraway seeds are sometimes added. Poppy seeds are also used, and either of these makes a snappier puff, especially tasty when served with soup.

A few drops of tabasco give this an extra tang.

☛ Cream Cheese Puffs

½ pound cream cheese
1 cup milk
4 eggs, lightly beaten
½ teaspoon salt
½ teaspoon dry mustard

Soften cheese by heating over hot water. Remove from heat and add milk, eggs and seasoning. Beat until well blended, then pour into custard cups, ramekins or any other individual baking dishes that are attractive enough to serve the puffs in.

RAMEKINS OR RAMEQUINS

Some Ramekin dishes are made so exquisitely that they may be collected like snuff bottles.

Ramekins are utterly French, both the cooked Puffs and the individual dishes in which they are baked. Essentially a Cheese Puff, this is also *au gratin* when topped with both cheese and browned bread crumbs. By a sort of poetic cook's license the name is also applied to any kind of cake containing cheese and cooked in the identifying one-portion ramekin. It is used chiefly in the plural, however, together with the name of the chief ingredient, such as "Chicken Ramekins" and:

☛ Cheese Ramekins I

2 eggs
2 tablespoons flour
⅛ pound butter, melted
⅛ pound grated cheese

Mix well and bake in individual molds for 15 minutes.

Cheese Ramekins II

3 tablespoons melted butter
½ teaspoon each, salt and pepper
¾ cup bread crumbs
½ cup grated cheese
2 eggs, lightly beaten
1½ cups milk

Mix the first four dry ingredients together, stir eggs into the milk and add. Stir to a smooth batter and bake in buttered ramekins, standing in water, in moderate oven. Serve piping hot, for like Soufflés and all associated Puffs, the hot air will puff out of them quickly; then they will sink and be inedible.

TWO ANCIENT ENGLISH RECIPES, STILL GOING STRONG

Cheese Ramekins III

Grate ½ pound of any dry, rich cheese. Butter a dozen small paper cases, or little boxes of stiff writing paper like Soufflé cases. Put a saucepan containing ½ pint of water over the fire, add 2 tablespoons of butter, and when the water boils, stir in 1 heaping tablespoonful of flour. Beat the mixture until it shrinks away from the sides of the saucepan; then stir in the grated cheese. Remove the paste thus made from the fire, and let it partly cool. In the meantime separate the yolks from the whites of three eggs, and beat them until the yolks foam and the whites make a stiff froth. Put the mixture at once into the buttered paper cases, only half-filling them (since they rise very high while being baked) with small slices of cheese, and bake in a moderate oven for about 15 minutes. As soon as the Puffs are done, put the cases on a hot dish covered with a folded napkin, and serve very hot.

The most popular cheese for Ramekins has always been, and still is, Gruyère. But because the early English also adopted Italian Parmesan, that followed as a close second, and remains there today.

Sharp Cheddar makes tangy Ramekins, as will be seen in this second oldster; for though it prescribes Gloucester and Cheshire "'arf-and-'arf," both are essentially Cheddars. Gloucester has been called "a glorified Cheshire" and the latter has long been known as a peculiarly rich and colorful elder brother of Cheddar, described in Kenelme Digby's *Closet Open'd* as a "quick, fat, rich, well-tasted cheese."

☛ Cheese Ramekins IV

Scrape fine ¼ pound of Gloucester cheese and ¼ pound of Cheshire cheese. Beat this scraped cheese in a mortar with the yolks of 4 eggs, ¼ pound of fresh butter, and the crumbs of a French roll boiled in cream until soft. When all this is well mixed and pounded to a paste, add the beaten whites of 4 eggs. Should the paste seem too stiff, 1 or 2 tablespoons of sherry may be added. Put the paste into paper cases, and bake in a Dutch oven till nicely browned. The Ramekins should be served very hot.

Since both Gloucester cheese and Cheshire cheese are not easily come by even in London today, it would be hard to reproduce this in the States. So the best we can suggest is to use half-and-half of two of our own great Cheddars, say half-Coon and half-Wisconsin Longhorn, or half-Tillamook and half-Herkimer County. For there's no doubt about it, contrasting cheeses tickle the taste buds, and as many as three different kinds put together make Puffs all the more perfect.

☛ Ramequins à la Parisienne

- 2 cups milk
- 1 cup cream
- 1 ounce salt butter
- 1 tablespoon flour
- ½ cup grated Gruyère
- Coarsely ground pepper
- An atom of nutmeg
- A *soupçon* of garlic
- A light touch of powdered sugar
- 8 eggs, separated

Boil milk and cream together. Melt butter, mix in the flour and stir over heat 5 minutes, adding the milk and cream mixture a little at a time. When thoroughly cooked, remove from heat and stir in cheese, seasonings and the yolks of all 8 eggs, well beaten, and the whites of 2 even better beaten. When well mixed, fold in the remaining egg whites, stiffly beaten, until you have a batter as smooth and thick as cream. Pour this into ramekins of paper, porcelain or earthenware, filling each about ⅔ full to allow for them to puff up as they bake in a very slow oven until golden-brown (or a little less than 20 minutes).

☛ Le Ramequin Morézien

This celebrated specialty of Franche-Comté is described as "a porridge of water, butter, seasoning, chopped garlic and toast; thickened with minced Gruyère and served very hot."

Several French provinces are known for distinctive individual Puffs usually served in the dainty fluted forms they are cooked in. In Jeanne d'Arc's Lorraine, for instance, there are the simply named *Les Ramequins,* made of flour, Gruyère and eggs.

☛ Swiss-Roquefort Ramekins

¼ pound Swiss cheese
¼ pound Roquefort cheese
½ pound butter
8 eggs, separated
4 breakfast rolls, crusts removed
½ cup cream

The batter is made in the usual way, with the soft insides of the rolls simmered in the cream and stirred in. The egg whites are folded in last, as always, the batter poured into ramekins part full and baked to a golden-brown. Then they are served instantaneously, lest they fall.

☛ Puff Paste Ramekins

Puff or other pastry is rolled out flat and sprinkled with fine tasty cheese or any cheese mixture, such as Parmesan with Gruyère and/or Swiss Sapsago for a piquant change, but in lesser quantity than the other cheeses used. Parmesan cheese has long been the favorite for these.

Fold paste into 3 layers, roll out again and dust with more cheese. Fold once more and roll this out and cut in small fancy shapes to bake 10 to 15 minutes in a hot oven. Brushing with egg yolk before baking makes these Ramekins shine.

☛ Frying Pan Ramekins

Melt 2 ounces of butter, let it cool a little and then mix with ½ pound of cheese. Fold in the whites of 3 eggs, beaten stiff but not dry. Cover frying pan with buttered papers, put slices of bread on this and cover with the cheese mixture. Cook about 5 minutes, take it off and brown it with a salamander.

There are two schools of salamandering among turophiles. One holds that it toughens the cheese and makes it less digestible; the other that it's simply swell. Some of the latter addicts have special cheese-branding irons made with their monograms, to identify their creations, whether they be burned on the skins of Welsh Rabbits or Frying Pan Ramekins. Salamandering with an iron that has a gay, carnivalesque design can make a sort of harlequin Ramekin.

☛ Casserole Ramekin

Here is the Americanization of a French original: In a deep casserole lay alternate slices of white bread and Swiss cheese, with the cheese slices a bit bigger all around. Beat 2 eggs with 2 cups of milk, season with salt and—of all things—nutmeg! Proceed to bake like individual Ramekins.

Chapter Eight

Pizzas, Blintzes, Pastes, Cheese Cakes, etc.

No matter how big or hungry your family, you can always appease them with pizza.

Pizza—The Tomato Pie of Sicily

DOUGH

1 package yeast, dissolved in warm water	2 cups sifted flour
	1 teaspoon salt

2 tablespoons olive oil

Make dough of this. Knead 12 to 20 minutes. Pat into a ball, cover it tight and let stand 3 hours in warm place until twice the size.

TOMATO PASTE

3 tablespoons olive oil
2 large onions, sliced thin
1 can Italian tomato paste
8 to 10 anchovy filets, cut small
½ teaspoon oregano
Salt
Crushed chili pepper
2½ cups water

In the oil fry onion tender but not too brown, stir in tomato paste and keep stirring 3 or 4 minutes. Season, pour water over and simmer slowly 25 to 30 minutes. Add anchovies when sauce is done.

CHEESE

½ cup grated Italian, Parmesan, Romano or Pecorino, depending on your pocketbook

Procure a low, wide and handsome tin pizza pan, or reasonable substitute, and grease well before spreading the well-raised dough ½ to ¾ inch thick. Poke your finger tips haphazardly into the dough to make marks that will catch the sauce when you pour it on generously. Shake on Parmesan or Parmesan-type cheese and bake in hot oven ½ hour, then ¼ hour more at lower heat until the pizza is golden-brown. Cut in wedges like any other pie and serve.

The proper pans come all tin and a yard wide, down to regular apple-pie size, but twelve-inch pans are the most popular.

☛ Miniature Pizzas

Miniature pizzas are split English muffins rubbed with garlic or onion and brushed with olive oil. Cover with tomato sauce and a slice of Mozzarella cheese, anchovy, oregano and grated Parmesan, and heat 8 minutes.

Italian-Swiss Scallopini

1 pound paper-thin veal cutlets
⅓ cup flour
⅓ cup grated Swiss and Parmesan, mixed
1 egg yolk, lightly beaten with water
Butter
Salt
Paprika

Moisten veal with egg and roll in flour mixed with cheese, quickly brown, lower flame and cook 4 to 5 minutes till tender. Dust with paprika and salt.

Neapolitan Baked Lasagne, or Stuffed Noodles

1 pound lasagne, or other wide noodles
1½ cups cooked thick tomato sauce with meat
½ pound Ricotta or cottage cheese
1 pound Mozzarella or American Cheddar
¼ pound grated Parmesan, Romano or Pecorino
Salt
Pepper, preferably crushed red pods
A shaker filled with grated Parmesan, or reasonable substitute

Cook wide or broad noodles 15 to 20 minutes in rapidly boiling salted water until tender, but not soft, and drain. Pour ½ cup of tomato sauce in baking dish or pan, cover with about ⅓ of the noodles, sprinkle with grated Parmesan, a layer of sauce, a layer of Mozzarella and dabs of Ricotta. Continue in this fashion, alternating layers and seasoning each, ending with a final spread of sauce, Parmesan and red pepper. Bake firm in moderate oven, about 15 minutes, and served in wedges like pizza, with canisters of grated Parmesan, crushed red pepper pods and more of the sauce to taste.

Little Hats, Cappelletti

Freshly made and still moist Cappelletti, little hats, contrived out of tasty paste, may be had in any Little Italy macaroni shop.

These may be stuffed sensationally in four different flavors with only two cheeses.

Brown slices of chicken and ham separately, in butter. Mince each very fine and divide in half, to make four mixtures in equal amounts. Season these with salt, pepper and nutmeg and a binding of 2 parts egg yolk to 1 part egg white.

With these meat mixtures you can make four different-flavored fillings:

Ham and Mozzarella
Chicken and Mozzarella
Ham and Ricotta
Chicken and Ricotta

Fill the little hats alternately, so you'll have the same number of each different kind. Pinch edges tight together to keep the stuffings in while boiling fast for 5 minutes in chicken broth (or salted water, if you must).

Since these Cappelletti are only a pleasing form and shape of ravioli, they are served in the same way on hot plates, with plain tomato sauce and Parmesan or reasonable substitute. If we count this final seasoning as an ingredient, this makes three cheeses, so that each of half a dozen taste buds can be getting individual sensations without letting the others know what it's doing.

☛ Dauphiny Ravioli

This French variant of the famous Italian pockets of pastry follows the Cappelletti pattern, with any fresh goat cheese and Gruyère melted with butter and minced parsley and boiled in chicken broth.

☛ Italian Fritters

¼ cup flour
2 tablespoons sugar
¼ pound fresh Ricotta
2 eggs, beaten
½ cup shredded Mozzarella
Rind of ½ lemon, grated
3 tablespoons brandy
Salt

Stir and mix well together in the order given and let stand 1 hour or more to thicken the batter so it will hold its shape while cooking.

Shape batter like walnuts and hold one at a time in the bowl of a long-handled spoon dipped for 10 seconds in boiling hot oil. Fritter the "walnuts" so, and serve at once with powdered sugar.

To make fascinating cheese croquettes, mix several contrasting cheeses in this batter.

☛ Italian Asparagus and Cheese

This gives great scope for contrasting cheeses in one and the same dish. In a shallow baking pan put a foundation layer of grated Cheddar and a little butter. Cover with a layer of tender parts of asparagus, lightly salted; next a layer of grated Gruyère with a bit of butter, and another of asparagus. From here you can go as far as you like with varied layers of melting cheeses alternating with asparagus, until you come to the top, where you add two more kinds of cheese, a mixture of powdered Parmesan with Sapsago to give the new-mown hay scent.

☛ Garlic on Cheese

For one sandwich prepare 30 or 40 garlic cloves by removing skins and frying out the fierce pungence in smoking olive oil. They skip in the hot pan like Mexican jumping beans. Toast one side of a thickish slice of bread, put this side down on a grilling pan, cover it with a slice of imported Swiss Emmentaler or Gruyère, of about the same size, shape and thickness. Stick the cooked garlic cloves, while still blistering hot, in a close pattern into the cheese and brown for a minute under the grill. Salt lightly and dash with paprika for the color. (Recipe by Bob Brown in Merle Armitage's collection *Fit for a King.*)

Spaniards call garlic cloves teeth, Englishmen call them toes. It was cheese and garlic together that inspired Shakespeare to Hotspur's declaration in *King Henry IV:*

I had rather live
With cheese and garlic in a windmill, far,
Than feed on cates and have him talk to me
In any summer-house in Christendom.

Some people can take a mere *soupçon* of the stuff, while others can down it by the soup spoon, so we feel it necessary in reprinting our recipe to point to the warning of another early English writer: "Garlic is very dangerous to young children, fine women and hot young men."

☛ Blintzes

This snow white member of the crêpes suzette sorority is the most popular deb in New York's fancy cheese dishes set. Almost unknown here a decade or two ago, it has joined blinis, kreplach and cheeseburgers as a quick and sustaining lunch for office workers.

2 eggs
1 cup water
1 cup sifted flour
Salt
Cooking oil
½ pound cottage cheese
2 tablespoons butter
2 cups sour cream

Beat 1 egg light and make a batter with the water, flour and salt to taste. Heat a well-greased small frying pan and make little pancakes with 2 tablespoons of batter each. Cook the cakes over low heat and on one side only. Slide each cake off on a white cloth, with the cooked side down. While these are cooling make the blintz-filling by beating together the second egg, cottage cheese and butter. Spread each pancake thickly with the mixture and roll or make into little pockets or envelopes with the end tucked in to hold the filling. Cook in foil till golden-brown and serve at once with sufficient sour cream to smother them.

☛ Vatroushki

Russia seems to have been the cradle of all sorts of blinis and blintzes, and perhaps the first of them to be made was vatroushki, a variant of the blintzes above. The chief difference is that rounds of puff paste dough are used instead of the hot cakes, 1 teaspoon of sugar is added to the cottage cheese filling, and the sour cream, ½ cup, is mixed into this instead of being served with it. Little cups filled with this mix are made by pinching the edges of the dough together. The tops are brushed with egg yolk and baked in a brisk oven.

☛ Cottage Cheese Pancakes

1 cup prepared pancake flour
4 tablespoons top milk or light cream
1 teaspoon salt
4 eggs, well beaten
1 tablespoon sugar
2 cups cottage cheese, put through ricer

Mix batter and stir in cheese last until smooth.

☛ Cheese Waffles

2 cups prepared waffle flour
3 egg yolks, lightly beaten
¼ cup melted butter
¾ cup grated sharp Cheddar
3 egg whites, beaten stiff

Stir up a smooth waffle batter of the first 4 ingredients and fold in egg whites last.

Today you can get imported canned Holland cheese waffles to heat quickly and serve.

☛ Napkin Dumpling

1 pound cottage cheese
⅛ pound butter, softened
3 eggs, beaten
¾ cup Farina
½ teaspoon salt
Cinnamon and brown sugar

Mix together all ingredients (except the cinnamon and sugar) to form a ball. Moisten a linen napkin with cold water and tie the ball of dough in it. Simmer 40 to 50 minutes in salted boiling water, remove from napkin, sprinkle well with cinnamon and brown sugar, and serve. This is on the style of Hungarian potato and other succulent dumplings and may be served with goulash or as a meal in itself.

BUTTER AND CHEESE

Where fish is scant
And fruit of trees,
Supply that want
With butter and cheese.

Thomas Tusser in
The Last Remedy

Butter and cheese are mixed together in equal parts for cheese butter. Serbia has a cheese called Butter that more or less matches Turkey's Durak, of which butter is an indispensable ingredient, and French Cancoillote is based on sour milk simmered with butter.

The English have a cheese called Margarine, made with the butter substitute. In Westphalia there are no two schools of thought about whether 'tis better to eat butter with cheese or not, for in Westphalia sour-milk cheese, butter is mixed in as part of the process of making. The Arabs press curds and butter together to store in vats, and the Scots have Crowdie or Cruddy Butter.

BUTTERMILK CHEESE

The value of buttermilk is stressed in an extravagant old Hindu proverb: "A man may live without bread, but without buttermilk he dies."

Cheese was made before butter, being the earliest form of

dairy manufacturing, so buttermilk cheese came well after plain milk cheese, even after whey cheese. It is very tasty, and a natural with potato salad. The curd is salted after draining and sold in small parchment packages.

German "leather" cheese has buttermilk mixed with the plain. The Danes make their Appetitost with sour buttermilk. Ricotta Romano, for a novelty, is made of sheep buttermilk.

COTTAGE CHEESE

In America cottage cheese is also called pot, Dutch and smearcase. It is the easiest and quickest to make of all cheeses, by simply letting milk sour, or adding buttermilk to curdle it, then stand a while on the back of the kitchen stove, since it is homemade as a rule. It is drained in a bag of cheesecloth and may be eaten the same day, usually salted.

The Pilgrims brought along the following two tried and true recipes from olde England, and both are still in use and good repute:

Cottage Cheese No. 1

Let milk sour until clotted. Pour boiling water over and it will immediately curd. Stir well and pour into a colander. Pour a little cold water on the curd, salt it and break it up attractively for serving.

Cottage Cheese No. 2

A very rich and tasty variety is made of equal parts whole milk and buttermilk heated together to just under the boiling point. Pour into a linen bag and let drain until next day. Then remove, salt to taste and add a bit of butter or cream to make a smooth, creamy consistency, and pat into balls the size of a Seville orange.

CREAM CHEESE

In England there are three distinct manners of making cream cheese:

1. Fresh milk strained and lightly drained.
2. Scalded cream dried and drained dry, like Devonshire.
3. Rennet curd ripened, with thin, edible rind, or none, packaged in small blocks or miniature bricks by dairy companies, as in the U.S. Philadelphia Cream cheese.

American cream cheeses follow the English pattern, being named from their region or established brands owned by Breakstone, Borden, Kraft, Shefford, etc.

Cream cheese such as the first listed above is easier to make than cottage cheese or any other. Technically, in fact, it is not a cheese but the dried curd of milk and is often called virginal. Fresh milk is simply strained through muslin in a perforated box through which the whey and extra moisture drains away for three or four days, leaving a residue as firm as fresh butter.

In America, where we mix cream cheese with everything, a popular assortment of twelve sold in New York bears these ingredients and names: Chives, Cherry, Garden, Caviar, Lachs, Pimiento, Olive and Pimiento, Pineapple, Relish, Scallion, Strawberry, and Triple Decker of Relish, Pimiento and Cream in layers.

In Italy there is Stracchino Cream, in Sweden Chantilly. Finally, to come to France, la Foncée or Fromage de Pau, a cream also known around the world as Crême d'Isigny, Double Crême, Fromage à la Crême de Gien, Pots de Crême St. Gervais, etc. etc.

The French go even farther by eating thick fresh cream with Chevretons du Beaujolais and Fromage Blanc in the style that adds *à la crême* to their already glorified names.

The English came along with Snow Cream Cheese that is more of a dessert, similar to Italian Cream Cheese.

We'd like to have a cheese ice cream to contrast with too sweet ones. Attempts at this have been made, both here and in England;

Scottish Caledonian cream came closest. We have frozen cheese with fruit, to be sure, but no true cheese ice cream as yet, though some cream cheeses seem especially suitable.

> The farmer's daughter hath soft brown hair
> (Butter and eggs and a pound of cheese)
> And I met with a ballad I can't say where,
> That wholly consisted of lines like these,
> (Butter and eggs and a pound of cheese.)

In this parody by Calverly, "The Farmer's Daughter," the ingredients suggest cheese cake, dating back to 1381 in England. From that year Kettner in his *Book of the Table* quotes this recipe:

> Take cream of almonds or of cow milk and beat them well together; and make small coffins (that is, cases of pastry), and do it (put it) therein; and do (put) thereto sugar and good powders. Or take good fat cheese and eggs and make them of divers colours, green, red or yellow, and bake them or serve them forth.

This primitive "receipt" grew up into Richmond maids of honor that caused Kettner to wax poetic with:

> At Richmond we are permitted to touch with our lips a countless number of these maids—light and airy as the "airy, fairy Lilian." What more can the finest poetry achieve in quickening the things of earth into tokens and foretastes of heaven, with glimpses of higher life and ethereal worlds.

CHEESE CAKES

Coronation Cheese Cake

The *Oxford Dictionary* defines cheese cake as a "tartlet filled with sweet curds, etc." This shows that the cheese is the main thing, and the and-so-forth just a matter of taste. We are delighted to record that the Lord Mayor of London picked traditional cheese tarts, the maids of honor mentioned earlier in this section, as the Coronation dessert with which to regale the second Queen Elizabeth at the city luncheon in Guildhall. This is most fitting, since these tarts were named after the maids of honor at the court of the first Queen Elizabeth. The original recipe is said to have sold for a thousand pounds. These Richmond maids of honor had the usual cheese cake ingredients: butter and eggs and pounds of cheese, but what made the subtle flavor: nutmeg, brandy, lemon, orange-flower water, or all four?

More than 2,000 years before this kind of Coronation cheese cake, the Greeks had a word for it—several in fact: Apician Cheese Cake, Aristoxenean, and Philoxenean among them. Then the Romans took it over and we read from an epistle of the period:

> Thirty times in this one year, Charinus, while you have been arranging to make your will, have I sent you cheese cakes dripping with Hyblaean Thyme. (Celestial honey, such as that of Mount Hymettus we still get from Greece.)

Plato mentioned cheese cake, and a town near Thebes was named for it before Christ was born, at a time when cheese cakes were widely known as "dainty food for mortal man."

Today cheese cakes come in a half dozen popular styles, of which the ones flavored with fresh pineapple are the most popular in New York. But buyers delight in every sort, including the one hundred percent American type called cheese pies.

Indeed, there seems to be no dividing line between cheese cakes and cheese pies. While most of them are sweet, some are made piquant with pimientos and olives. We offer a favorite of ours made from popcorn-style pot cheese put through a sieve:

☛ Pineapple Cheese Cake

- 2½ pounds sieved pot cheese
- ¼ pound sweet butter, melted
- 4 eggs
- 2 cups sugar
- 2 cups milk
- ⅓ cup flour
- 1-inch piece vanilla bean
- ½ small box graham crackers, crushed fine
- 1 small can crushed pineapple, drained

In a big bowl mix everything except the graham crackers and pineapple in the order given above. Butter a square Pyrex pan and put in the graham-cracker dust to make a crust. Cover this evenly with the pineapple and pour in the cheese-custard mixture. Bake 1 hour in a "quiet" oven, as the English used to say for a moderate one, and when done set aside for 12 hours before eating.

Because of the time and labor involved maybe you had better buy your cheese cakes, even though some of the truly fine ones cost a dime a bite, especially the pedigreed Jewish-American ones in Manhattan. Reuben's and Lindy's are two leaders at about five dollars a cake. Some are fruited with cherries or strawberries.

☛ Cheese Custard

4 eggs, slightly beaten
1 cup milk
3 tablespoons melted butter
4 tablespoons grated Swiss (imported)
½ teaspoon salt
A dash of pepper or paprika
A few drops of onion juice, if desired

Mix all together, set in molds in pan of hot water, and bake until brown.

☛ Open-faced Cheese Pie

3 eggs
1 cup sugar
2 pounds soft smearcase

Whip everything together and fill two pie crusts. Bake without any upper crust.

The Apple-pie Affinity

Hot apple pie was always accompanied with cheese in New England, even as every slice of apple pie in Wisconsin has cheese for a sidekick, according to law. Pioneer hot pies were baked in brick ovens and flavored with nutmeg, cinnamon and rose geranium. The cheese was Cheddar, but today all sorts of pie and cheese combinations are common, such as banana pie and Gorgonzola, mince with Danish Blue, pumpkin with cream cheese, peach pie with Hablé, and even a green dusting of Sapsago over raisin pie.

Apple pie *au gratin*, thickly grated over with Parmesan, Caciocavallo or Sapsago, is something special when served with black coffee. Cider, too, or applejack, is a natural accompaniment to any dessert of apple with its cheese.

☛ Apple Pie Adorned

Apple pie is adorned with cream and cheese by pressing cream cheese through a ricer and folding in plenty of double cream beaten thick and salted a little. Put the mixture in a pastry tube and decorate top of pie in fanciful fashion.

☛ Apple Pie á la Cheese

Lay a slice of melting cheese on top of apple (or any fruit or berry) pie, and melt under broiler 2 to 3 minutes.

☛ Cheese-crusty Apple Pie

In making an apple pie, roll out the top crust and sprinkle with sharp Cheddar, grated, dot with butter and bake golden-brown.

☛ Flan au Fromage

To make this Franche-Comté tart of crisp paste, simply mix coarsely grated Gruyère with beaten egg, fill the tart cases and bake.

For any cheese pastry or fruit and custard pie crusts, work in tasty shredded sharp Cheddar in the ratio of 1 to 4 parts of flour.

☛ Christmas Cake Sandwiches

A traditional Christmas carol begs for:

A little bit of spice cake
A little bit of cheese,
A glass of cold water,
A penny, if you please.

For a festive handout cut the spice cake or fruit cake in slices and sandwich them with slices of tasty cheese between.

To maintain traditional Christmas cheer for the elders, serve apple pie with cheese and applejack.

☛ Angelic Camembert

1 ripe Camembert, imported
1 cup Anjou dry white wine
½ pound sweet butter, softened
2 tablespoons finely grated toast crumbs

Lightly scrape all crusty skin from the Camembert and when its creamy interior stands revealed put it in a small, round covered dish, pour in the wine, cover tightly so no bouquet or aroma can possibly escape, and let stand overnight.

When ready to serve drain off and discard any wine left, dry the cheese and mash with the sweet butter into an angelic paste. Reshape in original Camembert form, dust thickly with the crumbs and there you are.

Such a delicate dessert is a favorite with the ladies, since some of them find a prime Camembert a bit too strong if taken straight.

Although A. W. Fulton's observation in *For Men Only* is going out of date, it is none the less amusing:

> In the course of a somewhat varied career I have only met one woman who appreciated cheese. This quality in her seemed to me so deserving of reward that I did not hesitate to acquire her hand in marriage.

Another writer has said that "only gourmets among women seem to like cheese, except farm women and foreigners." The association between gourmets and farm women is borne out by the following urgent plea from early Italian landowners:

Ai contadini non far sapere
Quanto è buono il cacio con le pere.
Don't let the peasants know
How good are cheese and pears.

Having found out for ourselves, we suggest a golden slice of Taleggio, Stracchino, or pale gold Bel Paese to polish off a good dinner, with a juicy Lombardy pear or its American equivalent, a Bartlett, let us say.

This celestial association of cheese and pears is further accented by the French:

Entre la poire et le fromage
Between the pear and the cheese.

This places the cheese after the fruit, as the last course, in accordance with early English usage set down by John Clarke in his *Paroemiologia:*

After cheese comes nothing.

But in his *Epigrams* Ben Jonson serves them together.

Digestive cheese, and fruit there sure will be.

That brings us back to cheese and pippins:

I will make an end of my dinner; there's
pippins and cheese to come.
Shakespeare's *Merry Wives of Windsor*

When should the cheese be served? In England it is served before or after the fruit, with or without the port.

Following *The Book of Keruynge* in modern spelling we note that when it was published in 1431 the proper thing "after meat" was "pears, nuts, strawberries, whortleberries (American huckleberries) and hard cheese." In modern practice we serve some suitable cheese like Camembert directly on slices of apple and pears, Gorgonzola on sliced banana, Hablé spread on pineapple, and a cheese dessert tray to match the Lazy Lou, with everything crunchy down to Crackerjacks. Good, too, are figs, both fresh and preserved, stuffed with cream cheese, kumquats, avocados, fruity dunking mixtures of Pineapple cheese, served in the scooped-out casque of the cheese itself, and apple or pear and Provolone creamed and put back in the rind it came in. Pots of liquored and wined cheeses, no end, those of your own making being the best.

☛ **Champagned Roquefort or Gorgonzola**

½ pound mellow Roquefort
¼ pound sweet butter, softened
A dash cayenne
¾ cup champagne

With a silver fork mix cheese and butter to a smooth paste, moistening with champagne as you go along, using a little more or less champagne according to consistency desired. Serve with the demitasse and cognac, offering, besides crackers, gilt gingerbread in the style of Holland Dutch cheese tasters, or just plain bread.

After dinner cheeses suggested by Phil Alpert are:

FROM FRANCE: Port-Salut, Roblochon, Coulommiers, Camembert, Brie, Roquefort, Calvados (try it with a spot of Calvados, apple brandy)

FROM THE U.S.: Liederkranz, Blue, Cheddar

FROM SWEDEN: Hablé Crême Chantilly

FROM ITALY: Taleggio, Gorgonzola, Provolone, Bel Paese

FROM HUNGARY: Kascaval

FROM SWITZERLAND: Swiss Gruyère

FROM GERMANY: Kümmelkäse

FROM NORWAY: Gjetost, Bondost

FROM HOLLAND: Edam, Gouda

FROM ENGLAND: Stilton

FROM POLAND: Warshawski Syr

Chapter Nine

Au Gratin, Soups, Salads and Sauces

He who says *au gratin* says Parmesan. Thomas Gray, the English poet, saluted it two centuries ago with:

> Parma, the happy country where huge cheeses grow.

On September 4, 1666, Pepys recorded the burying of his pet Parmesan, "as well as my wine and some other things," in a pit in Sir W. Batten's garden. And on the selfsame fourth of September, more than a century later, in 1784, Woodforde in his *Diary of a Country Parson* wrote:

> I sent Mr. Custance about 3 doz. more of apricots, and he sent me back another large piece of fine Parmesan cheese. It was very kind of him.

The second most popular cheese for *au gratin* is Italian Romano, and, for an entirely different flavor, Swiss Sapsago. The

French, who gave us this cookery term, use it in its original meaning for any dish with a browned topping, usually of bread crumbs, or crumbs and cheese. In America we think of *au gratin* as grated cheese only, although Webster says, "with a browned covering, often mixed with butter or cheese; as, potatoes *au gratin*." So let us begin with that.

☛ Potatoes au Gratin

- 2 cups diced cooked potatoes
- 2 tablespoons grated onion
- ½ cup grated American Cheddar cheese
- 2 tablespoons butter
- ½ cup milk
- 1 egg
- Salt
- Pepper
- More grated cheese for covering

In a buttered baking dish put a layer of diced potatoes, sprinkle with onion and bits of butter. Next, scatter on a thin layer of cheese and alternate with potatoes, onions and butter. Stir milk, egg, salt and pepper together and pour it on the mixture. Top everything with plenty of grated cheese to make it authentically American *au gratin*. Bake until firm in moderate oven, about ½ hour.

☛ Eggs au Gratin

Make a white sauce flavored with minced onion to pour over any desired number of eggs broken into a buttered baking dish. Begin by using half of the sauce and sprinkling on a lot of grated cheese. After the eggs are in, pour on the rest of the sauce, cover it with grated cheese and bread crumbs, drop in bits of butter, and cook until brown in oven (or about 12 minutes).

☛ Tomatoes au Gratin

Cover bottom of shallow baking pan with slices of tomato and sprinkle liberally with bread crumbs and grated cheese, season with salt, pepper and dots of butter, add another layer of tomato slices, season as before and continue this, alternating with cheese, until pan is full. Add a generous topping of crumbs, cheese and butter. Bake 50 minutes in moderate oven.

Onion Soup au Gratin

4 or 5 onions, sliced
4 or 5 tablespoons butter
1 quart stock or canned consommé
1 quart bouillon made from dissolving 4 or 5 cubes
Rounds of toasted French bread
1½ cups grated Parmesan cheese

Sauté onions in butter in a roomy saucepan until light golden, and pour the stock over. When heated put in a larger casserole, add the bouillon, season to taste and heat to boiling point. Let simmer 15 minutes and serve in deep well-heated soup plates, the bottoms covered with rounds of toasted French bread which have been heaped with freshly grated Parmesan and browned under the broiler. More cheese is served for guests to sprinkle on as desired.

At gala parties, where wine flows, a couple of glasses of champagne are often added to the bouillon.

In the famed onion soup *au gratin* at Les Halles in Paris, grated Gruyère is used in place of Parmesan. They are interchangeable in this recipe.

AMERICAN CHEESE SOUPS

In this era of fine canned soups a quick cheese soup is made by heating cream of tomato soup, ready made, and adding finely grated Swiss or Parmesan to taste. French bread toasted and topped with more cheese and broiled golden makes the best base to pour this over, as is done with the French onion soup above.

The same cheese toasts are the basis of a simple milk-cheese soup, with heated milk poured over and a seasoning of salt, pepper, chopped chives, or a dash of nutmeg.

☛ Chicken Cheese Soup

Heat together 1 cup milk, 1 cup water in which 2 chicken bouillon cubes have been dissolved, and 1 can of condensed cream of chicken soup. Stir in ¼ cup grated American Cheddar cheese and season with salt, pepper, and plenty of paprika until cheese melts.

Other popular American recipes simply add grated cheese to lima bean or split bean soup, peanut butter soup, or plain cheese soup with rice.

Imported French *marmites* are *de rigueur* for a real onion soup *au gratin,* and an imported Parmesan grinder might be used for freshly ground cheese. In preparing, it is well to remember that they are basically only melted cheese, melted from the top down.

CHEESE SALADS

> When a Frenchman reaches the salad he is
> resting and in no hurry. He eats the
> salad to prepare himself for the cheese.
>
> Henri Charpentier,
> *Life à la Henri.*

☛ Green Cheese Salad Julienne

Take endive, water cress and as many different kinds of crisp lettuce as you can find and mix well with Provolone cheese cut in thin julienne strips and marinated 3 to 4 hours in French dressing. Crumble over the salad some Blue cheese and toss everything thoroughly, with plenty of French dressing.

☛ American Cheese Salad

Slice a sweet ripe pineapple thin and sprinkle with shredded American Cheddar. Serve on lettuce dipped in French dressing.

☛ Cheese and Nut Salad

Mix American Cheddar with an equal amount of nut meats and enough mayonnaise to make a paste. Roll these in little balls and serve with fruit salads, dusting lightly with finely grated Sapsago.

☛ Brie or Camembert Salad

Fill ripe pear- or peach-halves with creamy imported Brie or Camembert, sprinkle with honey, serve on lettuce drenched with French dressing and scatter shredded almonds over. (Cream cheese will do in a pinch. If the Camembert isn't creamy enough, mash it with some sweet cream.)

☛ Three-in-One Mold

⅔ cup cream cheese
½ cup grated American Cheddar cheese
½ cup Roquefort cheese, crumbled
2 tablespoons gelatin, dissolved and stirred into
½ cup boiling water
Juice of 1 lemon
Salt
Pepper
2 cups cream, beaten stiff
½ cup minced chives

Mash the cheeses together, season gelatin liquid with lemon, salt and pepper and stir into cheese with the whipped cream. Add chives last. Put in ring mold or any mold you fancy, chill well and slice at table to serve on lettuce with a little mayonnaise, or plain.

☛ Swiss Cheese Salad

Dice ½ pound of cheese into ½-inch cubes. Slice one onion very thin. Mix well in a soup plate. Dash with German mustard, olive oil, wine vinegar, Worcestershire sauce. Salt lightly and grind in plenty of black pepper. Then stir, preferably with a wooden spoon so you won't mash the cheese, until every hole is drenched with the dressing.

☛ Rosie's Swiss Breakfast Cheese Salad

Often Emmentaler is cubed in a salad for breakfast, relished specially by males on the morning after. We quote the original recipe brought over by Rosie from the Swiss Tyrol to thrill the writers' and artists' colony of Ridgefield, New Jersey, in her brother Emil's White House Inn:

First Rosie cut a thick slice of prime imported Emmentaler into half-inch cubes. Then she mixed imported French olive oil, German mustard and Swiss white wine vinegar with salt and freshly ground pepper in a deep soup plate, sprinkled on a few drops of pepper sauce scattered in the chunks of Schweizer and stirred the cubes with a light hand, using a wooden fork and spoon to prevent bruising.

The salad was ready to eat only when each and every tiny, shiny cell of the Swiss from the homeland had been washed, oiled and polished with the soothing mixture.

"Drink down the juice, too, when you have finished mine Breakfast Cheese Salad," Rosie advised the customers. "It is the best cure in the world for the worst hangover."

☛ Gorgonzola and Banana Salad

Slice bananas lengthwise, as for a banana split. Sprinkle with lemon juice and spread with creamy Gorgonzola. Sluice with French dressing made with lemon juice in place of vinegar, to help bring out the natural banana flavor of ripe Gorgonzola.

Cheese and Pea Salad

Cube ½ pound of American Cheddar and mix with a can of peas, 1 cup of diced celery, 1 cup of mayonnaise, ½ cup of sour cream, and 2 tablespoons each of minced pimientos and sweet pickles. Serve in lettuce cups with a sprinkling of parsley and chopped radishes.

Apple and Cheese Salad

½ cup cream cheese
1 cup chopped pecans
Salt and pepper
Apples, sliced ½-inch thick
Lettuce leaves
Creamy salad dressing

Make tiny seasoned cheese balls, center on the apple slices standing on lettuce leaves, and sluice with creamy salad dressing.

Roquefort Cheese Salad Dressing

No cheese sauce is easier to make than the American favorite of Roquefort cheese mashed with a fork and mixed with French dressing. It is often made in a pint Mason jar and kept in the refrigerator to shake up on occasion and toss over lettuce or other salads.

Unfortunately, even when the Roquefort is the French import, complete with the picture of the sheep in red, and *garanti véritable,* the dressing is often ruined by bad vinegar and cottonseed oil (of all things). When bottled to sell in stores, all sorts of extraneous spice, oils and mustard flour are used where nothing more is necessary than the manipulation of a fork, fine olive oil and good vinegar—white wine, tarragon or malt. Some ardent amateurs must have their splash of Worcestershire sauce or lemon juice with salt and pepper. This Roquefort dressing is good on all green salads, but on endive it's something special.

☛ Sauce Mornay

Sauce Mornay has been hailed internationally as "the greatest culinary achievement in cheese."

Nothing is simpler to make. All you do is prepare a white sauce (the French Sauce Béchamel) and add grated Parmesan to your liking, stirring it in until melted and the sauce is creamy. This can be snapped up with cayenne or minced parsley, and when used with fish a little of the cooking broth is added.

☛ Plain Cheese Sauce

1 part of any grated cheese to 4 parts of white sauce

This is a mild sauce that is nice with creamed or hard-cooked eggs. When the cheese content is doubled, 2 parts of cheese to 4 of white sauce, it is delicious on boiled cauliflower, baked potatoes, macaroni and crackers soaked in milk.

The sauce may be made richer by mixing melted butter with the flour in making the white sauce, or by beating egg yolk in with the cheese.

From thin to medium to thick it serves divers purposes:

Thin: it may be used instead of milk to make a tasty milk toast, sometimes spiced with curry.

Medium: for baking by pouring over crackers soaked in milk.

Thick: serves as a sort of Welsh Rabbit when poured generously over bread toasted on one side only, with the untoasted side up, to let the sauce sink in.

☛ Parsleyed Cheese Sauce

This makes a mild, pleasantly pungent sauce, to enliven the cabbage family—hot cauliflower, broccoli, cabbage and Brussels sprouts. Croutons help when sprinkled over.

CORNUCOPIA OF CHEESE RECIPES

Since this is the Complete Book of Cheese we will fill a bounteous cornucopia here with more or less essential, if not indispensable, recipes and dishes not so easy to classify, or overlooked or crowded out of the main sections devoted to the classic Fondues, Rabbits, Soufflés, etc.

Stuffed Celery, Endive, Anise and Other Suitable Stalks

Use any soft cheese you like, or firm cheese softened by pressing through a sieve; at room temperature, of course, with any seasoning or relish.

SUGGESTIONS:

Cream cheese and chopped chives, pimientos, olives, or all three, with or without a touch of Worcestershire.

Cottage cheese and piccalilli or chili sauce.

Sharp Cheddar mixed with mayonnaise, mustard, cream, minced capers, pickles, or minced ham.

Roquefort and other Blues are excellent fillings for your favorite vegetable stalk, or scooped-out dill pickle. This last is specially nice when filled with snappy cheese creamed with sweet butter.

All canapé butters are ideally suited to stuffing stalks. Pineapple cheese, especially that part close to the pineapple-flavored rind, is perfect when creamed.

A masterpiece in the line of filled stalks: Cut the leafy tops off an entire head of celery, endive, anise or anything similarly suitable. Wash and separate stalks, but keep them in order, to reassemble in the head after each is stuffed with a different mixture, using any of the above, or a tangy mix of your own concoction.

After all stalks are filled, beginning with the baby center ones, press them together in the form of the original head, tie tight, and chill. When ready, slice in rolls about ½-inch thick and arrange as a salad on a bed of water cress or lettuce, moistened with French dressing.

☛ Cold Dunking

Besides hot dunking in Swiss Fondue, cold dunking may be had by moistening plenty of cream cheese with cream or lemon in a dunking bowl. When the cheese is sufficiently liquefied, it is liberally seasoned with chopped parsley, chives, onions, pimiento and/or other relish. Then a couple of tins of anchovies are macerated and stirred in, oil and all.

☛ Cheese Charlotte

Line a baking dish from bottom to top with decrusted slices of bread dipped in milk. Cream 1 tablespoon of sweet butter with 2 eggs and season before stirring in 2 cups of grated cheese. Bake until golden brown in slow oven.

☛ Straws

Roll pastry dough thin and cover with grated Cheddar, fold and roll at least twice more, sprinkling with cheese each time. Chill dough in refrigerator and cut in straw-size strips. Stiffly salt a beaten egg yolk and glaze with that to give a salty taste. Bake for several minutes until crisp.

☛ Supa Shetgia *

This is the famous cheese soup of the Engadine and little known in this country. One of its seasonings is nutmeg and until one has used it in cheese dishes, it is hard to describe how per-

* (from *Cheese Cookery*, by Helmut Ripperger)

fectly it gives that extra something. The recipe, as given, is for each plate, but there is no reason why the old-fashioned tureen could not be used and the quantities simply increased.

Put a slice of stale French bread, toasted or not, into a soup plate and cover it with 4 tablespoons of grated or shredded Swiss cheese. Place another slice of bread on top of this and pour over it some boiling milk. Cover the plate and let it stand for several minutes. Season with salt, pepper and nutmeg. Serve topped with browned, hot butter. Use whole nutmeg and grate it freshly.

WITH A CHEESE SHAKER ON THE TABLE

Italians are so dependent on cheese to enrich all their dishes, from soups to spaghetti—and indeed any vegetable—that a shaker of grated Parmesan, Romano or reasonable substitute stands ready at every table, or is served freshly grated on a side dish. Thus any Italian soup might be called a cheese soup, but we know of only one, the great minestrone, in which cheese is listed as an indispensable ingredient along with the pasta, peas, onion, tomatoes, kidney beans, celery, olive oil, garlic, oregano, potatoes, carrots, and so forth.

Likewise, a chunk of melting or toasting cheese is essential in the Fritto Misto, the finest mixed grill we know, and it's served up as a separate tidbit with the meats.

Italians grate on more cheese for seasoning than any other people, as the French are wont to use more wine in cooking.

☛ **Pfeffernüsse and Caraway**

The gingery little "pepper nuts," *pfeffernüsse,* imported from Germany in barrels at Christmastime, make one of the best accompaniments to almost any kind of cheese. For contrast try a dish of caraway.

Diablotins

Small rounds of buttered bread or toast heaped with a mound of grated cheese and browned in the oven is a French contribution.

CHEESE OMELETS

Cheddar Omelet

Make a plain omelet your own way. When the mixture has just begun to cook, dust over it evenly ½ cup grated Cheddar.

(a) Use young Cheddar if you want a mild, bland omelet.
(b) Use sharp, aged Cheddar for a full-flavored one.
(c) Sprinkle (b) with Worcestershire sauce to make what might be called a Wild Omelet.

Cook as usual. Fold and serve.

Parmesan Omelet (mild)

Cook as above, but use ¼ cup only of Parmesan, grated fine, in place of the ½ cup Cheddar.

Parmesan Omelet (full flavored)

As above, but use ½ cup Parmesan, finely grated, as follows: Sift ¼ cup of the Parmesan into your egg mixture at the beginning and dust on the second ¼ cup evenly, just as the omelet begins to set.

A Meal-in-One Omelet

Fry ½ dozen bacon slices crisp and keep hot while frying a cup of diced, boiled potatoes in the bacon fat, to equal crispness.

Meanwhile make your omelet mixture of 3 eggs, beaten, and 1½ tablespoons of shredded Emmentaler (or domestic Swiss) with 1 tablespoon of chopped chives and salt and pepper to taste.

☛ Tomato and

Make plain omelet, cover with thin rounds of fresh tomato and dust well with any grated cheese you like. Put under broiler until cheese melts to a golden brown.

☛ Omelet with Cheese Sauce

Make a plain French, fluffy or puffy omelet and when finished, cover with a hot, seasoned, reinforced white sauce in which ¼ pound of shredded cheese has been melted, and mixed well with ½ cup cooked, diced celery and 1 tablespoon of pimiento, minced.

The French use grated Gruyère for this with all sorts of sauces, such as the *Savoyar de Savoie,* with potatoes, chervil, tarragon and cream. A delicious appearance and added flavor can be had by browning with a salamander.

☛ Spanish Flan—Quesillo

FOR THE CARAMEL: ½ cup sugar
4 tablespoons water

FOR THE FLAN: 4 eggs, beaten separately
2 cups hot milk
⅓ cup sugar
Salt

Brown sugar and mix with water to make the caramel. Pour it into a baking mold.

Make Flan by mixing together all the ingredients. Add to carameled mold and bake in pan of water in moderate oven about ¾ hour.

☛ Italian Fritto Misto

The distinctive Italian Mixed Fry, Fritto Misto, is made with whatever fish, sweetbreads, brains, kidneys, or tidbits of meat are at hand, say a half dozen different cubes of meat and giblets, with as many hearts of artichokes, *finocchi,* tomato, and different vegetables as you can find, but always with a hunk of melting cheese, to fork out in golden threads with each mouthful of the mixture.

☛ Polish Piroghs (a pocketful of cheese)

Make noodle dough with 2 eggs and 2 cups of flour, roll out very thin and cut in 2-inch squares.

Cream a cupful of cottage cheese with a tablespoon of melted butter, flavor with cinnamon and toss in a handful of seedless currents.

Fill pastry squares with this and pinch edges tight together to make little pockets.

Drop into a lot of fast-boiling water, lightly salted, and boil steadily 30 minutes, lowering the heat so the pockets won't burst open.

Drain and serve on a piping hot platter with melted butter and a sprinkling of bread crumbs.

This is a cross between ravioli and blintzes.

☛ Cheesed Mashed Potatoes

Whip into a steaming hot dish of creamily mashed potatoes some old Cheddar with melted butter and a crumbling of crisp, cooked bacon.

If there's a chafing dish handy, a first-rate nightcap can be made via a

☛ Sautéed Swiss Sandwich

Tuck a slice of Swiss cheese between two pieces of thickly buttered bread, trim crusts, cut sandwich in two, surround it with one well-beaten egg, slide it into sizzling butter and fry on both sides. A chef at the New York Athletic Club once improved on this by first sandwiching the Swiss between a slice of ham and a slice of chicken breast, then beating up a brace of eggs with a jigger of heavy sweet cream and soaking his sandwich in this until it sopped up every drop. A final frying in sweet butter made strong men cry for it.

Chapter Ten

Appetizers, Crackers, Sandwiches, Savories, Snacks, Spreads and Toasts

In America cheese got its start in country stores in our cracker-barrel days when every man felt free to saunter in, pick up the cheese knife and cut himself a wedge from the big-bellied rattrap cheese standing under its glass bell or wire mesh hood that kept the flies off but not the free-lunchers. Cheese by itself being none too palatable, the taster would saunter over to the cracker barrel, shoo the cat off and help himself to the old-time crackers that can't be beat today.

At that time Wisconsin still belonged to the Indians and Vermont was our leading cheese state, with its Sage and Cheddar and Vermont Country Store Crackers, as Vrest Orton of Weston, Vermont, calls them. When Orton heard we were writing this book, he sent samples from the store his father started in 1897, which is still going strong. Together with the Vermont Good Old-fashioned Natural Cheese and the Sage came a handy handmade Cracker Basket, all wicker, ten crackers long and just one double cracker wide. A snug little casket for those puffy, old-time, two-in-one soda biscuits that have no salt to spoil the taste of the accompanying cheese. Each does double duty because it's made to split in the middle, so you can try one kind of cheese on one half and another on t'other, or sandwich them between.

Some Pied Piper took the country cheese and crackers to the corner saloon and led a free-lunch procession that never faltered till Prohibition came. The same old store cheese was soon pepped up as saloon cheese with a saucer of caraway seeds, bowls of pickles, peppers, pickled peppers and rye bread with plenty of mustard, pretzels or cheese straws, smearcase and schwarzbrot. Beer and cheese forever together, as in the free-lunch ditty of that great day:

> I am an Irish hunter;
> I am, I ain't.
> I do not hunt for deer
> But beer.
> Oh, Otto, wring the bar rag.
>
> I do not hunt for fleas
> But cheese.
> Oh, Adolph, bring the free lunch.

It was there and then that cheese came of age from coast to coast. In every bar there was a choice of Swiss, Cottage, Limburger—manly cheeses, walkie-talkie oldsters that could sit up and beg, golden yellow, tangy mellow, always cut in cubes.

Cheese takes the cube form as naturally as eggs take the oval and honeycombs the hexagon.

On the more elegant handout buffets, besides the shapely cubes, free Welsh Rabbit started at four every afternoon, to lead the tired businessman in by the nose; or a smear of Canadian Snappy out of a pure white porcelain pot in the classy places, on a Bent's water biscuit.

SANDWICHES AND SAVORY SNACKS

Next to nibbling cheese with crackers and appetizers, of which there is no end in sight, cheese sandwiches help us consume most of our country's enormous output of Brick, Cheddar and Swiss. To attempt to classify and describe all of these would be impossible, so we will content ourselves by picking a few of the cold and hot, the plain and the fancy, the familiar and the exotic. Let's use the alphabet to sum up the situation.

A Alpine Club Sandwich

Spread toasts with mayonnaise and fill with a thick slice of imported Emmentaler, well-mustarded and seasoned, and the usual club-sandwich toppings of thin slices of chicken or turkey, tomato, bacon and a lettuce leaf.

B Boston Beany, Open-face

Lightly butter a slice of Boston brown bread, cover it generously with hot baked beans and a thick layer of shredded Cheddar. Top with bacon and put under a slow broiler until cheese melts and the bacon crisps.

C Cheeseburgers

Pat out some small seasoned hamburgers exceedingly thin and, using them instead of slices of bread, sandwich in a nice slice of American Cheddar well covered with mustard. Crimp edges of the hamburgers all around to hold in the cheese when it melts and begins to run. Toast under a brisk boiler and serve on soft, toasted sandwich buns.

D Deviled Rye

Butter flat Swedish rye bread and heat quickly in hot oven. Cool until crisp again. Then spread thickly with cream cheese, bedeviled with catsup, paprika or pimiento.

E Egg, Open-faced

Sauté minced small onion and small green pepper in 2 tablespoons of butter and make a sauce by cooking with a cup of canned tomatoes. Season and reduce to about half. Fry 4 eggs and put one in the center of each of 4 pieces of hot toast spread with the red sauce. Sprinkle each generously with grated Cheddar, broil until melted and serve with crisp bacon.

F French-fried Swiss

Simply make a sandwich with a noble slice of imported Gruyère, soak it in beaten egg and milk and fry slowly till cheese melts and the sandwich is nicely browned. This is a specialty of Franche-Comté.

G Grilled Chicken-Ham-Cheddar

Cut crusts from 2 slices of white bread and butter them on both sides. Make a sandwich of these with 1 slice cooked chicken, ½ slice sharp Cheddar cheese, and a sprinkling of minced ham. Fasten tight with toothpicks, cut in half and dip thoroughly in a mixture of egg and milk. Grill golden on both sides and serve with lengthwise slices of dill pickle.

H He-man Sandwich, Open-faced

Butter a thick slice of dark rye bread, cover with a layer of mashed cold baked beans and a slice of ham, then one of Swiss cheese and a wheel of Bermuda onion topped with mustard and a sowing of capers.

I International Sandwich

Split English muffins and toast on the hard outsides, cover soft, untoasted insides with Swiss cheese, spread lightly with mustard, top that with a wheel of Bermuda onion and 1 or 2 slices of Italian-type tomato. Season with cayenne and salt, dot with butter, cover with Brazil nuts and brown under the broiler.

J Jurassiennes, or Croûtes Comtoises

Soak slices of stale buns in milk, cover with a mixture of onion browned in chopped lean bacon and mixed with grated Gruyère. Simmer until cheese melts, and serve.

K Kümmelkäse

If you like caraway flavor this is your sandwich: On well-buttered but lightly mustarded rye, lay a thickish slab of Milwaukee Kümmelkäse, which translates caraway cheese. For good measure sprinkle caraway seeds on top, or serve them in a saucer on the side. Then dash on a splash of kümmel, the caraway liqueur that's best when imported.

L Limburger Onion or Limburger Catsup

Marinate slices of Bermuda onion in a peppery French dressing for ½ hour. Then butter slices of rye, spread well with soft Limburger, top with onion and you will have something super duper—if you like Limburger.

When catsup is substituted for marinated onion the sandwich has quite another character and flavor, so true Limburger addicts make one of each and take alternate bites for the thrill of contrast.

M **Meringue, Open-faced** (from the Browns' *10,000 Snacks*)

Allow 1 egg and 4 tablespoons of grated cheese to 1 slice of bread. Toast bread on one side only, spread butter on untoasted side, put 2 tablespoons grated cheese over butter, and the yolk of an egg in the center. Beat egg white stiff with a few grains of salt and pile lightly on top. Sprinkle the other 2 tablespoons of grated cheese over that and bake in moderate oven until the egg white is firm and the cheese has melted to a golden-brown.

N **Neufchâtel and Honey**

We know no sandwich more ethereal than one made with thin, decrusted, white bread, spread with sweet butter, then with Neufchâtel topped with some fine honey—Mount Hymettus, if possible.

Any creamy Petit Suisse will do as well as the Neufchâtel, but nothing will take the place of the honey to make this heavenly sandwich that must have been the original ambrosia.

O **Oskar's Ham-Cam**

Oskar Davidsen of Copenhagen, whose five-foot menu lists 186 superb sandwiches and snacks, each with a character all its own, perfected the Ham-Cam base for a flock of fancy ham sandwiches, open-faced on rye or white, soft or crisp, sweet or sour, almost any one-way slice you desire. He uses as many contrasting kinds of bread as possible, and his butter varies from salt to fresh and whipped. The Ham-Cam base involves "a juicy, tender slice of freshly boiled, mild-cured ham" with imported Camembert spread on the ham as thick as velvet.

The Ham-Cam is built up with such splendors as "goose liver paste and Madeira wine jelly," "fried calves' kidney and *rémoulade*," "Bombay curry salad," "bird's liver and fried egg," " a slice of red roast beef" and more of that red Madeira jelly, with anything else you say, just so long as it does credit to Camembert on ham.

P **Pickled Camembert**

Butter a thin slice of rye or pumpernickel and spread with ripe imported Camembert, when in season (which isn't summer). Make a mixture of sweet, sour and dill pickles, finely chopped, and spread it on. Top this with a thin slice of white bread for pleasing contrast with the black.

Q **Queijo da Serra Sandwich**

On generous rounds of French "flute" or other crunchy, crusty white bread place thick portions of any good Portuguese cheese made of sheep's milk "in the mountains." This last translates back into Queijo da Serra, the fattest, finest cheese in the world —on a par with fine Greek Feta. Bead the open-faced creamy cheese lightly with imported capers, and you'll say it's scrumptious.

R **Roquefort Nut**

Butter hot toast and cover with a thickish slice of genuine Roquefort cheese. Sprinkle thickly with genuine Hungarian paprika. Put in moderate oven for about 6 minutes. Finish it off with chopped pine nuts, almonds, or a mixture thereof.

S **Smoky Sandwich and Sturgeon-smoked Sandwich**

Skin some juicy little, jolly little sprats, lay on thin rye, or a slice of miniature-loaf rye studded with caraway, spread with sweet butter and cover with a slice of smoked cheese.

Hickory is preferred for most of the smoking in America. In New York the best smoked cheese, whether from Canada or nearer home, is usually cured in the same room with sturgeon. Since this king of smoked fish imparts some of its regal savor to the Cheddar, there is a natural affinity peculiarly suited to sandwiching as above.

Smoked salmon, eel, whitefish or any other, is also good with cheese smoked with hickory or anything with a salubrious savor, while a sandwich of smoked turkey with smoked cheese is out of this world. We accompany it with a cup of smoky Lapsang Soochong China tea.

T Tangy Sandwich

On buttered rye spread cream cheese, and on this bed lay thinly sliced dried beef. In place of mustard dot the beef with horseradish and pearl onions or those reliable old chopped chives. And by the way, if you must use mustard on every cheese sandwich, try different kinds for a change: sharp English freshly mixed by your own hand out of the tin of powder, or Dijon for a French touch.

U Unusual Sandwich—of Flowers, Hay and Clover

On a sweet-buttered slice of French white bread lay a layer of equally sweet English Flower cheese (made with petals of rose, marigold, violet, etc.) and top that with French Fromage de foin. This French hay cheese gets its name from being ripened on hay and holds its new-mown scent. Sprinkle on a few imported capers (the smaller they are, the better), with a little of the luscious juice, and dust lightly with Sapsago.

V Vegetarian Sandwich

Roll your own of alternate leaves of lettuce, slices of store cheese, avocados, cream cheese sprinkled heavily with chopped chives, and anything else in the Vegetable or Caseous Kingdoms that suits your fancy.

W **Witch's Sandwich**

Butter 2 slices of sandwich bread, cover one with a thin slice of imported Emmentaler, dash with cayenne and a drop or two of tabasco. Slap on a sizzling hot slice of grilled ham and press it together with the cheese between the two bread slices, put in a hot oven and serve piping hot with a handful of "moonstones"—those outsize pearl onions.

X **Xochomilco Sandwich**

In spite of the "milco" in Xochomilco, there isn't a drop to be had that's native to the festive, floating gardens near Mexico City. For there, instead of the cow, a sort of century plant gives milky white *pulque,* the fermented juice of this cactuslike desert plant. With this goes a vegetable cheese curded by its own vegetable rennet. It's called tuna cheese, made from the milky juice of the prickly pear that grows on yet another cactuslike plant of the dry lands. This tuna cheese sometimes teams up in arid lands with the juicy thick cactus leaf sliced into a tortilla sandwich. The milky *pulque* of Xochomilco goes as well with it as beer with a Swiss cheese sandwich.

Y **Yolk Picnic Sandwich**

Hard-cooked egg yolk worked into a yellow paste with cream cheese, mustard, olive oil, lemon juice, celery salt and a touch of tabasco, spread on thick slices of whole wheat bread.

Z **Zebra**

Take a tip from Oskar over in Copenhagen and design your own Zebra sandwich as decoratively as one of those oft-photoed skins in El Morocco. Just alternate stripes of black bread with various white cheeses in between, to follow the black and white zebra pattern.

For good measure we will toss in a couple of toasted cheese sandwiches.

☛ Toasted Cheese Sandwich

Butter both sides of 2 thick slices of white bread and sandwich between them a seasoned mixture of shredded sharp cheese, egg yolk, mustard and chopped chives, together with stiffly beaten egg white folded in last to make a light filling. Fry the buttered sandwich in more butter until well melted and nicely gilded.

This toasted cheeser is so good it's positively sinful. The French, who outdo us in both cooking and sin, make one of their own in the form of fried fingers of stale bread doused in an 'arf and 'arf Welsh Rabbit and Fondue melting of Gruyère, that serves as a liaison to further sandwich the two.

Garlic is often used in place of chopped chives, and in contrast to this wild one there's a mild one made of Dutch cream cheese by the equally Dutch Pennsylvanians.

England, of course, together with Wales, holds all-time honors with such celebrated regional "toasting cheeses" as Devonshire and Dunlop. Even British Newfoundland is known for its simple version, that's quite as pleasing as its rich Prince Edward Island Oyster Stew.

☛ Newfoundland Toasted Cheese Sandwich

½ pound grated Cheddar	½ cup milk
1 egg, well beaten	1 tablespoon butter

Heat together and pour over well-buttered toast.

Chapter Eleven

"Fit for Drink"

A country without a fit drink for cheese has no cheese fit for drink.

Greece was the first country to prove its epicurean fitness, according to the old saying above, for it had wine to tipple and sheep's milk cheese to nibble. The classical Greek cheese has always been Feta, and no doubt this was the kind that Circe combined most suitably with wine to make a farewell drink for her lovers. She put further sweetness and body into the stirrup cup by stirring honey and barley meal into it. Today we might whip this up in an electric mixer to toast her memory.

While a land flowing with milk and honey is the ideal of many, France, Italy, Spain or Portugal, flowing with wine and honey, suit a lot of gourmets better. Indeed, in such vinous-caseous places cheese is on the house at all wine sales for prospective customers to snack upon and thus bring out the full flavor of the cellared vintages. But professional wine tasters are forbidden any cheese between sips. They may clear their palates with plain bread, but nary a crumb of Roquefort or cube of Gruyère in working hours, lest it give the wine a spurious nobility.

And, speaking of Roquefort, Romanée has the closest affinity for it. Such affinities are also found in Pont l'Evêque and Beaujolais, Brie and red champagne, Coulommiers and any good *vin rosé*. Heavenly marriages are made in Burgundy between red and white wines of both Côtes, de Nuits and de Baune, and Burgundian cheeses such as Époisses, Soumaintrin and Saint-Florentin. Pommard and Port-Salut seem to be made for each other, as do Château Margaux and Camembert.

A great cheese for a great wine is the rule that brings together in the neighboring provinces such notables as Sainte Maure, Valençay, Vendôme and the Loire wines—Vouvray, Saumur and Anjou. Gruyère mates with Chablis, Camembert with St. Emilion; and any dry red wine, most commonly claret, is a fit drink for the hundreds of other fine French cheeses.

Every country has such happy marriages, an Italian standard being Provolone and Chianti. Then there is a most unusual pair, French Neufchâtel cheese and Swiss Neuchâtel wine from just across the border. Switzerland also has another cheese favorite at home—Trauben (grape cheese), named from the Neuchâtel wine in which it is aged.

One kind of French Neufchâtel cheese, Bondon, is also uniquely suited to the company of any good wine because it is made in the exact shape and size of a wine barrel bung. A similar relation is found in Brinzas (or Brindzas) that are packed in miniature wine barrels, strongly suggesting what should be drunk with such excellent cheeses: Hungarian Tokay. Other foreign cheeses go to market wrapped in vine leaves. The affinity has clearly been laid down in heaven.

Only the English seem to have a *fortissimo* taste in the go-with wines, according to these matches registered by André Simon in *The Art of Good Living:*

Red Cheshire with Light Tawny Port
White Cheshire with Oloroso Sherry
Blue Leicester with Old Vintage Port
Green Roquefort with New Vintage Port

To these we might add brittle chips of Greek Casere with nips of Amontillado, for an eloquent appetizer.

The English also pour port into Stilton, and sundry other wines and liquors into Cheddars and such. This doctoring leads to fraudulent imitation, however, for either port or stout is put into counterfeit Cheshire cheese to make up for the richness it lacks.

While some combinations of cheeses and wines may turn out palatable, we prefer taking ours straight. When something more fiery is needed we can twirl the flecks of pure gold in a chalice of Eau de Vie de Danzig and nibble on legitimate Danzig cheese unadulterated. *Goldwasser,* or Eau de Vie, was a favorite liqueur of cheese-loving Franklin Roosevelt, and we can be sure he took the two separately.

Another perfect combination, if you can take it, is imported kümmel with any caraway-seeded cheese, or cream cheese with a handy saucer of caraway seeds. In the section of France devoted to gin, the juniper berries that flavor the drink also go into a local cheese, Fromage Fort. This is further fortified with brandy, white wine and pepper. One regional tipple with such brutally strong cheese is black coffee laced with gin.

French la Jonchée is another potted thriller with not only coffee and rum mixed in during the making, but orange flower water, too. Then there is la Petafina, made with brandy and absinthe; Hazebrook with brandy alone; and la Cachat with white wine and brandy.

In Italy white Gorgonzola is also put up in crocks with brandy. In Oporto the sharp cheese of that name is enlivened by port. Cider and the greatest of applejacks, Calvados, seem made to go with the regional Calvados cheese. This is also true of our native Jersey Lightning and hard cider with their accompanying New

York State cheese. In the Auge Valley of France, farmers also drink homemade cider with their own Augelot, a piquant kind of Pont l'Evêque.

The English sip pear cider (perry) with almost any British cheese. Milk would seem to be redundant, but Sage cheese and buttermilk do go well together.

Wine and cheese have other things in common. Some wines and some cheeses are aged in caves, and there are vintage cheeses no less than vintage wines, as is the case with Stilton.

Chapter Twelve

Lazy Lou

Once, so goes the sad story, there was a cheesemonger unworthy of his heritage. He exported a shipload of inferior "Swiss" made somewhere in the U.S.A. Bad to begin with, it had worsened on the voyage. Rejected by the health authorities on the other side, it was shipped back, reaching home in the unhappy condition known as "cracked." To cut his losses the rascally cheesemonger had his cargo ground up and its flavor disguised with hot peppers and chili sauce. Thus there came into being the abortion known as the "cheese spread."

The cheese spread or "food" and its cousin, the processed cheese, are handy, cheap and nasty. They are available everywhere and some people even like them. So any cheese book is bound to take formal notice of their existence. I have done so—and now, an unfond farewell to them.

My academic cheese education began at the University of Wisconsin in 1904. I grew up with our great Midwest industry; I have read with profit hundreds of pamphlets put out by the learned Aggies of my Alma Mater. Mostly they treat of honest, natural cheeses: the making, keeping and enjoying of authentic Longhorn Cheddars, short Bricks and naturalized Limburgers.

At the School of Agriculture the students still, I am told, keep their hand in by studying the classical layout on a cheese board. One booklet recommends the following for freshman contemplation:

CARAWAY BRICK	SELECT BRICK	EDAM
WISCONSIN SWISS	LONGHORN AMERICAN	SHEFFORD

These six sturdy samples of Wisconsin's best will stimulate any amount of classroom discussion. Does the Edam go better with German-American black bread or with Swedish Ry-Krisp? To butter or not to butter? And if to butter, with which cheese? Salt or sweet? How close do we come to the excellence of the genuine Alpine Swiss? Primary school stuff, but not unworthy of thought.

Pass on down the years. You are now ready to graduate. Your cheese board can stand a more sophisticated setup. Try two boards; play the teams against each other.

The All-American Champs

NEW YORK COON
VERMONT SAGE
PHILADELPHIA CREAM
KENTUCKY TRAPPIST
OHIO LIEDERKRANZ
WISCONSIN LIMBURGER
PINEAPPLE
BRICK
CALIFORNIA JACK
MINNESOTA BLUE
TILLAMOOK

VS.

The European Giants

PORTUGUESE TRAZ-OS MONTES
YUGOSLAVIAN KACKAVALJ
DUTCH GOUDA
FRENCH ROQUEFORT
ITALIAN PARMESAN
SWISS EMMENTALER
ENGLISH STILTON
GERMAN MÜNSTER
DANISH BLUE
GREEK FETA
HABLÉ

The postgraduate may play the game using as counters the great and distinctive cheeses of more than fifty countries. Your Scandinavian board alone, just to give an idea of the riches available, will shine with blues, yellows, whites, smoky browns, and chocolates representing Sweden, Norway, Denmark, Finland, Iceland and Lapland.

For the Britisher only blue-veined Stilton is worthy to crown the banquet. The Frenchman defends Roquefort, the Dane his own regal Blue; the Swiss sticks to Emmentaler before, during and after all three meals. You may prefer to finish with a delicate Brie, a smoky slice of Provolone, a bit of Baby Gouda, or some Liptauer Garniert, about which more later.

We load them all on Lazy Lou, Lazy Susan's big twin brother, a giant roulette wheel of cheese, every number a winner. A second Lazy Lou will bear the savories and go-withs. For these tidbits the English have a divine genius; think of the deviled shrimps, smoked oysters, herring roe on toast, snips of broiled sausage . . . But we will make do with some olives and radishes, a few pickles, nuts, capers. With our two trusty Lazy Lous on hand plus wine or beer, we can easily dispense with the mere dinner itself.

Perhaps it is an Italian night. Then Lazy Lou is happily burdened with imported Latticini; Incanestrato, still bearing the imprint of its wicker basket; Pepato, which is but Incanestrato peppered; Mel Fina; deep-yellow, buttery Scanno with its slightly burned flavor; tangy Asiago; Caciocavallo, so called because the cheeses, tied in pairs and hung over a pole, look as though they were sitting in a saddle—cheese on horseback, or "*cacio a cavallo.*" Then we ring in Lazy Lou's first assistant, an old, silver-plated, revolving Florentine magnum-holder. It's designed to spin a gigantic flask of Chianti. The flick of a finger and the bottle is before you. Gently pull it down and hold your glass to the spout.

True, imported wines and cheeses are expensive. But native American products and reasonably edible imitations of the real thing are available as substitutes. Anyway, protein for protein, a cheese party will cost less than a steak barbecue. And it can be more fun.

Encourage your guests to contribute their own latest discoveries. One may bring along as his ticket of admission a Primavera from Brazil; another some cubes of an Andean specialty just flown in from Colombia's mountain city, Mérida, and still wrapped in its aromatic leaves of *Frailejón Lanudo;* another a few wedges of savory sweet English Flower cheese, some flavored with rose petals, others with marigolds; another a tube of South American Kräuterkäse.

Provide your own assortment of breads and try to include some of those fat, flaky old-fashioned crackers that country stores in New England can still supply. Mustard? Sure, if you like it. If you want to be fancy, use a tricky little gadget put out by the Maille condiment-makers in France and available here in the food specialty shops. It's a miniature painter's palate holding five mustards of different shades and flavors and two mustard paddles. The mustards, in proper chromatic order, are: jonquil yellow "Strong Dijon"; "Green Herbs"; brownish "Tarragon"; golden "Ora"; crimson "Tomato-flavored."

And, just to keep things moving, we have restored an antique whirling cruet-holder to deliver Worcestershire sauce, soy sauce, A-1, Tap Sauce and Major Grey's Chutney. Salt shakers and pepper mills are handy, with a big-holed tin canister filled with crushed red-pepper pods, chili powder, Hungarian paprika and such small matters. Butter, both sweet and salt, is on hand, together with saucers or bowls of curry, capers, chives (sliced, not chopped), minced onion, fresh mint leaves, chopped pimientos, caraway, quartered lemons, parsley, fresh tarragon, tomato slices, red and white radishes, green and black olives, pearl onions and assorted nutmeats.

Some years ago, when I was collaborating with my mother, Cora, and my wife, Rose, in writing *10,000 Snacks* (which, by the way, devotes nearly forty pages to cheeses), we staged a rather elaborate tasting party just for the three of us. It took a two-tiered Lazy Lou to twirl the load.

The eight wedges on the top round were English and French samples and the lower one carried the rest, as follows:

ENGLISH CHEDDAR	CHESHIRE	ENGLISH STILTON	CANADIAN CHEDDAR (rum flavored)
FRENCH MÜNSTER	FRENCH BRIE	FRENCH CAMEMBERT	FRENCH ROQUEFORT
SWISS SAPSAGO	SWISS GRUYÈRE	ITALIAN PROVOLONE	ITALIAN GORGONZOLA
SWISS EDAM	DUTCH GOUDA	CZECH OSTIEPKI	NORWEGIAN GJETOST

HUNGARIAN LIPTAUER

The tasting began with familiar English Cheddars, Cheshires and Stiltons from the top row. We had cheese knives, scoops, graters, scrapers and a regulation wire saw, but for this line of crumbly Britishers fingers were best.

The Cheddar was a light, lemony-yellow, almost white, like our best domestic "bar cheese" of old.

The Cheshire was moldy and milky, with a slightly fermented flavor that brought up the musty dining room of Fleet Street's Cheshire cheese and called for draughts of beer. The Stilton was strong but mellow, as high in flavor as in price.

Only the rum-flavored Canadian Cheddar from Montreal (by courtesy English) let us down. It was done up as fancy as a bridegroom in waxed white paper and looked as smooth and glossy as a gardenia. But there its beauty ended. Either the rum that flavored it wasn't up to much or the mixture hadn't been allowed to ripen naturally.

The French Münster, however, was hearty, cheery, and better made than most German Münster, which at that time wasn't being exported much by the Nazis. The Brie was melting prime, the Camembert was so perfectly matured we ate every scrap of the crust, which can't be done with many American "Camemberts" or, indeed, with the dead, dry French ones sold out of season. Then came the Roquefort, a regal cheese we voted the best buy of the lot, even though it was the most expensive. A plump piece, pleasantly unctuous but not greasy, sharp in scent, stimulatingly bittersweet in taste—unbeatable. There is no American pretender to the Roquefort throne. Ours is invariably chalky and tasteless. That doesn't mean we have no good Blues. We have. But they are not Roquefort.

The Sapsago or Kräuterkäse from Switzerland (it has been made in the Canton of Glarus for over five hundred years) was the least expensive of the lot. Well-cured and dry, it lent itself to grating and tasted fine on an old-fashioned buttered soda cracker. Sapsago has its own seduction, derived from the clover-leaf powder with which the curd is mixed and which gives it its haunting flavor and spring-like sage-green color.

Next came some truly great Swiss Gruyère, delicately rich, and nutty enough to make us think of the sharp white wines to be drunk with it at the source.

As for the Provolone, notable for the water-buffalo milk that makes it, there's an example of really grown-up milk. Perfumed as spring flowers drenched with a shower of Anjou, having a bouquet all its own and a trace of a winelike kick, it made us vow never to taste another American imitation. Only a smooth-cheeked, thick slab cut from a pedigreed Italian Provolone of medium girth, all in one piece and with no sign of a crack, will satisfy the gourmet.

The second Italian classic was Gorgonzola, gorgeous Gorgonzola, as fruity as apples, peaches and pears sliced together. It smells so much like a ripe banana we often eat them together, plain or with the crumbly *formaggio* lightly forked into the fruit, split lengthwise.

After that the Edam tasted too lipsticky, like the red-paint job on its rind, and the Gouda seemed only half-hearted. Both too obviously ready-made for commerce with nothing individual or custom-made about them, rolled or bounced over from Holland by the boat load.

The Ostiepki from Czechoslovakia might have been a link of smoked ostrich sausage put up in the skin of its own red neck. In spite of its pleasing lemon-yellow interior, we couldn't think of any use for it except maybe crumbling thirty or forty cents' worth into a ten-cent bowl of bean soup. But that seemed like a waste of money, so we set it aside to try in tiny chunks on crackers as an appetizer some other day, when it might be more appetizing.

We felt much the same about the chocolate-brown Norwegian Gjetost that looked like a slab of boarding-school fudge and which had the same cloying cling to the tongue. We were told by a native that our piece was entirely too young. That's what made it so insipid, undeveloped in texture and flavor. But the next piece we got turned out to be too old and decrepit, and so strong it would have taken a Paul Bunyan to stand up under it. When we complained to our expert about the shock to our palates, he only laughed, pointing to the nail on his little finger.

"You should take just a little bit, like that. A pill no bigger than a couple of aspirins or an Alka-Seltzer. It's only in the morning you take it when it's old and strong like this, for a pick-me-up, a cure for a hangover, you know, like a prairie oyster well soused in Worcestershire."

That made us think we might use it up to flavor a Welsh Rabbit, *instead* of the Worcestershire sauce, but we couldn't melt it with anything less than a blowtorch.

To bring the party to a happy end, we went to town on the

Hungarian Liptauer, garnishing that fine, granulating buttery base after mixing it well with some cream cheese. We mixed the mixed cheese with sardine and tuna mashed together in a little of the oil from the can. We juiced it with lemon, sluiced it with bottled sauces, worked in the leftovers, some tarragon, mint, spicy seeds, parsley, capers and chives. We peppered and paprikaed it, salted and spiced it, then spread it thicker than butter on pumpernickel and went to it. *That's* Liptauer Garniert.

Appendix

The A-B-Z of Cheese

Each cheese is listed by its name and country of origin, with any further information available. Unless otherwise indicated, the cheese is made of cow's milk.

A

Aberdeen *Scotland*	Soft; creamy mellow.
Abertam *Bohemia (Made near Carlsbad)*	Hard; sheep; distinctive, with a savory smack all its own.
Absinthe	*see* Petafina.
Acidophilus	*see* Saint-Ivel.
Aettekees *Belgium*	November to May—winter-made and eaten.

Affiné, Carré	*see* Ancien Impérial.
Affumicata, Mozzarella	*see* Mozzarella.
After-dinner cheeses	*see* Chapter 8.
Agricultural school cheeses	*see* College-educated.
Aiguilles, Fromage d' *Alpine France*	Named "Cheese of the Needles" from the sharp Alpine peaks of the district where it is made.
Aizy, Cendree d'	*see* Cendrée.
Ajacilo, Ajaccio *Corsica*	Semihard; piquant; nut-flavor. Named after the chief city of French Corsica where a cheese-lover, Napoleon, was born.
à la Crème	*see* Fromage, Fromage Blanc, Chevretons.
à la Main	*see* Vacherin.
à la Pie	*see* Fromage.
à la Rachette	*see* Bagnes.
Albini *Northern Italy*	Semihard; made of both goat and cow milk; white, mellow, pleasant-tasting table cheese.
Albula *Switzerland*	Rich with the flavor of cuds of green herbs chewed into creamy milk that makes tasty curds. Made in the fertile Swiss Valley of Albula whose proud name it bears.
Alderney *Channel Islands*	The French, who are fond of this special product of the very special breed of cat-

tle named after the Channel Island of Alderney, translate it phonetically—Fromage d'Aurigny.

Alemtejo
Portugal

Called in full Queijo de Alemtejo, cheese of Alemtejo, in the same way that so many French cheeses carry along the *fromage* title. Soft; sheep and sometimes goat or cow; in cylinders of three sizes, weighing respectively about two ounces, one pound, and four pounds. The smaller sizes are the ones most often made with mixed goat and sheep milk. The method of curdling without the usual animal rennet is interesting and unusual. The milk is warmed and curdled with vegetable rennet made from the flowers of a local thistle, or cardoon, which is used in two other Portuguese cheeses—Queijo da Cardiga and Queijo da Serra da Estrella—and probably in many others not known beyond their locale. In France la Caillebotte is distinguished for being clabbered with *chardonnette,* wild artichoke seed. In Portugal, where there isn't so much separating of the sheep from the goats, it takes several weeks for Alemtejos to ripen, depending on the lactic content and difference in sizes.

Alfalfa

see Sage.

Alise Saint-Reine
France

Soft; summer-made.

Allgäuer Bergkäse, Allgäuer Rundkäse, or Allgäuer Emmentaler
Bavaria

Hard; Emmentaler type. The small district of Allgäu names a mountain of cheeses almost as fabulous as our "Rock-candy Mountain." There are two principal kinds, vintage Allgäuer Bergkäse and soft Allgäuer Rahmkäse, described below. This celebrated cheese section runs through rich pasture lands right down and into the Swiss Valley of the Emme that gives the name Emmentaler to one of the world's greatest. So it is no wonder that Allgäuer Bergkäse can compete with the best Swiss. Before the Russian revolution, in fact, all vintage cheeses of Allgäu were bought up by wealthy Russian noblemen and kept in their home caves in separate compartments for each year, as far back as the early 1900's. As with fine vintage wines, the price of the great years went up steadily. Such cheeses were shipped to their Russian owners only when the chief cheese-pluggers of Allgäu found they had reached their prime.

Allgäuer Rahmkäse
Bavaria

Full cream, similar to Romadur and Limburger, but milder than both. This sets a high grade for similar cheeses made in the Bavarian mountains, in monasteries such as Andechs. It goes exquisitely with the rich dark Bavarian beer. Some of it is as slippery as the stronger, smellier Bierkäse, or the old-time Slipcoat of England. Like so many North Europeans, it is often flavored with caraway. Although entirely different from its big brother, vintage Bergkäse, Rahmkäse can stand proudly at its side as one of the finest cheeses in Germany.

Alpe

see Fiore di Alpe.

Al Pepe
Italy

Hard and peppery, like its name. Similar to Pepato (*see*).

Alpes *France*	Similar to Bel Paese.
Alpestra *Austria*	A smoked cheese that tastes, smells and inhales like whatever fish it was smoked with. The French Alps has a different Alpestre; Italy spells hers Alpestro.
Alpestre, Alpin, or Fromage de Briançon *France*	Hard; goat; dry; small; lightly salted. Made at Briançon and Gap.
Alpestro *Italy*	Semisoft; goat; dry; lightly salted.
Alpin or Clérimbert *Alpine France*	The milk is coagulated with rennet at 80° F. in two hours. The curd is dipped into molds three to four inches in diameter and two and a half inches in height, allowed to drain, turned several times for one day only, then salted and ripened one to two weeks.
Altenburg, or Altenburger Ziegenkäse *Germany*	Soft; goat; small and flat—one to two inches thick, eight inches in diameter, weight two pounds.
Alt Kuhkäse **Old Cow Cheese** *Germany*	Hard; well-aged, as its simple name suggests.
Altsohl	*see* Brinza.
Ambert, or Fourme d' Ambert *Limagne, Auvergne, France*	A kind of Cheddar made from November to May and belonging to the Cantal —Fourme–La Tome tribe.
American, American Cheddar *U.S.A.*	Described under their home states and distinctive names are a dozen fine American Cheddars, such as Coon, Wiscon-

sin, Herkimer County and Tillamook, to name only a few. They come in as many different shapes, with traditional names such as Daisies, Flats, Longhorns, Midgets, Picnics, Prints and Twins. The ones simply called Cheddars weigh about sixty pounds. All are made and pressed and ripened in about the same way, although they differ greatly in flavor and quality. They are ripened anywhere from two months to two years and become sharper, richer and more flavorsome, as well as more expensive, with the passing of time. *See* Cheddar states and Cheddar types in Chapter 4.

Americano Romano
U.S.A.

Hard; brittle; sharp.

Amou
Béarn, France

Winter cheese, October to May.

Anatolian
Turkey

Hard; sharp.

Anchovy Links
U.S.A.

American processed cheese that can be mixed up with anchovies or any fish from whitebait to whale, made like a sausage and sold in handy links.

Ancien Impérial
Normandy, France

Soft; fresh cream; white, mellow and creamy like Neufchâtel and made in the same way. Tiny bricks packaged in tin foil, two inches square, one-half inch thick, weighing three ounces. Eaten both fresh and when ripe. It is also called Carré and has separate names for the new and the old: (a) Petit Carré when newly made; (b) Carré Affiné, when it has reached a ripe old age, which doesn't take long—about the same time as Neufchâtel.

Ancona — *see* Pecorino.

Andean
Venezuela

A cow's-milker made in the Andes near Mérida. It is formed into rough cubes and wrapped in the pungent, aromatic leaves of *Frailejón Lanudo* (*Espeletia Schultzii*) which imparts to it a characteristic flavor. (Description given in *Buen Provecho!* by Dorothy Kamen-Kaye.)

Andechs
Bavaria

A lusty Allgäuer type. Monk-made on the monastery hill at Andechs on Ammersee. A superb snack with equally monkish dark beer, black bread and blacker radishes, served by the brothers in dark brown robes.

Antwerp
Belgium

Semihard; nut-flavored; named after its place of origin.

Appenzeller
Switzerland, Bavaria and Baden

Semisoft Emmentaler type made in a small twenty-pound wheel—a pony-cart wheel in comparison to the big Swiss. There are two qualities: (a) Common, made of skim milk and cured in brine for a year; (b) Festive, full milk, steeped in brine with wine, plus white wine lees and pepper. The only cheese we know of that is ripened with lees of wine.

Appetitost
Denmark

Semisoft; sour milk; nutlike flavor. It's an appetizer that lives up to its name, eaten fresh on the spot, from the loose bottom pans in which it is made.

Appetost
Denmark

Sour buttermilk, similar to Primula, with caraway seeds added for snap. Imitated in U.S.A.

Apple
U.S.A.

A small New York State Cheddar put up in the form of a red-cheeked apple for New York City trade. Inspired by the pear-shaped Provolone and Baby Gouda, no doubt.

Arber
Bohemia

Semihard; sour milk; yellow; mellow and creamy. Made in mountains between Bohemia and Silesia.

Argentine
Argentina

Argentina is specially noted for fine reproductions of classical Italian hard-grating cheeses such as Parmesan and Romano, rich and fruity because of the lush pampas-grass feeding.

Armavir
Western Caucasus

Soft; whole sour sheep milk; a hand cheese made by stirring cold, sour buttermilk or whey into heated milk, pressing in forms and ripening in a warm place. Similar to Hand cheese.

Arnauten

see Travnik.

Arovature
Italy

Water-buffalo milk.

Arras, Coeurs d'

see Coeurs.

Arrigny
Champagne, France

Made only in winter, November to May. Since gourmet products of the same province often have a special affinity, Arrigny and champagne are specially well suited to one another.

Artichoke, Cardoon or Thistle for Rennet

see Caillebotte.

Artificial Dessert Cheese

In the lavish days of olde England Artificial Dessert Cheese was made by mixing one quart of cream with two of milk and spiking it with powdered cinnamon, nutmeg and mace. Four beaten eggs were then stirred in with one-half cup of white vinegar and the mixture boiled to a curd. It was then poured into a cheesecloth and hung up to drain six to eight hours. When taken out of the cloth it was further flavored with rose water, sweetened with castor sugar, left to ripen for an hour or two and finally served up with more cream.

Asadero, or Oaxaca
Jalisco and Oaxaca, Mexico

White; whole-milk. Curd is heated, and hot curd is cut and braided or kneaded into loaves from eight ounces to eleven pounds in weight. Asadero means "suitable for roasting."

Asco
Corsica, France

Made only in the winter season, October to May.

Asiago I, II and III
Vicenza, Italy

Sometimes classed as medium and mild, depending mostly on age. Loaves weigh about eighteen pounds each and look like American Cheddar but have a taste all their own.

I. Mild, nutty and sharp, used for table slicing and eating.
II. Medium, semihard and tangy, also used for slicing until nine months old.
III. Hard, old, dry, sharp, brittle. When over nine months old, it's fine for grating.

Asin, or Water cheese
Northern Italy

Sour-milk; washed-curd; whitish; soft; buttery. Made mostly in spring and eaten in summer and autumn. Dessert

	cheese, frequently eaten with honey and fruit.
Au Cumin	*see* Münster.
Au Fenovil	*see* Tome de Savoie.
Au Foin and de Foin	A style of ripening "on the hay." *See* Pithiviers au Foin and Fromage de Foin.
Augelot *Valée d'Auge, Normandy, France*	Soft; tangy; piquant Pont l'Evêque type.
d'Auray	*see* Sainte-Anne.
Aurigny, Fromage d'	*see* Alderney.
Aurillac	*see* Bleu d'Auvergne.
Aurore and Triple Aurore *Normandy, France*	Made and eaten all year.
Australian and New Zealand *Australia and New Zealand*	Enough cheese is produced for local consumption, chiefly Cheddar; some Gruyère, but unfortunately mostly processed.
Autun *Nivernais, France*	Produced and eaten all year. Fromage de Vache is another name for it and this is of special interest in a province where the chief competitors are made of goat's milk.
Auvergne, Bleu d'	*see* Bleu.
Au Vin Blanc, Confits	*see* Epoisses.
Avesnes, Boulette d'	*see* Boulette.
Aydes, les *Orléanais, France*	Not eaten during July, August or September. Season, October to June.

Azeitão, Queijo do
Portugal

Soft, sheep, sapid and extremely oily as the superlative *ão* implies. There are no finer, fatter cheeses in the world than those made of rich sheep milk in the mountains of Portugal and named for them.

Azeitoso
Portugal

Soft; mellow, zestful and as oily as it is named.

Azuldoch Mountain
Turkey

Mild and mellow mountain product.

B

Backsteiner
Bavaria

Resembles Limburger, but smaller, and translates Brick, from the shape. It is aromatic and piquant and not very much like the U.S. Brick.

Bagnes, or Fromage à la Raclette
Switzerland

Not only hard but very hard, named from *racler,* French for "scrape." A thick, one-half-inch slice is cut across the whole cheese and toasted until runny. It is then scraped off the pan it's toasted in with a flexible knife, spread on bread and eaten like an open-faced Welsh Rabbit sandwich.

Bagozzo, Grana Bagozzo, Bresciano
Italy

Hard; yellow; sharp. Surface often colored red. Parmesan type.

Bakers' cheese

Skim milk, similar to cottage cheese, but softer and finer grained. Used in making bakery products such as cheese cake, pie, and pastries, but may also be eaten like creamed cottage cheese.

Ball
U.S.A.
Made from thick sour milk in Pennsylvania in the style of the original Pennsylvania Dutch settlers.

Ballakäse or Womelsdorf
Similar to Ball.

Balls, Dutch Red
English name for Edam.

Banbury
England
Soft, rich cylinder about one inch thick made in the town of Banbury, famous for its spicy, citrus-peel buns and its equestrienne. Banbury cheese with Banbury buns made a sensational snack in the early nineteenth century, but both are getting scarce today.

Banick
Armenia
White and sweet.

Banjaluka
Bosnia
Port-Salut type from its Trappist monastery.

Banon, or les Petits Banons
Provence, France
Small, dried, sheep-milker, made in the foothills of the Alps and exported through Marseilles in season, May to November. This sprightly summer cheese is generously sprinkled with the local brandy and festively wrapped in fresh green leaves.

Bar cheese
U.S.A.
Any saloon Cheddar, formerly served on every free-lunch counter in the U.S. Before Prohibition, free-lunch cheese was the backbone of America's cheese industry.

Barbacena
Minas Geraes, Brazil
Hard, white, sometimes chalky. Named from its home city in the leading cheese state of Brazil.

Barberey, or Fromage de Troyes
Champagne, France

Soft, creamy and smooth, resembling Camembert, five to six inches in diameter and 1¼ inches thick. Named from its home town, Barberey, near Troyes, whose name it also bears. Fresh, warm milk is coagulated by rennet in four hours. Uncut curd then goes into a wooden mold with a perforated bottom, to drain three hours, before being finished off in an earthenware mold. The cheeses are salted, dried and ripened three weeks in a cave. The season is from November to May and when made in summer they are often sold fresh.

Barboux
France

Soft.

Baronet
U.S.A.

A natural product, mild and mellow.

Barron
France

Soft.

Bassilac

see Bleu.

Bath
England

Gently made, lightly salted, drained on a straw mat in the historic resort town of Bath. Ripened in two weeks and eaten only when covered with a refined fuzzy mold that's also eminently edible. It is the most delicate of English-speaking cheeses.

Battelmatt
Switzerland, St. Gothard Alps, northern Italy, and western Austria

An Emmentaler made small where milk is not plentiful. The "wheel" is only sixteen inches in diameter and four inches high, weighing forty to eighty pounds. The cooking of the curd is done at a little lower temperature than Emmentaler, it ripens more rapidly—in four months

—and is somewhat softer, but has the same holes and creamy though sharp, full nutty flavor.

Bauden (*see also* Koppen)
Germany, Austria, Bohemia and Silesia

Semisoft, sour milk, hand type, made in herders' mountain huts in about the same way as Harzkäse, though it is bigger. In two forms, one cup shape (called Koppen), the other a cylinder. Strong and aromatic, whether made with or without caraway.

Bavarian Beer cheese

see Bayrischer Bierkäse.

Bavarian Cream
German

Very soft; smooth and creamy. Made in the Bavarian mountains. Especially good with sweet wines and sweet sauces.

Bavarois à la Vanille

see Fromage Bavarois.

Bayonne

see Fromage de Bayonne.

Bayrischer Bierkäse
Bavaria

Bavarian beer cheese from the Tyrol is made not only to eat with beer, but to dunk in it.

Beads of cheese
Tibet

Beads of hard cheese, two inches in diameter, are strung like a necklace of cowrie shells or a rosary, fifty to a hundred on a string. *Also see* Money Made of Cheese.

Beagues

see Tome de Savoie.

Bean Cake, Tao-foo, or Tofu
China, Japan, the Orient

Soy bean cheese imported from Shanghai and other oriental ports, and also imitated in every Chinatown around the world. Made from the milk of beans and curdled with its own vegetable rennet.

Beaujolais — *see* Chevretons.

Beaumont, or Tome de Beaumont
Savoy, France

A more or less successful imitation of Trappist Tamie, a trade-secret triumph of Savoy. At its best from October to June.

Beaupré de Roybon
Dauphiné, France

A winter specialty made from November to April.

Beckenried
Switzerland

A good mountain cheese from goat milk.

Beer cheese
U.S.A.

While our beer cheese came from Germany and the word is merely a translation of Bierkäse, we use it chiefly for a type of strong Limburger made mostly in Milwaukee. This fine, aromatic cheese is considered by many as the very best to eat while drinking beer. But in Germany Bierkäse is more apt to be dissolved in a glass or stein of beer, much as we mix malted powder in milk, and drunk with it, rather than eaten.

Beer-Regis
Dorsetshire, England

This sounds like another beer cheese, but it's only a mild Cheddar named after its hometown in Dorsetshire.

Beist-Cheese
Scotland

A curiosity of the old days. "The first milk after a calving, boiled or baked to a thick consistency, the result somewhat resembling new-made cheese, though this is clearly not a true cheese." (MacNeill)

Belarno
Italy

Hard; goat; creamy dessert cheese.

Belgian Cooked
Belgium

The milk, which has been allowed to curdle spontaneously, is skimmed and allowed to drain. When dry it is thoroughly kneaded by hand and is allowed to undergo fermentation, which takes ordinarily from ten to fourteen days in winter and six to eight days in summer. When the fermentation is complete, cream and salt are added and the mixture is heated slowly and stirred until homogeneous, when it is put into molds and allowed to ripen for eight days longer. A cheese ordinarily weighs about three-and-a-half pounds. It is not essentially different from other forms of cooked cheese.

Beli Sir

see Domaci.

Bellelay, Tête de Moine, or Monk's Head
Switzerland

Soft, buttery, semisharp spread. Sweet milk is coagulated with rennet in twenty to thirty minutes, the curd cut fairly fine and cooked not so firm as Emmentaler, but firmer than Limburger. After being pressed, the cheeses are wrapped in bark for a couple of weeks until they can stand alone. Since no eyes are desired in the cheeses, they are ripened in a moist cellar at a lowish temperature. They take a year to ripen and will keep three or four years. The diameter is seven inches, the weight nine to fifteen pounds. The monk's head after cutting is kept wrapped in a napkin soaked in white wine and the soft, creamy spread is scraped out to "butter" bread and snacks that go with more white wine. Such combinations of old wine and old cheese suggest monkish influence, which began here in the fifteenth century with the jolly friars of the Canton of Bern. There it is still made exclusively and not exported, for there's never quite enough to go around

Bel Paese
Italy

see under Foreign Greats, Chapter 3. *Also see* Mel Fino, a blend, and Bel Paese types—French Boudanne and German Saint Stefano. The American imitation is not nearly so good as the Italian original.

Bel Paesino
U.S.A.

A play on the Bel Paese name and fame. Weight one pound and diminutive in every other way.

Bergkäse

see Allgäuer.

Bergquara
Sweden

Semihard, fat, resembles Dutch Gouda. Tangy, pleasant taste. Gets sharper with age, as they all do. Molded in cylinders of fifteen to forty pounds. Popular in Sweden since the eighteenth century.

Berkeley
England

Named after its home town in Gloucester, England.

Berliner Kuhkäse
Berlin, Germany

Cow cheese, pet-named turkey cock cheese by Berlin students. Typical German hand cheese, soft; aromatic with caraway seeds, and that's about the only difference between it and Alt Kuhkäse, without caraway.

Bernarde, Formagelle Bernarde
Italy

Cow's whole milk, to which about 10% of goat's milk is added for flavor. Cured for two months.

Berques
France

Made of skim milk.

Berry Rennet

see Withania.

Bessay, le
Bourbonnais, France

Soft, mild, and creamy.

Bexhill
England

Cream cheeses, small, flat, round. Excellent munching.

Bierkäse
Germany

There are several of these unique beer cheeses that are actually dissolved in a stein of beer and drunk down with it in the Bierstubes, notably Bayrischer, Dresdener, and Olmutzer. Semisoft; aromatic; sharp. Well imitated in *echt Deutsche* American spots such as Milwaukee and Hoboken.

Bifrost
Norway

Goat; white; mildly salt. Imitated in a process spread in 4¼-ounce package.

Binn
Wallis, Switzerland

Exceptionally fine Swiss from the great cheese canton of Wallis.

Bitto
Northern Italy

Hard Emmentaler type made in the Valtellina. It is really two cheeses in one. When eaten fresh, it is smooth, sapid, big-eyed Swiss. When eaten after two years of ripening, it is very hard and sharp and has small eyes.

Blanc à la crème

see Fromage Blanc.

Blanc

see Fromage Blanc I and II.

Bleu
France

Brittle; blue-veined; smooth; biting.

Bleu d'Auvergne or Fromage Bleu
Auvergne, France

Hard; sheep or mixed sheep, goat or cow; from Pontgibaud and Laqueuille ripening caves. Similar to better-known Cantal of the same province. Akin to Roquefort and Stilton, and to Bleu de Laqueuille.

Bleu de Bassillac
Limousin, France

Blue mold of Roquefort type that's prime from November to May.

Bleu de Laqueuille *France*	Similar to Bleu d'Auvergne, but with a different savor. Named for its originator, Antoine Roussel-Laqueuille, who first made it a century ago, in 1854.
Bleu de Limousin, Fromage *Lower Limousin*	Practically the same as Bleu de Bassillac, from Lower Limousin.
Bleu de Salers *France*	A variety of Bleu d'Auvergne from the same province distinguished for its blues that are green. With the majority, this is at its best only in the winter months, from November to May.
Bleu, Fromage	*see* Bleu d'Auvergne.
Bleu-Olivet	*see* Olivet.
Blind	The name for cheeses lacking the usual holes of the type they belong to, such as blind Swiss.
Block Edam *U.S.A.*	U.S. imitation of the classical Dutch cheese named after the town of Edam.
Block, Smoked *Austria*	The name is self-explanatory and suggests a well-colored meerschaum.
Bloder, or Schlicker Milch *Switzerland*	Sour-milker.
Blue Cheddar	*see* Cheshire-Stilton.
Blue, Danish	*see* Danish Blue.
Blue Dorset	*see* Dorset.
Blue, Jura	*see* Jura Bleu and Septmoncel.
Blue, and Blue with Port Links *U.S.A.*	One of the modern American process sausages.

Blue, Minnesota — *see* Minnesota.

Blue Moon
U.S.A.
A process product.

Blue Vinny, Blue Vinid, Blue-veined Dorset, or Double Dorset
Dorsetshire, England
A unique Blue that actually isn't green-veined. Farmers make it for private consumption, because it dries up too easily to market. An epicurean esoteric match for Truckles No. 1 of Wiltshire. It comes in a flat form, chalk-white, crumbly and sharply flavored, with a "royal Blue" vein running right through horizontally. The Vinny mold, from which it was named, is different from all other cheese molds and has a different action.

Bocconi Geganti
Italy
Sharp and smoky specialty.

Bocconi Provoloni — *see* Provolone.

Boîte — *see* Fromage de Boîte.

Bombay
India
Hard; goat; dry; sharp. Good to crunch with a Bombay Duck in place of a cracker.

Bondes — *see* Bondon de Neufchâtel.

Bondon de Neufchâtel, or Bondes
Normandy, France
Nicknamed *Bonde à tout bien,* from resemblance to the bung in a barrel of Neuchâtel wine. Soft, small loaf rolls, fresh and mild. Similar to Gournay, but sweeter because of 2% added sugar.

Bondon de Rouen
France
A fresh Neufchâtel, similar to Petit Suisse, but slightly salted, to last up to ten days.

Bondost *Sweden*	When caraway seed is added this is called Kommenost, spelled Kuminost in Norway.
Bond Ost *U.S.A.*	Imitation of Scandinavian cheese, with small production in Wisconsin.
Bon Larron *France*	Romantically named "the penitent thief."
Borden's *U.S.A.*	A full line of processed and naturals, of which Liederkranz is the leader.
Borelli *Italy*	A small water-buffalo cheese.
Bossons Maceres *Provence, France*	A winter product, December, January, February and March only.
Boudanne *France*	Whole or skimmed cow's milk, ripens in two to three months.
Boudes, Boudon *Normandy, France*	Soft, fresh, smooth, creamy, mild child of the Neufchâtel family.
Bougon Lamothe	*see* Lamothe.
Bouillé, la *Normandy France*	One of this most prolific province's thirty different notables. In season October to May.
Boule de Lille *France*	Name given to Belgian Oude Kaas by the French who enjoy it.
Boulette d'Avesnes, or Boulette de Cambrai *Flanders, France*	Made from November to May, eaten all year.
Bourgain *France*	Type of fresh Neufchâtel made in France. Perishable and consumed locally.

Bourgognes

see Petits Bourgognes.

Box
Württemberg, Germany

Similar to U.S. Brick. It comes in two styles; firm, and soft:

I. Also known as Schachtelkäse, Boxed Cheese; and Hohenheim, where it is made. A rather unimportant variety. Made in a copper kettle, with partially skim milk, colored with saffron and spiked with caraway, a handful to every two hundred pounds. Salted and ripened for three months and shipped in wooden boxes.

II. Also known by names of localities where made: Hohenburg, Mondess and Weihenstephan. Made of whole milk. Mild but piquant.

Bra No. I
Piedmont, Italy

Hard, round form, twelve inches in diameter, three inches high, weight twelve pounds. A somewhat romantic cheese, made by nomads who wander with their herds from pasture to pasture in the region of Bra.

Bra No. II
Turin and Cuneo, Italy

Soft, creamy, small, round and mild although cured in brine.

Brand or Brandkäse
Germany

Soft, sour-milk hand cheese, weighing one-third of a pound. The curd is cooked at a high temperature, then salted and set to ferment for a day. Butter is then mixed into it before pressing into small bricks. After drying it is put in used beer kegs to ripen and is frequently moistened with beer while curing.

Brandy

see Caledonian Cream.

Branja de Brailia
Rumania

Hard; sheep; extra salty because always kept in brine.

Branja de Cosulet
Rumania

Described by Richard Wyndham in *Wine and Food* (Winter, 1937): A creamy sheep's cheese which is encased in pine bark. My only criticism of this most excellent cheese is that the center must always remain a gastronomical second best. It is no more interesting than a good English Cheddar, while the outer crust has a scented, resinous flavor which must be unique among cheeses.

Bratkäse
Switzerland

Strong; specially made to roast in slices over coal. Fine, grilled on toast.

Breakfast, Frühstuck, Lunch, Delikat, and other names
Germany

Soft and delicate, but with a strong tang. Small round, for spreading. Lauterbach is a well-known breakfast cheese in Germany, while in Switzerland Emmentaler is eaten at all three meals.

Breakstone
U.S.A.

Like Borden and other leading American cheesemongers and manufacturers, Breakstone offer a full line, of which their cream cheese is an American product to be proud of.

Brésegaut
Savoy, France

Soft, white.

Breslau
Germany

A proud Prussian dessert cheese.

Bressans

see les Petits.

Bresse
France

Lightly cooked.

Bretagne

see Montauban.

Brevine
Switzerland

Emmentaler type.

Briançon

see Alpin.

Brick

see Chapter 4.

Brickbat
Wiltshire, England

A traditional Wiltshire product since early in the eighteenth century. Made with fresh milk and some cream, to ripen for one year before "it's fit to eat." The French call it Briqueton.

Bricotta
Corsica

Semisoft, sour sheep, sometimes mixed with sugar and rum and made into small luscious cakes.

Brie

see Chapter 3; *also see* Cendré and Coulommiers.

Brie Façon
France

The name of imitation Brie or Brie type made in all parts of France. Often it is dry, chalky, and far inferior to the finest Brie *véritable* that is still made best in its original home, formerly called La Brie, now Seine et Marne, or Ile-de-France.

see Nivernais Decize, Le Mont d'Or, and Ile-de-France.

Brie de Meaux
France

This genuine Brie from the Meaux region has an excellent reputation for high quality. It is made only from November to May.

Brie de Melun
France

This Brie *véritable* is made not only in the seasonal months, from November to May, but practically all the year around. It is not always prime. Summer Brie, called Maigre, is notably poor and thin.

Spring Brie is merely Migras, half-fat, as against the fat autumn Gras that ripens until May.

Brillat-Savarin
Normandy, France
Soft, and available all year. Although the author of *Physiologie du Gout* was not noted as a caseophile and wrote little on the subject beyond *Le Fondue* (*see* Chapter 6), this savory Normandy produce is named in his everlasting praise.

Brina Dubreala
Rumania
Semisoft, sheep, done in brine.

Brindza
U.S.A.
Our imitation of this creamy sort of fresh, white Roquefort is as popular in foreign colonies in America as back in its Hungarian and Greek homelands. On New York's East Side several stores advertise "Brindza fresh daily," with an extra "d" crowded into the original Brinza.

Brine
see Italian Bra, Caucasian Ekiwani, Brina Dubreala, Briney.

Briney, or Brined
Syria
Semisoft, salty, sharp. So-called from being processed in brine. Turkish Tullum Penney is of the same salt-soaked type.

Brinza, or Brinsen
Hungary, Rumania, Carpathian Mountains
Goes by many local names: Altsohl, Klencz, Landoch, Liptauer, Neusohl, Siebenburgen and Zips. Soft, sheep milk or sheep and goat; crumbly, sharp and biting, but creamy. Made in small lots and cured in a tub with beech shavings. Ftinoporino is its opposite number in Macedonia.

Brioler
see Westphalia.

Briquebec — *see* Providence

Briqueton
England

The French name for English Wiltshire Brickbat, one of the very few cheeses imported into France. Known in France in the eighteenth century, it may have influenced the making of Trappist Port-Salut at the Bricquebec Monastery in Manche.

Brittle — *see* Greek Cashera, Italian Ricotta, Turkish Rarush Durmar, and U.S. Hopi.

Brizecon
Savoy, France

Imitation Reblochon made in the same Savoy province.

Broccio, or le Brocconis
Corsica, France

Soft, sour sheep milk or goat, like Bricotta and a first cousin to Italian Chiavari. Cream white, slightly salty; eaten fresh in Paris, where it is as popular as on its home island. Sometimes salted and half-dried, or made into little cakes with rum and sugar. Made and eaten all year.

Broodkaas
Holland

Hard, flat, nutty.

Brousses de la Vézubie, les
Nice, France

Small; sheep; long narrow bar shape, served either with powdered sugar or salt, pepper and chopped chives. Made in Vézubie.

Brussels or Bruxelles
Belgium

Soft, washed skim milk, fermented, semisharp, from Louvain and Hal districts.

Budapest
Hungary

Soft, fresh, creamy and mellow, a favorite at home in Budapest and abroad in Vienna.

Buderich *Germany*	A specialty in Dusseldorf.
Bulle *Switzerland*	A Swiss Gruyère.
Bundost *Sweden*	Semihard; mellow; tangy.
Burgundy *France*	Named after the province, not the wine, but they go wonderfully together.
Bushman *Australia*	Semihard; yellow; tangy.
Butter and Cheese	*see* Chapter 8.
"Butter," Serbian	*see* Kajmar.
Buttermilk *U. S. & Europe*	Resembles cottage cheese, but of finer grain.

C

Cabeçou, le *Auvergne, France*	Small; goat; from Maurs.
Cabrillon *Auvergne, France*	So much like the Cabreçon they might be called sister nannies under the rind.
Cachet d'Entrechaux, le, or Fromage Fort du Ventoux *Provence Mountains, France*	Semihard; sheep; mixed with brandy, dry white wine and sundry seasonings. Well marinated and extremely strong. Season May to November.
Caciocavallo *Italy*	"Horse Cheese." The ubiquitous cheese of classical greats, imitated all around the world and back to Italy again. *See* Chapter 3.

Caciocavallo Siciliano
Sicily, also in U.S.A.

Essentially a pressed Provolone. Usually from cow's whole milk, but sometimes from goat's milk or a mixture of the two. Weight between 17½ and 26 pounds. Used for both table cheese and grating.

Cacio Fiore, or Caciotta
Italy

Soft as butter; sheep; in four-pound square frames; sweetish; eaten fresh.

Cacio Pecorino Romano

see Pecorino.

Cacio Romano

see Chiavari.

Caerphilly
Wales and England—Devon, Dorset, Somerset & Wiltshire

Semihard; whole fresh milk; takes three weeks to ripen. Also sold "green," young and innocent, at the age of ten to eleven days when weighing about that many pounds. Since it has little keeping qualities it should be eaten quickly. Welsh miners eat a lot of it, think it specially suited to their needs, because it is easily digested and does not produce so much heat in the body as long-keeping cheeses.

Caillebottes (Curds)
France—Anjou, Poitou, Saintonge & Vendée

Soft, creamy, sweetened fresh or sour milk clabbered with chardonnette, wild artichoke seed, over slow fire. Cut in lozenges and served cold not two hours after cooking. Smooth, mellow and aromatic. A high type of this unusual cheese is Jonchée (*see*). Other cheeses are made with vegetable rennet, some from similar thistle or cardoon juice, especially in Portugal.

Caille de Poitiers

see Petits pots.

Caille de Habas
Gascony, France

Clabbered or clotted sheep milk.

Cajassou
Périgord, France

A notable goat cheese made in Cubjac.

Calabrian
Italy

The Calabrians make good sheep cheese, such as this and Caciocavallo.

Calcagno
Sicily

Hard; ewe's milk. Suitable for grating.

Caledonian Cream
Scotland

More of a dessert than a true cheese. We read in *Scotland's Inner Man:* "A sort of fresh cream cheese, flavored with chopped orange marmalade, sugar brandy and lemon juice. It is whisked for about half an hour. Otherwise, if put into a freezer, it would be good ice-pudding."

Calvados
France

Medium-hard; tangy. Perfect with Calvados applejack from the same province.

Calvenzano
Italy

Similar to Gorgonzola, made in Bergamo.

Cambrai

see Boulette.

Cambridge, or York
England

Soft; fresh; creamy; tangy. The curd is quickly made in one hour and dipped into molds without cutting to ripen for eating in thirty hours.

Camembert

see Chapter 3.

"Camembert"
Germany, U.S. & elsewhere

A West German imitation that comes in a cute little heart-shaped box which nevertheless doesn't make it any more like the Camembert *véritable* of Normandy.

Camosun
U.S.A.

Semisoft; open-textured, resembling Monterey. Drained curd is pressed in hoops, cheese is salted in brine for thirty hours, then coated with paraffin and cured for one to three months in humid room at 50° to 60° F.

Canadian Club

see Cheddar Club.

Cancoillotte, Cancaillotte, Canquoillotte, Quincoillotte, Cancoiade, Fromagère, Tempête and "Purée" de fromage très fort
Franche-Comté, France

Soft; sour milk; sharp and aromatic; with added eggs and butter and sometimes brandy or dry white wine. Sold in attractive small molds and pots. Other sharp seasonings besides the brandy or wine make this one of the strongest of French strong cheeses, similar to Fromage Fort.

Canestrato
Sicily, Italy

Hard; mixed goat and sheep; yellow and strong. Takes one year to mature and is very popular both in Sicily where it is made to perfection and in Southern Colorado where it is imitated by and for Italian settlers.

Cantal, Fromage de Cantal, Auvergne or Auvergne Bleu; also Fourme and La Tome
Auvergne, France

Semihard; smooth; mellow; a kind of Cheddar, lightly colored lemon; yellow; strong, sharp taste but hardly any smell. Forty to a hundred-twenty pound cylinders. The rich milk from highland pastures is more or less skimmed and, being a very old variety, it is still made most primitively. Cured six weeks or six months, and when very old it's very hard and very sharp. A Cantal type is Laguiole or Guiole.

Capitanata
Italy

Sheep.

Caprian
Capri, Italy

Made from milk of goats that still overrun the original Goat Island, and tangy as a buck.

Caprino (Little Goat)
Argentina

Semihard; goat; sharp; table cheese.

Caraway Loaf
U.S.A.

This is just one imitation of dozens of German caraway-seeded cheeses that roam the world. In Germany there is not only Kümmel loaf cheese but a loaf of caraway-seeded bread to go with it. Milwaukee has long made a good Kümmelkäse or hand cheese and it would take more than the fingers on both hands to enumerate all of the European originals, from Dutch Komynkaas through Danish King Christian IX and Norwegian Kuminost, Italian Freisa, Pomeranian Rinnen and Belgian Leyden, to Pennsylvania Pot.

Cardiga, Queijo da
Portugal

Hard; sheep; oily; mild flavor. Named from cardo, cardoon in English, a kind of thistle used as a vegetable rennet in making several other cheeses, such as French Caillebottes curdled with chardonette, wild artichoke seed. Only classical Greek sheep cheeses like Casera can compare with the superb ones from the Portuguese mountain districts. They are lusciously oily, but never rancidly so.

Carlsbad
Bohemia

Semihard; sheep; white; slightly salted; expensive.

Carré Affine
France

Soft, delicate, in small square forms; similar to Petit Carré and Ancien Impérial (*see*).

Carré de l'Est
France

Similar to Camembert, and imitated in the U.S.A.

Cascaval Penir
Turkey

Cacciocavallo imitation consumed at home.

Caseralla *Greece*	Semisoft; sheep; mellow; creamy.
Casere *Greece*	Hard; sheep; brittle; gray and greasy. But wonderful! Sour-sweet tongue tickle. This classical though greasy Grecian is imitated with goat milk instead of sheep in Southern California.
Cashera *Armenia and Greece*	Hard; goat or cow's milk; brittle; sharp; nutty. Similar to Casere and high in quality.
Cashera *Turkey*	Semihard; sheep.
Casher Penner	*see* Kasher.
Cashkavalio *Syria*	Mellow but sharp imitation of the ubiquitous Italian Cacciocavallo.
Casigiolu, Panedda, Pera di vacca *Sardinia*	Plastic-curd cheese, made by the Caciocavallo method.
Caskcaval or Kaschcavallo	*see* Feta.
Caspian *Caucasus*	Semihard. Sheep or cow, milked directly into cone-shaped cloth bag to speed the making. Tastes tangy, sharp and biting.
Cassaro *Italy*	Locally consumed, seldom exported.
Castelmagno *Italy*	Blue-mold, Gorgonzola type.
Castelo Branco, White Castle *Portugal*	Semisoft; goat or goat and sheep; fermented. Similar to Serra da Estrella (*see*).

Castillon, or Fromage de Gascony *France*	Fresh cream cheese.
Castle, Schlosskäse *North Austria*	Limburger type.
Catanzaro *Italy*	Consumed locally, seldom exported.
Cat's Head	*see* Katzenkopf.
Celery *Norway*	Flavored mildly with celery seeds, instead of the usual caraway.
Cendrée, la *France—Orléanais, Blois & Aube*	Hard; sheep; round and flat. Other Cendrées are Champenois or Ricey, Brie, d'Aizy and Olivet.
Cendré d'Aizy *Burgundy, France*	Available all year. *See* la Cendrée.
Cendré de la Brie *Ile-de-France, France*	Fall and winter Brie cured under the ashes, season September to May.
Cendré Champenois or Cendré des Riceys *Aube & Marne, France*	Made and eaten from September to June, and ripened under the ashes.
Cendré Olivet	*see* Olivet.
Cenis	*see* Mont Cenis.
Certoso Stracchino *Italy, near Milan*	A variety of Stracchino named after the Carthusian friars who have made it for donkey's years. It is milder and softer and creamier than the Taleggio because it's made of cow instead of goat milk, but it has less distinction for the same reason.

Ceva
Italy

Soft veteran of Roman times named from its town near Turin.

Chabichou
Poitou, France

Soft; goat; fresh; sweet and tasty. A vintage cheese of the months from April to December, since such cheeses don't last long enough to be vintaged like wine by the year.

Chaingy
Orléans, France

Season September to June.

Cham
Switzerland

One of those eminent Emmentalers from Cham, the home town of Mister Pfister (*see* Pfister).

Chamois milk

Aristotle said that the most savorous cheese came from the chamois. This small goatlike antelope feeds on wild mountain herbs not available to lumbering cows, less agile sheep or domesticated mountain goats, so it gives, in small quantity but high quality, the richest, most flavorsome of milk.

Champenois or Fromage des Riceys
Aube & Marne, France

Season from September to June. The same as Cendre Champenois and des Riceys.

Champoléon de Queyras
Hautes-Alpes, France

Hard; skim-milker.

Chantelle
U.S.A.

Natural Port du Salut type described as "zesty" by some of the best purveyors of domestic cheeses. It has a sharp taste and little odor, perhaps to fill the demand for a "married man's Limburger."

Chantilly

see Hablé.

Chaourec
Champagne, France

Soft, nice to nibble with the bottled product of this same high-living Champagne Province. A kind of Camembert.

Chapelle
France

Soft.

Charmey Fine
Switzerland

Gruyère type.

Chaschol, or Chaschosis
Canton of Grisons, Switzerland

Hard; skim; small wheels, eighteen to twenty-two inches in diameter by three to four inches high, weight twenty-two to forty pounds.

Chasteaux

see Petits Fromages.

Chateauroux

see Fromage de Chèvre.

Chaumont
Champagne, France

Season November to May.

Chavignol

see Crottin.

Chechaluk
Armenia

Soft; pot; flaky; creamy.

Cheddar

see Chapter 3.

Cheese bread
Russia and U.S.A.

For centuries Russia has excelled in making a salubrious cheese bread called Notruschki and the cheese that flavors it is Tworog. (*See both.*) Only recently Schrafft's in New York put out a yellow, soft and toothsome cheese bread that has become very popular for toasting. It takes heat to bring out its full cheesy savor. Good when overlaid with cheese butter of contrasting piquance, say one mixed with Sapsago.

Cheese butter

Equal parts of creamed butter and finely grated or soft cheese and mixtures thereof. The imported but still cheap green Sapsago is not to be forgotten when mixing your own cheese butter.

Cheese food
U.S.A.

"Any mixtures of various lots of cheese and other solids derived from milk with emulsifying agents, coloring matter, seasonings, condiments, relishes and water, heated or not, into a homogeneous mass." (A long and kind word for a homely, tasteless, heterogeneous mess.) From an advertisement.

Cheese hoppers

see Hoppers.

Cheese mites

see Mites.

Cheshire and Cheshire imitations

see with Cheddar in Chapter 3.

Cheshire-Stilton
England

In making this combination of Cheshire and Stilton, the blue mold peculiar to Stilton is introduced in the usual Cheshire process by keeping out each day a little of the curd and mixing it with that in which the mold is growing well. The result is the Cheshire in size and shape and general characteristics but with the blue veins of Stilton, making it really a Blue Cheddar. Another combination is Yorkshire-Stilton, and quite as distinguished.

Chester
England

Another name for Cheshire, used in France where formerly some was imported to make the visiting Britishers feel at home.

Chevalier *France*	Curds sweetened with sugar.
Chevelle *U.S.A.*	A processed Wisconsin.
Chèvre	*see* Fromages.
Chèvre de Chateauroux	*see* Fromages.
Chèvre petit	*see* Petits Fromages.
Chèvre, Tome de	*see* Tome.
Chevretin *Savoy, France*	Goat; small and square. Named after the mammy nanny, as so many are.
Chevrets, Ponta & St. Remy *Bresse & Franche-Comté, France*	Dry and semi-dry; crumbly; goat; small squares; lightly salted. Season December to April. Such small goat cheeses are named in the plural in France.
Chevrettons du Beaujolais à la crème, les *Lyonnais, France*	Small goat-milkers served with cream. This is a fair sample of the railroad names some French cheeses stagger under.
Chevrotins *Savoy, France*	Soft, dried goat milk; white; small; tangy and semi-tangy. Made and eaten from March to December.
Chhana *Asia*	All we know is that this is made of the whole milk of cows, soured, and it is not as unusual as the double "h" in its name.
Chiavari *Italy*	There are two different kinds named for the Chiavari region, and both are hard: I. Sour cow's milk, also known as Cacio Romano. II. Sweet whole milker, similar to Corsican Broccio. Chiavari, the historic

little port between Genoa and Pisa, is more noted as the birthplace of the barbaric "chivaree" razzing of newlyweds with its raucous serenade of dishpans, sour-note bugling and such.

Chives cream cheese

Of the world's many fine fresh cheeses further freshened with chives, there's Belgian Hervé and French Claqueret (with onion added). (*See both.*) For our taste it's best when the chives are added at home, as it's done in Germany, in person at the table or just before.

Christalinna
Canton Graubünden, Switzerland

Hard; smooth; sharp; tangy.

Christian IX
Denmark

A distinguished spiced cheese.

Ciclo
Italy

Soft, small cream cheese.

Cierp de Luchon
France

Made from November to May in the Comté de Foix, where it has the distinction of being the only local product worth listing with France's three hundred notables.

Citeaux
Burgundy, France

Trappist Port-Salut.

Clabber cheese
England

Simply cottage cheese left in a cool place until it grows soft and automatically changes its name from cottage to clabber.

Clairvaux
France

Formerly made in a Benedictine monastery of that name.

Claqueret, le
Lyonnais, France

Fresh cream whipped with chives, chopped fine with onions. *See* Chives.

Clérimbert

see Alpin.

Cleves
France

French imitation of the German imitation of a Holland-Dutch original.

Cloves

see Nagelkäse.

Club, Potted Club, Snappy, Cold-pack and Comminuted cheese
U.S.A. and Canada

Probably McLaren's Imperial Club in pots was first to be called club, but others credit club to the U.S. In any case McLaren's was bought by an American company and is now all-American.

Today there are many clubs that may sound swanky but taste very ordinary, if at all. They are made of finely ground aged, sharp Cheddar mixed with condiments, liquors, olives, pimientos, etc., and mostly carry come-on names to make the customers think they are getting something from Olde England or some aristocratic private club. All are described as "tangy."

Originally butter went into the better clubs which were sold in small porcelain jars, but in these process days they are wrapped in smaller tin foil and wax-paper packets and called "snappy."

Cocktail Cheeses

Recommended from stock by Phil Alpert's "Cheeses of all Nations" stores:
Argentine aged Gruyère
Canadian d'Oka

French Bleu
Brie
Camembert
Fontainebleu
Pont l'Evêque
Port du Salut
Roblochon
Roquefort
Grecian Feta
Hungarian Brinza
Polish Warshawski Syr
Rumanian Kaskaval
Swiss Schweizerkäse
American Cheddar in brandy
Hopi Indian

Coeur à la Crème
Burgundy, France

This becomes Fromage à la Crème II (*see*) when served with sugar, and it is also called a heart of cream after being molded into that romantic shape in a wicker or willow-twig basket.

Coeurs d'Arras
Artois, France

These hearts of Arras are soft, smooth, mellow, caressingly rich with the cream of Arras.

Coffee-flavored cheese

Just as the Dutch captivated coffee lovers all over the world with their coffee-flavored candies, Haagische Hopjes, so the French with Jonchée cheese and Italians with Ricotta satisfy the universal craving by putting coffee in for flavor.

Coimbra
Portugal

Goat or cow; semihard; firm; round; salty; sharp. Not only one of those college-educated cheeses but a postgraduate one, bearing the honored name of Portugal's ancient academic center.

Colby
U.S.A.

Similar to Cheddar, but of softer body and more open texture. Contains more moisture, and doesn't keep as well as Cheddar.

College-educated

Besides Coimbra several countries have cheeses brought out by their colleges. Even Brazil has one in Minas Geraes and Transylvania another called Kolos-Monoster, while our agricultural colleges in every big cheese state from California through Ames in Iowa, Madison in Wisconsin, all across the continent to Cornell in New York, vie with one another in turning out diploma-ed American Cheddars and such of high degree. It is largely to the agricultural colleges that we owe the steady improvement in both quality and number of foreign imitations since the University of Wisconsin broke the curds early in this century by importing Swiss professors to teach the high art of Emmentaler.

Colwick

see Slipcote.

Combe-air
France

Small; similar to Italian Stracchino in everything but size.

Commission
Holland

Hard; ball-shaped like Edam and resembling it except in being darker in color and packed in a ball weighing about twice as much, around eight pounds. It is made in the province of North Holland and in Friesland. It is often preferred to Edam for size and nutty flavor.

Compiègne
France

Soft.

Comté

see Gruyère.

Conches
France

Emmentaler type.

Condrieu, Rigotte de la
Rhone Valley below Lyons, France

Semihard; goat; small; smooth; creamy; mellow; tasty. A cheese of cheeses for epicures, only made from May to November when pasturage is rich.

Confits au Marc de Bourgogne

see Epoisses.

Confits au Vin Blanc

see Epoisses.

Cooked, or Pennsylvania pot
U.S.A.

Named from cooking sour clabbered curd to the melting point. When cool it is allowed to stand three or four days until it is colored through. Then it is cooked again with salt, milk, and usually caraway. It is stirred until it's as thick as molasses and strings from a spoon. It is then put into pots or molds, whose shape it retains when turned out.

All cooked cheese is apt to be tasteless unless some of the milk flavor cooked out is put back in, as wheat germ is now returned to white bread. Almost every country has a cooked cheese all its own, with or without caraway, such as the following:

Belgium—Kochtounkäse
Germany—Kochkäse, Topfen
Luxembourg—Kochenkäse
France—Fromage Ouit & Le P'Teux
Sardinia—Pannedas, Freisa

Coon

see Chapter 4.

Cornhusker
U.S.A.

A Nebraska product similar to Cheddar and Colby, but with softer body and more moisture.

Cornimont
Vosges, France

A splendid French version of Alsatian Münster spiked with caraway, in flattish cylinders with mahogany-red coating. It is similar to Géromé and the harvest cheese of Gérardmer in the same lush Vosges Valley.

Corse, Roquefort de
Corsica, France

Corsican imitation of the real Roquefort, and not nearly so good, of course.

Cossack
Caucasus

Cow or sheep. There are two varieties:

I. Soft, cured in brine and still soft and mild after two months in the salt bath.

II. Semihard and very sharp after aging in brine for a year or more.

Cotherstone
Yorkshire, England

Also known as Yorkshire-Stilton, and Wensleydale No. I. (*See both.*)

Cotrone, Cotronese

see Pecorino.

Cotta

see Pasta.

Cottage cheese

Made in all countries where any sort of milk is obtainable. In America it's also called pot, Dutch, and smearcase. The English, who like playful names for homely dishes, call cottage cheese smearcase from the German Schmierkäse. It is also called Glumse in Deutschland, and, together with cream, formed the basis of all of our fine Pennsylvania Dutch cuisine.

Cottenham or Double Cottenham
English Midlands

Semihard; double cream; blue mold. Similar to Stilton but creamier and richer, and made in flatter and broader forms.

Cottslowe
Cotswold, England

A brand of cream cheese named for its home in Cotswold, Gloucester. Although soft, it tastes like hard Cheddar.

Coulommiers Frais, or Petit-Moule
Ile-de-France, France

Fresh cream similar to Petit Suisse. (*See.*)

Coulommiers, le, or Brie de Coulommiers
France

Also called Petit-moule, from its small form. This genuine Brie is a pocket edition, no larger than a Camembert, standing only one inch high and measuring five or six inches across. It is made near Paris and is a great favorite from the autumn and winter months, when it is made, on until May. The making starts in October, a month earlier than most Brie, and it is off the market by July, so it's seldom tasted by the avalanche of American summer tourists.

Cow cheese

Sounds redundant, and is used mostly in Germany, where an identifying word is added, such as Berliner Kuhkäse and Alt Kuhkäse: old cow cheese.

Cream cheese
International

England, France and America go for it heavily. English cream begins with Devonshire, the world-famous, thick fresh cream that is sold cool in earthenware pots and makes fresh berries—especially the small wild strawberries of rural England—taste out of this world. It is also drained on straw mats and formed into fresh hardened cheeses in small molds. (*See* Devonshire cream.) Among regional specialties are the following, named from their place of origin or commercial brands:

Cambridge
Cottslowe

Cornwall
Farm Vale
Guilford
Horner's
"Italian"
Lincoln
New Forest
Rush (from being made on rush or straw mats—*see* Rush)
St. Ivel (distinguished for being made with acidophilus bacteria)
Scotch Caledonian
Slipcote (famous in the eighteenth century)
Victoria
York

Crème Chantilly — *see* Hablé.

Crème de Gien — *see* Fromage.

Crème de Gruyère
Franche-Comté, France — Soft Gruyère cream cheese, arrives in America in perfect condition in tin foil packets. Expensive but worth it.

Crème des Vosges
Alsace, France — Soft cream. Season October to April.

Crème Double — *see* Double-Crème.

Crème, Fromage à la — *see* Fromage.

Crème, Fromage Blanc à la — *see* Fromage Blanc.

Crème St. Gervais — *see* Pots de Crème St. Gervais.

Crèmet Nantais
Lower Loire, France — Soft fresh cream of Nantes.

Crèmets, les
Anjou, France

A fresh cream equal to English Devonshire, served more as a dessert than a dessert cheese. The cream is whipped stiff with egg whites, drained and eaten with more fresh cream, sprinkled with vanilla and sugar.

Cremini
Italy

Soft, small cream cheese from Cremona, the violin town. And by the way, art-loving Italians make ornamental cheeses in the form of musical instruments, statues, still life groups and everything.

Creole
Louisiana, U.S.A.

Soft, rich, unripened cottage cheese type, made by mixing cottage-type curd and rich cream.

Crescenza, Carsenza, Stracchino Crescenza, Crescenza Lombardi
Lombardy, Italy

Uncooked; soft; creamy; mildly sweet; fast-ripening; yellowish; whole milk. Made from September to April.

Creuse
Creuse, France

A two-in-one farm cheese of skimmed milk, resulting from two different ways of ripening, after the cheese has been removed from perforated earthen molds seven inches in diameter and five or six inches high, where it has drained for several days:

I. It is salted and turned frequently until very dry and hard.

II. It is ripened by placing in tightly closed mold, lined with straw. This softens, flavors, and turns it golden-yellow. (*See* Hay or Fromage de Foin.)

Creusois, or Guéret
Limousin, France

Season, October to June.

Croissant Demi-sel
France

Soft, double cream, semisalty. All year.

Crottin de Chavignol
Berry, France

Semihard; goat's milk; small; lightly salted; mellow. In season April to December. The name is not exactly complimentary.

Crowdie, or Cruddy butter
Scotland

Named from the combination of fresh sweet milk curds pressed together with fresh butter. A popular breakfast food in Inverness and the Ross Shires. When kept for months it develops a high flavor. A similar curd and butter is made by Arabs and stored in vats, the same as in India, the land of ghee, where there's no refrigeration.

Crying Kebbuck

F. Marion MacNeill, in *The Scots Kitchen* says that this was the name of a cheese that used to be part of the Kimmers feast at a lying-in.

Cuajada

see Venezuela.

Cubjac

see Cajassou.

Cuit

see Fromage Cuit.

Cumin, Münster au

see Münster.

Cup

see Koppen.

Curd

see Granular curd, Sweet curd and York curd.

Curds and butter
Arabia

Fresh sweet milk curd and fresh butter are pressed together as in making Crowdie or Cruddy butter in Scotland. The Arabs put this strong mixture away in vats to get it even stronger than East Indian ghee.

Curé, Fromage de

see Nantais.

D

Daisies, fresh
A popular type and packaging of mild Cheddar, originally English. Known as an "all-around cheese," to eat raw, cook, let ripen, and use for seasoning.

Dalmatian
Austria
Hard ewe's-milker.

Dambo
Denmark
Semihard and nutty.

Damen, or Glory of the Mountains (Gloires des Montagnes)
Hungary
Soft, uncured, mild ladies' cheese, as its name asserts. Popular Alpine snack in Viennese cafés with coffee gossip in the afternoon.

Danish Blue
Denmark
Semihard, rich, blue-veined, piquant, delicate, excellent imitation of Roquefort. Sometimes called "Danish Roquefort," and because it is exported around the world it is Denmark's best-known cheese. Although it sells for 20% to 30% less than the international triumvirate of Blues, Roquefort, Stilton and Gorgonzola, it rivals them and definitely leads lesser Blues.

Danish Export
Denmark
Skim milk and buttermilk. Round and flat, mild and mellow. A fine cheese, as many Danish exports are.

Dansk Schweizerost
Denmark
Danish Swiss cheese, imitation Emmentaler, but with small holes. Nutty, sweet dessert or "picnic cheese," as Swiss is often called.

Danzig
Poland
A pleasant cheese to accompany a glass of the great liqueur, Goldwasser, Eau de Vie de Danzig, from the same celebrated city.

Darling *U.S.A.*	One of the finest Vermont Cheddars, handled for years by one of America's finest fancy food suppliers, S. S. Pierce of Boston.
Dauphin *Flanders, France*	Season, November to May.
d'Aurigny, Fromage	*see* Alderney.
Daventry *England*	A Stilton type, white, small, round, flat and very rich, with "blue" veins of a darker green.
Decize *Nivernaise, France*	In season all year. Soft, creamy, mellow, resembles Brie.
de Foin, Fromage	*see* Hay.
de Fontine *Spain*	Crumbly, sharp, nutty.
de Gascony, Fromage	*see* Castillon.
de Gérardmer	*see* Récollet.
Delft *Holland*	About the same as Leyden. (*See.*)
Délicieux	The brand name of a truly delicious Brie.
Delikat *U.S.A.*	A mellow breakfast spread, on the style of the German Frühstück original. (*See.*)
de Lile, Boule	French name for Belgian Oude Kaas.
Demi-Étuve	Half-size Étuve. (*See.*)
Demi Petit Suisse	The name for an extra small Petit Suisse to distinguish it from the Gros.

Demi-Sel
Normandy, France

Soft, whole, creamy, lightly salted, resembles Gournay but slightly saltier; also like U.S. cream cheese, but softer and creamier.

Demi-Sel, Croissant

see Croissant Demi-Sel.

Derby, or Derbyshire
England

Hard; shape like Austrian Nagelkassa and the size of Cheshire though sometimes smaller. Dry, large, flat, round, flaky, sharp and tangy. A factory cheese said to be identical with Double Gloucester and similar to Warwickshire, Wiltshire and Leicester. The experts pronounce it "a somewhat inferior Cheshire, but deficient in its quality and the flavor of Cheddar." So it's unlikely to win in any cheese derby in spite of its name.

Devonshire cream and cheese
England

Devonshire cream is world famous for its thickness and richness. Superb with wild strawberries; almost a cream cheese by itself. Devonshire cream is made into a luscious cheese ripened on straw, which gives it a special flavor, such as that of French Foin or Hay cheese.

Dolce Verde
Italy

This creamy blue-vein variety is named Sweet Green, because cheesemongers are color-blind when it comes to the blue-greens and the green-blues.

Domaci Beli Sir
Yugoslavia

"Sir" is not a title but the word for cheese. This is a typical ewe's-milker cured in a fresh sheep skin.

Domestic Gruyère
U.S.A.

An imitation of a cheese impossible to imitate.

Domestic Swiss
U.S.A.

Same as domestic Gruyère, maybe more so, since it is made in ponderous 150- to 200-pound wheels, chiefly in Wisconsin and Ohio. The trouble is there is no Alpine pasturage and Emmentaler Valley in our country.

Domiati
Egypt

Whole or partly skimmed cow's or buffalo's milk. Soft; white; no openings; mild and salty when fresh and cleanly acid when cured. It's called "a pickled cheese" and is very popular in the Near East.

Dorset, Double Dorset, Blue Dorset, or Blue Vinny
England

Blue mold type from Dorsetshire; crumbly, sharp; made in flat forms. "Its manufacture has been traced back 150 years in the family of F. E. Dare, who says that in all probability it was made longer ago than that."
(*See* Blue Vinny.)

Dotter
Nürnberg, Germany

An entirely original cheese perfected by G. Leuchs in Nürnberg. He enriched skim milk with yolk of eggs and made the cheese in the usual way. When well ripened it is splendid.

Doubles

The English name cheese made of whole milk "double," such as Double Cottenham, Double Dorset, Double Gloucester. "Singles" are cheeses from which some of the cream has been removed.

Double-cream
England

Similar to Wensleydale.

Double-crème
France

There are several of this name, made in the summer when milk is richest in cream. The full name is Fromage à la

Double-crême, and Pommel is one well known. They are made throughout France in season and are much in demand.

Dresdener Bierkäse
Germany

A celebrated hand cheese made in Dresden. The typical soft, skim milker, strong with caraway and drunk dissolved in beer, as well as merely eaten.

Drinking cheeses

Not only Dresdener, but dozens of regional hand cheeses in Germanic countries are melted in steins of beer or glasses of wine to make distinctive cheesed drinks for strong stomachs and noses. This peps up the drinks in somewhat the same way as ale and beer are laced with pepper sauce in some parts.

Dry
Germany

From the drinking cheese just above to dry cheese is quite a leap. "This cheese, known as Sperrkäse and Trockenkäse, is made in the small dairies of the eastern part of the Bavarian Alps and in the Tyrol. It is an extremely simple product, made for home consumption and only in the winter season, when the milk cannot be profitably used for other purposes. As soon as the milk is skimmed it is put into a large kettle which can be swung over a fire, where it is kept warm until it is thoroughly thickened from souring. It is then broken up and cooked quite firm. A small quantity of salt and sometimes some caraway seed are added, and the curd is put into forms of various sizes. It is then placed in a drying room, where it becomes very hard, when it is ready for eating." (From U.S. Department of Agriculture *Bulletin* No. 608.)

Dubreala	*see* Brina.
Duel *Austria*	Soft; skim milk; hand type; two by two by one-inch cube.
Dunlop *Scotland*	One of the national cheeses of Scotland, but now far behind Cheddar, which it resembles, although it is closer in texture and moister. Semihard; white; sharp; buttery; tangy and rich in flavor. It is one of the "toasting cheeses" resembling Lancashire, too, in form and weight. Made in Ayr, Lanark and Renfrew and sold in the markets of Kilmarnock, Kirkcudbright and Wigtown.
Durak *Turkey*	Mixed with butter; mellow and smoky. Costs three dollars a pound.
Duralag, or Bgug-Panir *Armenia*	Sheep; semisoft to brittle hard; square; sharp but mellow and tangy with herbs. Sometimes salty from lying in a brine bath from two days to two months.
Durmar, Rarush	*see* Rarush.
Dutch *Holland*	Cream cheese of skim milk, very perishable spread.
Dutch cheese	American vernacular for cottage or pot cheese.
Dutch Cream Cheese *England*	Made in England although called Dutch. Contains eggs, and is therefore richer than Dutch cream cheese in Holland itself. In America we call the original Holland-kind Dutch, cottage, pot, and farmer.
Dutch Mill *U.S.A.*	A specialty of Oakland, California.
Dutch Red Balls	English name for Edam.

E

Echourgnac, Trappe d'
Périgord, France
Trappist monastery Port-Salut made in Limousin.

Edam
see Chapter 3.

Egg
Finland
Semihard. One of the few cheeses made by adding eggs to the curds. Others are Dutch Cream Cheese of England; German Dotter; French Fromage Cuit (cooked cheese), and Westphalian. Authorities agree that these should be labeled "egg cheese" so the buyers won't be fooled by their richness. The Finns age their eggs even as the Chinese ripen their hundred-year-old eggs, by burying them in grain, as all Scandinavians do, and the Scotch as well, in the oat bin. But none of them is left a century to ripen, as eggs are said to be in China.

Elbinger, or Elbing
West Prussia
Hard; crumbly; sharp. Made of whole milk except in winter when it is skimmed. Also known as Werderkäse and Niederrungkäse.

Ekiwani
Caucasus
Hard; sheep; white; sharp; salty with some of the brine it's bathed in.

Elisavetpolen, or Eriwani
Caucasus
Hard; sheep; sweetish-sharp and slightly salty when fresh from the brine bath. Also called Kasach (Cossack), Tali, Kurini and Karab in different locales.

Elmo Table
Italy
Soft, mellow, tasty.

Emiliano
Italy
Hard; flavor varies from mild to sharp. Parmesan type.

Emmentaler *Switzerland*	There are so many, many types of this celebrated Swiss all around the world that we're not surprised to find Lapland reindeer milk cheese listed as similar to Emmentaler of the hardest variety. (*See* Chapter 3, *also* Vacherin Fondu.)
"En enveloppe"	French phrase of packaged cheese, "in the envelope." Similar to English packet and our process. Raw natural cheese the French refer to frankly as *nu,* "in the nude."
Engadine *Graubünden, Switzerland*	Semihard; mild; tangy-sweet.
English Dairy *England and U.S.A.*	Extra-hard, crumbly and sharp. Resembles Cheddar and has long been imitated in the States, chiefly as a cooking cheese.
Entrechaux, le Cachat d'	*see* Cachat.
Epoisses, Fromage d' *Côte d'Or, Upper Burgundy, France*	Soft, small cylinder with flattened end, about five inches across. The season is from November to July. Equally proud of their wine and cheese, the Burgundians marry white wine or *marc* to d'Epoisses in making *confits* with that name.
Erbo *Italy*	Similar to Gorgonzola. The Galvani cheesemakers of Italy who put out both Bel Paese and Taleggio also export Erbo to our shores.
Erce *Languedoc, France*	Soft, smooth and sharp. A winter cheese in season only from November to May.
Eriwani	*see* Elisavetpolen.

Ervy
Champagne, France
Soft; yellow rind; smooth; tangy; piquant; seven by two-and-a-half inches, weight four pounds. Resembles Camembert. A washed cheese, also known as Fromage de Troyes. In season November to May.

Essex
U.S.A.
Imitation of an extinct or at least dormant English type.

Estrella
see Serra da Estrella.

Etuve and Demi-Etuve
Holland
Semihard; smooth; mellow. In full size and demi (half) size. In season all year.

Evarglice
Yugoslavia
Sharp, nutty flavor.

Excelsior
Normandy, France
Season all year.

F

Factory Cheddar
U.S.A.
Very Old Factory Cheddar is the trade name for well-aged sharp Cheddar. New Factory is just that—mild, young and tractable—too tractable, in fact.

Farm
France
Known as Ferme; Maigre (thin); Fromage à la Pie (nothing to do with apple pie); and Mou (weak). About the same as our cottage cheese.

Farmer
U.S.A.
This is curd only and is nowadays mixed with pepper, lachs, nuts, fruits, almost anything. A very good base for your own fancy spread, or season a slab to fancy and bake it like a hoe cake, but in the oven.

Farmhouse
see Herrgårdsost.

Farm Vale *England*	Cream cheese of Somerset wrapped in tin foil and boxed in wedges, eight to a box.
Fat cheese	*see* Fromage Gras and Maile Pener.
Fenouil	*see* Tome de Savoie.
Ferme	*see* Farm.
Feta	*see* Chapter 3.
Feuille de Dreux *Béaun, France*	November to May.
"Filled cheese" *England*	Before our processed and food cheese era some scoundrels in the cheese business over there added animal fats and margarine to skimmed milk to make it pass as whole milk in making cheese. Such adulteration killed the flavor and quality, and no doubt some of the customers. Luckily in America we put down this vicious counterfeiting with pure food laws. But such foreign fats are still stuffed into the skimmed milk of many foreign cheeses. To take the place of the natural butterfat the phony fats are whipped in violently and extra rennet is added to speed up coagulation.
Fin de Siècle *Normandy, France*	Although this is an "all year" cheese its name dates it back to the years at the close of the nineteenth century.
Fiore di Alpe *Italy*	Hard; sharp; tangy. Romantically named "Flowers of the Alps."
Fiore Sardo *Italy*	Ewe's milk. Hard. Table cheese when immature; a condiment when fully cured.

Flandre, Tuile de
France

A kind of Marolles.

Fleur de Deauville
France

A type of Brie, in season December to May.

Fleur des Alpes

see Bel Paese and Millefiori.

Floedeost
Norway

Like Gjedeost, but not so rich because it's made of cow's milk.

Fløtost
Norway

Although the name translates Cream Cheese it is made of boiled whey. Similar to Mysost, but fatter.

Flower
England

Soft and fragrant with petals of roses, violets, marigolds and such, delicately mixed in. Since the English are so fond of oriental teas scented with jasmine and other flowers, perhaps they imported the idea of mixing petals with their cheese, since there is no oriental cheese for them to import except bean curd.

Fodder cheese

A term for cheese made from fodder in seasons when there is no grass. Good fresh grass is the essence of all fine cheese, so silo or barn-fed cows can't give the kind of milk it takes.

Foggiano
Apulia, Italy

A member of the big Pecorino family because it's made of sheep's milk.

Foin, Fromage de

see Hay.

Fondu, Vacherin

see Vacherin Fondu.

Fontainebleau
France

Named after its own royal commune. Soft; fresh cream; smooth; mellow; summer variety.

Fontina *Val d'Acosta, Italy*	Soft; goat; creamy; with a nutty flavor and delightful aroma.
Fontine, de *Franche-Comté, France*	A favorite all-year product.
Fontinelli *Italy*	Semidry; flaky; nutty; sharp.
Fontini *Parma, Italy*	Hard; goat; similar to Swiss, but harder and sharper. From the same region as Parmesan.
Food cheese *U.S.A.*	An unattractive type of processed mixes, presumably with some cheese content to flavor it.
Forez, also called d'Ambert *France*	The process of making this is said to be very crude, and the ripening unusual. The cheeses are cylindrical, ten inches in diameter and six inches high. They are ripened by placing them on the floor of the cellar, covering with dirt, and allowing water to trickle over them. Many are spoiled by the unusual growths of mold and bacteria. The flavor of the best of these is said to resemble Roquefort. (From *Bulletin* No. 608 of the U.S. Department of Agriculture, to which we are indebted for descriptions of hundreds of varieties in this alphabet.)
Formagelle *Northwest Italy*	Soft, ripened specialty put up in half-pound packages.
Formaggi di Pasta Filata *Italy*	A group of Italian cheeses made by curdling milk with rennet, warming and fermenting the curd, heating it until it is plastic, drawing it into ropes and then kneading and shaping while hot. Provolone, Caciocavallo and Mozzarella are in this group.

Formaggini, and Formaggini di Lecco *Italy*	Several small cheeses answer to this name, of which Lecco is typical. A Lombardy dessert cheese measuring 1¼ by two inches, weighing two ounces. It is eaten from the time it is fresh and sweet until it ripens to piquance. Sometimes made of cow and goat milk mixed, with the addition of oil and vinegar, as well as salt, pepper, sugar and cinnamon.
Formaggio d'Oro *Northwest Italy*	Hard, sharp, mountain-made.
Formaggio Duro (Dry) and Formaggio Tenero	*see* Nostrale.
Fort	*see* Fromage Fort.
Fourme, Cantal, and la Tome *Auvergne, France*	This is a big family in the rich cheese province of Auvergne, where many mountain varieties are baptized after their districts, such as Aubrac, Aurilla, Grand Murol, Rôche and Salers. (*See* Fourme d'Ambert and Cantal.)
Fourme de Montebrison *Auvergne, France*	This belongs to the Fourme clan and is in season from November to May.
Fourme de Salers	*see* Cantal, which it resembles so closely it is sometimes sold under that name.
Fresa, or Pannedas *Sardinia, Italy*	A soft, mild and sweet cooked cheese.
Fribourg *Italy and Switzerland*	Hard; cooked-curd, Swiss type very similar to Spalen. (*See*)
Frissche Kaas, Fresh cheese *Holland*	Dutch generic name for any soft, fresh spring cheese, although some is made in winter, beginning in November.
Friesian	*see* West Friesian.

Fromage à la Crème
France

I. Sour milk drained and mixed with cream. Eaten with sugar. That of Gien is a noted produce, and so is d'Isigny.

II. Franche-Comté—fresh sheep milk melted with fresh thick cream, whipped egg whites and sugar.

III. Morvan—homemade cottage cheese. When milk has soured solid it is hung in cheesecloth in a cool place to drain, then mixed with a little fresh milk and served with cream.

IV. When Morvan or other type is put into a heart-shaped wicker basket for a mold, and marketed in that, it becomes Coeur à la Crème, heart of cream, to be eaten with sugar.

Fromage à la Pie

see Fromage Blanc just below, and Farm

Fromage Bavarois à la Vanille
France

Dessert cheese sweetened and flavored with vanilla and named after Bavaria where it probably originated.

Fromage Blanc
France

Soft cream or cottage cheese, called à la Pie, too, suggesting pie à la mode; also Farm from the place it's made. Usually eaten with salt and pepper, in summer only. It is the ascetic version of Fromage à la Crème, usually eaten with salt and pepper and without cream or sugar, except in the Province of Bresse where it is served with cream and called Fromage Blanc à la Crème.

Every milky province has its own Blanc. In Champagne it's made of fresh ewe milk. In Upper Brittany it is named after Nantes and also called Fromage de

Curé. Other districts devoted to it are Alsace-Lorraine, Auvergne, Languedoc, and Ile-de-France.

Fromage Bleu — *see* Bleu d'Auvergne.

Fromage Cuit (cooked cheese)
Thionville, Lorraine, France
Although a specialty of Lorraine, this cooked cheese is produced in many places. First it is made with fresh whole cow milk, then pressed and potted. After maturing a while it is de-potted, mixed with milk and egg yolk, re-cooked and re-potted.

Fromage d'Aurigny — *see* Alderney.

Fromage de Bayonne
Bayonne, France
Made with ewe's milk.

Fromage de Bôite
Doubs, France
Soft, mountain-made, in the fall only. Resembles Pont l'Evêque.

Fromage de Bourgogne — *see* Burgundy.

Fromage de Chèvre de Chateauroux
Berry, France
A seasonal goat cheese.

Fromage de Curé — *see* Nantais.

Fromage de Fontenay–le Comté
Poitou, France
Half goat and half cow milk.

Fromage de Gascony — *see* Castillon.

Fromage de Pau — *see* La Foncée.

Fromage de St. Rémy — *see* Chevrets.

Fromage de Serac
Savoy, France

Half and half, cow and goat, from Serac des Allues.

Fromage de Troyes
France

Two cheeses have this name. (*See* Barberry and Ervy.)

Fromage de Vache

Another name for Autun.

Fromage de Monsieur Fromage
Normandy, France

This Cheese of Mr. Cheese is as exceptional as its name. Its season runs from November to June. It comes wrapped in a green leaf, maybe from a grape vine, suggesting what to drink with it. It is semidry, mildly snappy with a piquant pungence all its own. The playful name suggests the celebrated dish, Poulette de Madame Poulet, Chick of Mrs. Chicken.

Fromage Fort
France

Several cooked cheeses are named Fort (strong) chiefly in the department of Aisne. Well-drained curd is melted, poured into a cloth and pressed, then buried in dry ashes to remove any whey left. After being fermented eight to ten days it is grated, mixed with butter, salt, pepper, wine, juniper berries, butter and other things, before fermenting some more.

Similar extra-strong cheeses are the one in Lorraine called Fondue and Fromagère of eastern France, classed as the strongest cheeses in all France.

Fort No. I: That of Flanders, potted with juniper berries, as the gin of this section is flavored, plus pepper, salt and white wine.

Fort No. II: That from Franche-Comté. Small dry goat cheeses pounded and potted with thyme, tarragon, leeks, pepper and brandy. (*See* Hazebrook.)

Fort No. III: From Provence, also called Cachat d'Entrechaux. In production from May to November. Semihard, sheep milk, mixed with brandy, white wine, strong herbs and seasonings and well marinated.

Fromage Gras (fat cheese)
Savoy, France

Soft, round, fat ball called *tête de mort,* "death's head." Winter Brie is also called Gras but there is no relation. This macabre name incited Victor Meusy to these lines:

Les gens à l'humeur morose
Prennent la Tête-de-Mort.

People of a morose disposition
Take the Death's Head.

Fromage Mou

Any soft cheese.

Fromage Piquant

see Remoudon.

Fromagère

see Canquillote.

Fromages de Chèvre
Orléanais, France

Small, dried goat-milkers.

Frühstück

Also known as breakfast and lunch cheese. Small rounds two-and-a-half to three inches in diameter. Limburger type. Cheeses on which many Germans and Americans break their fast.

Ftinoporino
Macedonia, Greece

Sheep's-milker similar to Brinza.

G

Gaiskäsli
Germany and Switzerland

A general name for goat's milk cheese. Usually a small cylinder three inches in diameter and an inch-and-a-half thick, weighing up to a half pound. In making, the curds are set on a straw mat in molds, for the whey to run away. They are salted and turned after two days to salt the other side. They ripen in three weeks with a very pleasing flavor.

Gammelost
Norway

Hard, golden-brown, sour-milker. After being pressed it is turned daily for fourteen days and then packed in a chest with wet straw. So far as we are concerned it can stay there. The color all the way through is tobacco-brown and the taste, too. It has been compared to medicine, chewing tobacco, petrified Limburger, and worse. In his *Encyclopedia of Food* Artemas Ward says that in Gammelost the ferments absorb so much of the curd that "in consequence, instead of eating cheese flavored by fungi, one is practically eating fungi flavored with cheese."

Garda
Italy

Soft, creamy, fermented. A truly fine product made in the resort town on Gardasee where d'Annunzio retired. It is one of those luscious little ones exported in tin foil to America, and edible, including the moldy crust that could hardly be called a rind.

Garden
U.S.A.

Cream cheese with some greens or vegetables mixed in.

Garlic
U.S.A.

A processed Cheddar type flavored with garlic.

Garlic-onion Link
U.S.A.

A strong processed Cheddar put up to look like links of sausage, nobody knows why.

Gascony, Fromage de

see Castillon.

Gautrias
Mayenne, France

Soft, cylinder weighing about five pounds and resembling Port-Salut.

Gavot
Hautes-Alpes, France

A good Alpine cheese whether made of sheep, goat or cow milk.

Geheimrath
Netherlands

A factory cheese turned out in small quantities. The color is deep yellow and it resembles a Baby Gouda in every way, down to the weight.

Gérardmer, de

see Récollet.

German-American adopted types

Bierkäse
Delikat
Grinnen
Hand
Harzkäse
Kümmelkäse
Koppen
Lager
Liederkranz
Mein Kaese
Münster
Old Heidelberg
Schafkäse (sheep)
Silesian
Stein
Tilsit
Weisslack (piquant like Bavarian Allgäuer)

Géromé, la
Vosges, France

Semihard; cylinders up to eleven pounds; brick-red rind; like Münster, but larger. Strong, fragrant and flavorsome, sometimes with aniseed. It stands high at home, where it is in season from October to April.

Gervais
Ile-de-France, France

Cream cheese like Neufchâtel, long made by Maison Gervais, near Paris. Sold in tiny tin-foil squares not much larger than old-time yeast. Like Petit Suisse, it makes a perfect luncheon dessert with honey.

Gesundheitkäse, Holsteiner

see Holstein Health.

Getmesost
Sweden

Soft; goat; whey; sweet.

Gex
Pays de Gex, France

Semihard; skim milk; blue-veined. A "little" Roquefort in season from November to May.

Gex Marbré
France

A very special type marbled with rich milks of cow, goat and sheep, mixed. A full-flavored ambassador of the big international Blues family, that are green in spite of their name.

Gien

see Fromage à la Crème.

Gislev
Scandinavia

Hard; mild, made from skimmed cow's milk.

Gjetost
Norway

A traditional chocolate-colored companion piece to Gammelost, but made with goat's milk.

Glavis
Switzerland

The brand name of a cone of Sapsago. (*See.*)

Glattkäse, or Gelbkäse
Germany

Smooth cheese or yellow cheese. A classification of sour-milkers that includes Olmützer Quargel.

Gloire des Montagnes — *see* Damen.

Gloucester
Gloucestershire, England

There are two types:

I. Double, the better of the two Gloucesters, is eaten only after six months of ripening. "It has a pronounced, but mellow, delicacy of flavor . . . the tiniest morsel being pregnant with savour. To measure its refinement, it can undergo the same comparison as that we apply to vintage wines. Begin with a small piece of Red Cheshire. If you then pass to a morsel of Double Gloucester, you will find that the praises accorded to the latter have been no whit exaggerated." *A Concise Encyclopedia of Gastronomy*, by André L. Simon.

II. Single. By way of comparison, the spring and summer Single Gloucester ripens in two months and is not as big as its "large grindstone" brother. And neither is it "glorified Cheshire." It is mild and "as different in quality of flavour as a young and crisp wine is from an old vintage."

Glumse
West Prussia, Germany

A common, undistinguished cottage cheese.

Glux
Nivernais, France

Season, all year.

Goat
France

A frank and fair name for a semihard, brittle mouthful of flavor. Every country has its goat specialties. In Norway the milk is boiled dry, then fresh milk or cream added. In Czechoslovakia the peasants smoke the cheese up the kitchen chimney. No matter how you slice it, goat cheese is always notable or noble.

Gold-N-Rich
U.S.A.

Golden in color and rich in taste. Bland, as American taste demands. Like Bel Paese but not so full-flavored and a bit sweet. A good and deservedly popular cheese none the less, easily recognized by its red rind.

Gomost
Norway

Usually made from cow's milk, but sometimes from goat's. Milk is curdled with rennet and condensed by heating until it has a butter-like consistency. (*See* Mysost.)

Gorgonzola
Italy

Besides the standard type exported to us (*See* Chapter 3.) there is White Gorgonzola, little known outside Italy where it is enjoyed by local caseophiles, who like it put up in crocks with brandy, too.

Gouda

see Chapter 3.

Gouda, Kosher
Holland

The same semihard good Gouda, but made with kosher rennet. It is a bit more mellow than most and, like all kosher products, is stamped by the Jewish authorities who prepare it.

Goya
Corrientes, Argentine

Hard, dry, Italian type for grating. Like all fine Argentine cheeses the milk of pedigreed herds fed on prime pampas grass distinguishes Goya from lesser Parmesan types, even back in Italy.

It is interesting that the nitrate in Chilean soil makes their wines the best in America, and the richness of Argentine milk does the same for their cheeses, most of which are Italian imitations and some of which excel the originals.

Gournay
Seine, France

Soft, similar to Demi-sel, comes in round and flat forms about ¼ pound in weight. Those shaped like Bondons resemble corks about ¾ of an inch thick and four inches long.

Grana
Italy

Another name for Parmesan. From "grains," the size of big shot, that the curd is cut into.

Grana Lombardo
Lombardy

The same hard type for grating, named after its origin in Lombardy.

Grana Reggiano
Reggio, Italy

A brand of Parmesan type made near Reggio and widely imitated, not only in Lombardy and Mantua, but also in the Argentine where it goes by a pet name of its own—Regianito.

Grande Bornand, la
Switzerland

A luscious half-dried sheep's milker.

Granular curd

see Stirred curd.

Gras, or Volvet Kaas
Holland

Named from its butterfat content and called "Moor's Head," *Tête de Maure,* in France, from its shape and size. The same is true of Fromage de Gras in France, called *Tête de Mort,* "Death's Head." Gras is also the popular name for Brie that's made in the autumn in France and sold from November to May. (*See* Brie.)

Gratairon
France

Goat milk named, as so many are, from the place it is made.

Graubünden
Switzerland

A luscious half-dried sheep's milker.

Green Bay
U.S.A.

Medium-sharp, splendid White Cheddar from Green Bay, Wisconsin, the Limburger county.

Grey
Germany and Austrian Tyrol

Semisoft; sour skim milk with salty flavor from curing in brine bath. Named from the gray color that pervades the entire cheese when ripe. It has a very pleasant taste.

Gruyère

see Chapter 3.

Güssing, or Land-l-kas
Austria

Similar to Brick. Skim milk. Weight between four and eight pounds.

H

Habas

see Caille.

Hablé Crème Chantilly
Ösmo, Sweden

Soft ripened dessert cheese made from pasteurized cream by the old Walla Creamery. Put up in five-ounce wedge-shaped boxes for export and sold for a high price, well over two dollars a pound, in fancy big city groceries. Truly an aristocrat of cheeses to compare with the finest French Brie or Camembert. *See* Chapter 3.

Hand

see Chapter 3.

Hard
Puerto Rico

Dry; tangy.

Harzkäse, Harz
Harz Mountains, Germany

Tiny hand cheese. Probably the world's smallest soft cheese, varying from 2½ inches by 1½ down to ¼ by 1½. Packed in little boxes, a dozen together, rubbing rinds, as close as sardines. And like Harz canaries, they thrive on seeds, chiefly caraway.

Harzé *Belgium*
Port-Salut type from the Trappist monastery at Harzé.

Hasandach *Turkey*
Bland; sweet.

Hauskäse *Germany*
Limburger type. Disk-shaped.

Haute Marne *France*
Soft; square.

Hay, or Fromage au Foin *Seine, France*
A skim-milker resembling "a poor grade of Livarot." Nothing to write home about, except that it is ripened on new-mown hay.

Hazebrook
There are two kinds:

I. Flemish; a Fromage Fort type with white wine, juniper, salt and pepper. Excessively strong for bland American tasters.

II. Franche-Comté, France; small dry goat's milker, pounded, potted and marinated in a mixture of thyme, tarragon, leeks, pepper and brandy.

Head
Four cheeses are called Head:

The French Death's Head.
Swiss Monk's Head.
Dutch Cat's Head.
Moor's Head.

There's headcheese besides but that's made of a pig's head and is only a cheese by discourtesy.

Health
see Holstein.

Herbesthal *Germany*
Named from a valley full of rich *herbes* for grazing.

Herkimer *U.S.A.*	Cheddar type; nearly white. *See* Chapter 4.
Herrgårdsost, Farm House or Manor House *West Gothland and Jamtland, Sweden*	Hard Emmentaler type in two qualities: full cream and half cream. Weighs 25 to 40 pounds. It is the most popular cheese in all Sweden and the best is from West Gothland and Jutland.
Herrgårdstyp	*see* Hushållsost.
Hervé *Belgium*	Soft; made in cubes and peppered with *herbes* such as tarragon, parsley and chives. It flourishes from November to May and comes in three qualities: extra cream, cream, and part skim milk.
Hickory Smoked *U.S.A.*	Good smoke is often wasted on bad cheese.
Hohenburg	*see* Box No. II.
Hohenheim *Germany*	Soft; part skimmed milk; half-pound cylinders. (*See* Box No. I.)
Hoi Poi *China*	Soybean cheese, developed by vegetable rennet. Exported in jars.
Hoja	*see* Queso de.
Hollander *North Germany*	Imitation Dutch Goudas and Edams, chiefly from Neukirchen in Holstein.
Holstein Dairy	*see* Leather.
Holsteiner, or Old Holsteiner *Germany*	Eaten best when old, with butter, or in the North, with dripping.
Holstein Health, or Holsteiner Gesundheitkäse *Germany*	Sour-milk curd pressed hard and then cooked in a tin kettle with a little cream and salt. When mixed and melted it is poured into half-pound molds and cooled.

Holstein Skim Milk or Holstein Magerkäse
Germany
Skim-milker colored with saffron. Its name, "thin cheese," tells all.

Hop, Hopfen
Germany
Small, one inch by 2½ inches, packed in hops to ripen. An ideal beer cheese, loaded with lupulin.

Hopi
U.S.A.
Hard; goat; brittle; sharp; supposed to have been made first by the Hopi Indians out west where it's still at home.

Horner's
England
An old cream cheese brand in Redditch where Worcestershire sauce originated.

Horse Cheese
Not made of mare's milk, but the nickname for Caciocavallo because of the horse's head used to trademark the first edition of it.

Hum
Holland
Brand name of one of those mild little red Baby Goudas that make you say "Ho-hum."

Hushållsost, Household Cheese
Sweden
Popular in three types:
Herrgårdstyp—Farmhouse
Västgötatyp—Westgotland
Sveciatyp—Swedish

Hvid Gjetost
Norway
A strong variety of Gjetost, little known and less liked outside of Scandinavia.

I

Icelandic
In *Letters from Iceland,* W. H. Auden says: "The ordinary cheese is like a strong Dutch and good. There is also a brown sweet cheese, like the Norwegian." Doubtless the latter is Gjetost.

Ihlefield
Mecklenburg, Germany

A hand cheese.

Ilha, Queijo de
Azores

Semihard "Cheese of the Isle," largely exported to mother Portugal, measuring about a foot across and four inches high. The one word, *Ilha,* Isle, covers the several Azorian Islands whose names, such as *Pico,* Peak, and *Terceiro,* Third, are sometimes added to their cheeses.

Impérial, Ancien

see Ancien.

Imperial Club
Canada

Potted Cheddar; snappy; perhaps named after the famous French Ancien Impérial.

Incanestrato
Sicily, Italy

Very sharp; white; cooked; spiced; formed into large round "heads" from fifteen to twenty pounds. *See* Majocchino, a kind made with the three milks, goat, sheep and cow, and enriched with olive oil besides.

Irish Cheeses

Irish Cheddar and Irish Stilton are fairly ordinary imitations named after their native places of manufacture: Ardagh, Galtee, Whitehorn, Three Counties, etc.

Isigny
France

Full name Fromage à la Crème d'Isigny. (*See.*) Cream cheese. The American cheese of this name never amounted to much. It was an attempt to imitate Camembert in the Gay Nineties, but it turned out to be closer to Limburger. (*See* Chapter 2.)

In France there is also Crème d'Isigny, thick fresh cream that's as famous as England's Devonshire and comes as close to being cheese as any cream can.

Island of Orléans
Canada

This soft, full-flavored cheese was doubtless brought from France by early emigrés, for it has been made since 1869 on the Orléans Island in the St. Lawrence River near Quebec. It is known by its French name, Le Fromage Raffiné de l'Ile d'Orléans, and lives up to the name "refined."

J

Jack

see Monterey

Jochberg
Tyrol, Germany

Cow and goat milk mixed in a fine Tyrolean product, as all mountain cheeses are. Twenty inches in diameter and four inches high, it weighs in at forty-five pounds with the rind on.

Jonchée
Santonge, France

A superior Caillebotte, flavored with rum, orange-flower water or, uniquely, black coffee.

Josephine
Silesia, Germany

Soft and ladylike as its name suggests. Put up in small cylindrical packages.

Journiac

see Chapter 3.

Julost
Sweden

Semihard; tangy.

Jura Bleu, or Septmoncel
France

Hard: blue-veined; sharp; tangy.

K

Kaas, Oude
Belgium

Flemish name for the French Boule de Lille.

Kackavalj *Yugoslavia*	Same as Italian Caciocavallo.
Kaiser-käse *Germany*	This was an imperial cheese in the days of the kaisers and is still made under that once awesome name. Now it's just a jolly old mellow, yellow container of tang.
Kajmak, or Serbian Butter *Serbia and Turkey*	Cream cheese, soft and bland when young but ages to a tang between that of any goat's-milker and Roquefort.
Kamembert *Yugoslavia*	Imitation Camembert.
Karaghi La-La *Turkey*	Nutty and tangy.
Kareish *Egypt*	A pickled cheese, similar to Domiati.
Karut *India*	Semihard; mellow; for grating and seasoning.
Karvi *Norway*	Soft; caraway-seeded; comes in smallish packages.
Kash *Rumania*	Soft, white, somewhat stringy cheese named cheese.
Kashcavallo, Caskcaval *Greece*	A good imitation of Italian Caciocavallo.
Kasher, or Caher, Penner *Turkey*	Hard; white; sharp.
Kash Kwan *Bulgaria and the Balkans*	An all-purpose goat's milk, Parmesan type, eaten sliced when young, grated when old. An attempt to imitate it in Chicago failed. It is sold in Near East quarters in New York, Washington and all big American cities.

Kaskaval *Rumania*	Identical with Italian Caciocavallo, widely imitated, and well, in Greece, Yugoslavia, Bulgaria, Transylvania and neighboring lands. As popular as Cheddar in England, Canada and U.S.A.
Kasseri *Greece*	Hard; ewe's milk, usually.
Katschkawalj *Serbia*	Just another version of the international Caciocavallo.
Katzenkopf, Cat's Head *Holland*	Another name for Edam. (*See* Chapter 3.)
Kaukauna Club *U.S.A.*	Widely advertised processed cheese food.
Kauna *Lithuania*	A hearty cheese that's in season all the year around.
Kefalotir, Kefalotyi *Yugoslavia, Greece and Syria*	Both of these hard, grating cheeses are made from either goat's or ewe's milk and named after their shape, resembling a Greek hat, or Kefalo.
Keg-ripened	*see* Brand.
King Christian IX *Denmark*	Sharp with caraway. Popular with everybody.
Kingdom Farm *U.S.A., near Ithaca, N.Y.*	The Rutherfordites or Jehovah's Witnesses make Brick, Limburger and Münster that are said to be most delectable by those mortals lucky enough to get into the Kingdom Farm. Unfortunately their cheese is not available elsewhere.
Kirgischerkäse	*see* Krutt.

Kjarsgaard
Denmark
Hard; skim; sharp; tangy.

Klatschkäse, Gossip Cheese
Germany
A rich "ladies' cheese" corresponding to Damen; both designed to promote the flow of gossip in afternoon *Kaffeeklatsches* in the *Konditories.*

Kloster, Kloster Käse
Bavaria
Soft; ripe; finger-shaped, one by one by four inches. In Munich this was, and perhaps still is, carried by brew masters on their tasting tours "to bring out the excellence of a freshly broached tun." Named from being made by monks in early cloisters, down to this day.

Kochenkäse
Luxembourg
Cooked white dessert cheese. Since it is salt-free it is recommended for diets.

Koch Käse
Germany
This translates "cooked cheese."

Kochtounkäse
Belgium
Semisoft, cooked and smoked. Bland flavor.

Kolos-monostor
Rumania
Sheep; rectangular four-pounder, 8½ by five by three inches. One of those college-educated cheeses turned out by the students and professors at the Agricultural School of Transylvania.

Kolosvarer
Rumania
A Trappist Port-Salut imitation made with water-buffalo milk, as are so many of the world's fine cheeses.

Komijnekaas, Komynekass
North Holland
Spiked with caraway seeds and named after them.

Konigskäse
Germany
A regal name for a German imitation of Bel Paese.

Kopanisti
Greece

Blue-mold cheese with sharp, peppery flavor.

Koppen, Cup, or Bauden
Germany

Semihard; goat; made in a cup-shaped mold that gives both its shape and name. Small, three to four ounces; sharp; pungent; somewhat smoky. Imitated in U.S.A. in half-pound packages.

Korestin
Russia

Semisoft; mellow; cured in brine.

Kosher

This cheese appears in many countries under several names. Similar to Limburger, but eaten fresh. It is stamped genuine by Jewish authorities, for the use of religious persons. (*See* Gouda, Kosher.)

Krauterkäse
Brazil

Soft-paste herb cheese put up in a tube by German Brazilians near the Argentine border. A rich, full-flavored adaptation of Swiss Krauterkäse even though it is processed.

Kreuterkäse, Herb Cheese
Switzerland

Hard, grating cheese flavored with herbs; like Sapsago or Grunkäse.

Krutt, or Kirgischerkäse
Asian Steppes

A cheese turned out en route by nomadic tribes in the Asiatic Steppes, from sour skim milk of goat, sheep, cow or camel. The salted and pressed curd is made into small balls and dried in the sun.

Kühbacher
Bavaria

Soft, ripe, and chiefly interesting because of its name, Cow Creek, where it is made.

Kuminost
Norway

Semihard; caraway-seeded.

Kumminost
Sweden

This is Bondost with caraway added.

Kummin Ost
Wisconsin, U.S.A.

Imitation of the Scandinavian, with small production in Wisconsin where so many Swedes and Norwegians make their home and their *ost*.

Kummel, Leyden, or Leidsche Kaas
Holland

Caraway-seeded and named.

Kümmelkäse
Germany and U.S.A.

Semihard; sharp with caraway. Milwaukee Kümmelkäse has made a name for itself as a nibble most suitable with most drinks, from beer to imported kümmel liqueur.

L

Labneh
Syria

Sour-milk.

La Foncée, or Fromage de Pau
France

Cream cheese.

Lager Käse
U.S.A.

Semidry and mellow. While *lager* means merely "to store," there is more than a subtle suggestion of lager beer here.

Laguiole, Fromage de, and Guiole
Aveyron, France

An ancient Cantal type said to have flourished since the Roman occupation. Many consider Laguiole superior to Cantal. It is in full season from November to May.

Lamothe-Bougon, La Mothe St. Heray
Poitou

Goat cheese made from May to November.

Lancashire, or Lancaster
North England

White; crumbly; sharp; a good Welsh Rabbit cheese if you can get it. It is more like Cheshire than Cheddar. This most popular variety in the north of England is turned out best at Fylde, near the Irish Sea. It is a curiosity in manufacture, for often the curds used are of different ages, and this is accountable for a loose, friable texture. Deep orange in color.

Land-l-kas, or Güssing
Austria

Skim-milker, similar to U.S. Brick. Square loaves, four to eight pounds.

Langlois Blue
U.S.A.

A Colorado Blue with an excellent reputation, though it can hardly compete with Roquefort.

Langres
Haute-Marne, France

Semihard; fermented whole milk; farm-made; full-flavored, high-smelling Limburger type, similar to Maroilles. Ancient of days, said to have been made since the time of the Merovingian kings. Cylindrical, five by eight inches, they weigh one and a half to two pounds. Consumed mostly at home.

Lapland
Lapland

Reindeer milk. Resembles hard Swiss. Of unusual shape, both round and flat, so a cross-section looks like a dumbbell with angular ends.

Laredo
Mexico

Soft; creamy; mellow, made and named after the North Mexico city.

Larron
France

A kind of Maroilles.

Latticini
Italy

Trade name for a soft, water-buffalo product as creamy as Camembert.

Laumes, les
Burgundy, France

Made from November to July.

Lauterbach
Germany

Breakfast cheese.

Leaf

see Tschil.

Leather, Leder, or Holstein Dairy
Germany

A skim-milker with five to ten percent buttermilk, all from the great *milch* cows up near Denmark in Schleswig-Holstein. A technical point in its making is that it's "broken up with a harp or a stirring stick and stirred with a Danish stirrer."

Lebanie
Syria

Dessert cottage cheese often served with yogurt.

Lecco, Formaggini di
Italy

Soft; cow or goat; round dessert variety; representative of a cheese family as big as the human family of most Italians.

Lees

see Appenzeller, Festive, No. II.

Le Guéyin
Lorraine, France

Half-dried; small; salted; peppered and sharp. The salt *and* pepper make it unusual, though not as peppery as Italian Pepato.

Leicester
England

Hard; shallow; flat millstone of Cheddar-like cheese weighing forty pounds. Dark orange and mild to red and strong, according to age. With Wiltshire and Warwickshire it belongs to the Derbyshire type.

An ancient saying is: "Leicester cheese and water cress were just made for each other."

Leidsche Kaas

see Leyden.

Leonessa
A kind of Pecorino.

Leroy
U.S.A.
Notable because it's a natural cheese in a mob of modern processed.

Lerroux
France
Goat; in season from February to September and not eaten in fall or winter months.

Lescin
Caucasus
Curious because the sheep's milk that makes it is milked directly into a sack of skin. It is made in the usual way, rennet added, curd broken up, whey drained off, curd put into forms and pressed lightly. But after that it is wrapped in leaves and ropes of grass. After curing two weeks in the leaves, they are discarded, the cheese salted and wrapped up in leaves again for another ripening period.

The use of a skin sack again points the association of cheese and wine in a region where wine is still drunk from skin bags with nozzles, as in many wild and mountainous parts.

Les Petits Bressans
Bresse, France
Small goat cheeses named from food-famous Bresse, of the plump pullets, and often stimulated with brandy before being wrapped in fresh vine leaves, like Les Petits Banons.

Les Petits Fromages
see Petits Fromages and Thiviers.

Le Vacherin
Name given to two entirely different varieties:
I. Vacherin à la Main
II. Vacherin Fondu.
(*See* Vacherin.)

Levroux
Berry, France

A goat cheese in season from May to December.

Leyden, Komijne Kaas, Caraway Cheese
Holland

Semihard, tangy with caraway. Similar to Delft. There are two kinds of Leyden that might be called Farm Fat and Factory Thin, for those made on the farms contain 30 to 35% fat, against 20% in the factory product.

Liederkranz

see Chapter 4.

Limburger

see Chapter 3.

Lincoln
England

Cream cheese that keeps two to three weeks. This is in England, where there is much less refrigeration than in the U.S.A., and that's a big break for most natural cheeses.

Lindenhof
Belgium

Semisoft; aromatic; sharp.

Liptau, Liptauer, Liptoi
Hungary

A classic mixture with condiments, especially the great peppers from which the world's best paprika is made. Liptauer is the regional name for Brinza, as well, and it's made in the same manner, of sheep milk and sometimes cow. Salty and spready, somewhat oily, as most sheep-milkers are. A fairly sharp taste with a suggestion of sour milk. It is sold in various containers and known as "pickled cheese." (*See* Chapter 3.)

Lipto
Hungary

Soft; sheep; white; mild and milky taste. A close relative of both Liptauer and Brinza.

Little Nippy
U.S.A.

Processed cheese with a cute name, wrapped up both plain and smoky, to "slice and serve for cheese trays, mash or whip for spreading," but no matter how you slice, mash and whip it, it's still processed.

Livarot
Calvados, France

Soft paste, colored with annatto-brown or deep red (also, uncommonly, fresh and white). It has the advantage over Camembert, made in the same region, in that it may be manufactured during the summer months when skim milk is plentiful and cheap. It is formed in cylinders, six by two inches, and ripened several months in the even temperature of caves, to be eaten at its best only in January, February and March. By June and afterward it should be avoided. Similar to Mignot II. Early in the process of making, after ripening ten to twelve days, the cheeses are wrapped in fresh *laiche* leaves, both to give flavor and help hold in the ammonia and other essentials for making a strong, piquant Livarot.

Livlander
Russia

A popular hand cheese. A most unusual variety because the cheese itself is red, not the rind.

Locatelli
Italy

A brand of Pecorino differing slightly from Romano Pecorino.

Lodigiano, or Lombardo
Lodi, Italy

Sharp; fragrant; sometimes slightly bitter; yellow. Cylindrical; surface colored dark and oiled. Used for grating. Similar to Parmesan but not as fine in quality.

Longhorn
Wisconsin, U.S.A.

This fine American Cheddar was named from its resemblance to the long horn of a popular milking breed of cattle, or just from the Longhorn breed of cow that furnished the makings.

Lorraine
Lorraine, Germany

Hard; small; delicate; unique because it's seasoned with pistachio nuts besides salt and pepper. Eaten while quite young, in two-ounce portions that bring a very high price.

Lumburger
Belgium

Semisoft and tangy dessert cheese. The opposite of Limburger because it has no odor.

Lunch
Germany and U.S.A.

The same as Breakfast and Frühstück. A Limburger type of eye-opener.

Lüneberg
West Austria

Swiss type; saffron-colored; made in a copper kettle; not as strong as Limburger, or as mild as Emmentaler, yet piquant and aromatic, with a character of its own.

Luxembourg
U.S.A.

Tiny tin-foiled type of Liederkranz. A mild, bland, would-be Camembert.

M

Maconnais
France

Soft; goat's milk; two inches square by one and a half inches thick.

Macqueline
Oise, France

Soft Camembert type, made in the same region, but sold at a cheaper price.

Madridejos
Spain

Named for Madrid where it is made.

Magdeburger-kuhkäse
Germany

"Cow cheese" made in Magdeburg.

Magerkäse — *see* Holstein Skim Milk

Maggengo, Sorte
Italy
A term for Parmesan types made between April and September.

Maguis
Belgium
Also called Fromage Mou. Soft; white; sharp; spread.

Maigre
France
A name for Brie made in summer and inferior to both the winter Gras and spring Migras.

Maile
Crimea
Sheep; cooked; drained; salted; made into forms and put into a brine bath where it stays sometimes a year.

Maile Pener (Fat Cheese)
Crimea
Sheep; crumbly; open texture and pleasing flavor when ripened.

Mainauer
German
Semihard; full cream; round; red outside, yellow within. Weight three pounds.

Mainzer Hand
German
Typical hand cheese, kneaded by hand thoroughly, which makes for quality, pressed into flat cakes by hand, dried for a week, packed in kegs or jars and ripened in the cellar six to eight weeks. As in making bread, the skill in kneading Mainzer makes a worthy craft.

Majocchino
Sicily, Italy
An exceptional variety of the three usual milks mixed together: goat, sheep and cow, flavored with spices and olive oil. A kind of Incanestrato.

Malakoff
France
A form of Neufchâtel about a half inch by two inches, eaten fresh or ripe.

Manicamp
French Flanders
In season from October to July.

Mano, Queso de
Venezuela
A kind of Venezuelan hand cheese, as its Spanish name translates. (*See* Venezuelan.)

Manor House
see Herrgårdsost.

Manteca, Butter
Italy
Cheese and butter combined in a small brick of butter with a covering of Mozzarella. This is for slicing—not for cooking—which is unusual for any Italian cheese.

Manur, or Manuri
Yugoslavia
Sheep or cow's milk heated to boiling, then cooled "until the fingers can be held in it." A mixture of fresh whey and buttermilk is added with the rennet. "The curd is lifted from the whey in a cloth and allowed to drain, when it is kneaded like bread, lightly salted, and dried."

Maquée
Belgium
Another name for Fromage Mou, Soft Cheese.

Marches
Tuscany, Italy
Ewe's milk; hard.

Margarine
England
An oily cheese made with oleomargarine.

Margherita
Italy
Soft; cream; small.

Marienhofer
Austria
Limburger type. About 4⅜ inches square and 1½ inches thick; weight about a pound. Wrapped in tin foil.

Märkisch, or Märkisch Hand
Germany
Soft; smelly; hand type.

Maroilles, Marolles, Marole *Flanders, France*	Semisoft and semihard, half way between Pont l'Evêque and Limburger. Full flavor, high smell, reddish brown rind, yellow within. Five inches square and 2¼ inches thick; some larger.
Martha Washington Aged Cheese *U.S.A.*	Made by Kasper of Bear Creek, Wisconsin. (*See under* Wisconsin in Chapter 4.)
Mascarpone, or Macherone *Italy*	Soft; white; delicate fresh cream from Lombardy. Usually packed in muslin or gauze bags, a quarter to a half pound.
McIntosh *Alaska*	An early Klondike Cheddar named by its maker, Peter McIntosh, and described as being as yellow as that "Alaskan gold, which brought at times about ounce for ounce over mining-camp counters." *The Cheddar Box* by Dean Collins.
McLaren's *U.S.A.*	Pioneer club type of snappy Cheddar in a pot, originally made in Canada, now by Kraft in the U.S.A.
Meadowbloom *U.S.A.*	Made by the Iowa State College at Ames.
Mecklenburg Skim *Germany*	No more distinguished than most skim-milkers.
Meilbou *France*	Made in the Champagne district.
Mein Käse *U.S.A.*	Sharp; aromatic; trade-marked package.
Melfa *U.S.A.*	Excellent for a processed cheese. White; flavorsome. Packed in half moons.

Melun *France*	Brown-red rind, yellow inside; high-smelling. There is also a Brie de Melun.
Mentelto *Italy*	Sharp; goat; from the Mentelto mountains.
Merignac *France*	Goat.
Merovingian *Northeast France*	Semisoft; white; creamy; sharp; historic since the time of the Merovingian kings.
Mersem *France*	Lightly cooked.
Mesitra *Crimea*	Eaten when fresh and unsalted; also when ripened. Soft, ewe's milk.
Mesost *Sweden*	Whey; sweetish.
Metton *Franche-Comté, France*	Season October to June.
Meuse *France*	Soft; piquant; aromatic.
Midget Salami Provolone *U.S.A.*	This goes Baby Goudas and Edams one better by being a sort of sausage, too.
Mignot *Calvados, France*	*White, No. I:* Soft; fresh; in small cubes or cylinders; in season only in summer, April to September. *Passe, No. II:* Soft but ripened, and in the same forms, but only seasonal in winter, October to March. Similar to Pont l'Evêque and popular for more than a century. It goes specially well with Calvados cider, fresh, hard or distilled.

Migras — Name given to spring Brie—midway between fat winter Gras and thin summer Maigre.

Milano, Stracchino di Milano, Fresco, Quardo
Italy — Similar to Bel Paese. Yellow, with thin rind. 1½ to 2¾ inches thick, 3 to 6½ pounds.

Milk Mud — *see* Schlickermilch.

Millefiori
Milan, Italy — A Thousand Flowers—as highly scented as its sentimental name. Yet no cheeses are so freshly fragrant as these flowery Alpine ones.

Milltown Bar
U.S.A. — Robust texture and flavor reminiscent of free-lunch and old-time bars.

Milk cheeses — Milks that make cheese around the world:

- Ass
- Buffalo
- Camel
- Chamois
- Elephant
- Goat
- Human (*see* Mother's milk)
- Llama
- Mare
- Reindeer
- Sea cow (Amazonian legend)
- Sheep
- Whale (legendary; see Whale Cheese)
- Yak
- Zebra
- Zebu

U.S. pure food laws prohibit cheeses made of unusual or strange animal's milk, such as camel, llama and zebra.

Milwaukee Kümmelkäse and Hand Käse
U.S.A.

Aromatic with caraway, brought from Germany by early emigrants and successfully imitated.

Minas
Brazil

Name for the Brazilian state of Minas Geraes, where it is made. Semihard; white; round two-pounder; often chalky. The two best brands are one called Primavera, Spring, and another put out by the Swiss professors who teach the art at the Agricultural University in the State Capital, Bello Horizonte.

Minnesota Blue
U.S.A.

A good national product known from coast to coast. Besides Blue, Minnesota makes good all-American Brick and Cheddar, natural nationals to be proud of.

Mintzitra
in Macedonia; and
Mitzithra
in Greece

Sheep; soft; succulent; and as pleasantly greasy as other sheep cheeses from Greece. It's a by-product of the fabulous Feta.

Modena, Monte
U.S.A.

Made in U.S.A. during World War II. Parmesan-type.

Mohawk Limburger Spread
U.S.A.

A brand that comes in one-pound jars.

Moliterno
Italy

Similar to Caciocavallo. (*See.*)

Monceau
Champagne, France

Semihard, similar to Maroilles.

Moncenisio
Italy

Similar to Gorgonzola.

Mondseer, Mondseer Schachtelkäse, Mondseer Schlosskäse
Austria

This little family with a lot of long names is closely related to the Münster tribe, with very distant connections with the mildest branch of the Limburgers.

The Schachtelkäse is named from the wooden boxes in which it is shipped, while the Schlosskäse shows its class by being called Castle Cheese, probably because it is richer than the others, being made of whole milk.

Money made of cheese
China

In the Chase National Bank collection of moneys of the world there is a specimen of "Cheese money" about which the curator, Farran Zerbee, writes: "A specimen of the so-called 'cheese money' of Northern China, 1850–70, now in the Chase Bank collection, came to me personally some thirty years ago from a woman missionary, who had been located in the field where she said a cake form of condensed milk, and referred to as 'cheese,' was a medium of exchange among the natives. It, like other commodities, particularly compressed tea, was prized as a trading medium in China, in that it had value as nutriment and was sufficiently appreciated by the population as to be exchangeable for other articles of service."

Monk's Head

see Tête de Moine.

Monostorer
Transylvania, Rumania

Ewe's milk.

Monsieur
France

Soft; salted; rich in flavor.

Monsieur Fromage — *see* Fromage de Monsieur Fromage.

Montana
Catalonia
A mountain cheese.

Montasio
Austria and Italy
Usually skimmed goat and cow milk mixed. When finished, the rind is often rubbed with olive oil or blackened with soot. It is eaten both fresh, white and sweet, and aged, when it is yellow, granular and sharp, with a characteristic flavor. Mostly used when three to twelve months old, but kept much longer and grated for seasoning. Widely imitated in America.

Montauban de Bretagne, Fromage de
Brittany, France
A celebrated cheese of Brittany.

Montavoner
Austria
Sour and sometimes sweet milk, made tasty with dried herbs of the *Achillea* family.

Mont Blanc
France
An Alpine cheese.

Mont Cenis
Southeastern France
Usually made of all three available milks, cow, goat and sheep; it is semi-hard and blue-veined like the other Roquefort imitations, Gex and Septmoncel. Primitive methods are still used in the making and sometimes the ripening is done by *penicillium* introduced in moldy bread. Large rounds, eighteen by six to eight inches, weighing twenty-five pounds.

Mont-des-Cats
French Flanders
Trappist monk-made Port-Salut.

Montdidier *France*	A fresh cream.
Mont d'or, le, or Mont Dore *Lyonnais, France*	Soft; whole milk; originally goat, now cow; made throughout the Rhone Valley. Fat, golden-yellow and "relished by financiers" according to Victor Meusy. Between Brie and Pont l'Evêque but more delicate than either, though not effeminate. Alpin and Riola are similar. The best is still turned out at Mont d'Or, with runners-up in St. Cyr and St. Didier.
Montavoner *Austria*	A sour-milker made fragrant with herbs added to the curd.
Monterey *Mexico*	Hard; sharp; perhaps inspired by Monterey Jack that's made in California and along the Mexican border.
Monterey Jack	*see* Chapter 4.
Monthéry *Seine-et-Oise, France*	Whole or partly skimmed milk; soft in quality and large in size, weighing up to 5½ pounds. Notable only for its patriotic tri-color in ripening, with whitish mold that turns blue and has red spots.
Montpellier *France*	Sheep.
Moravian *Czechoslovakia*	Semihard and sharp.
Morbier *Bresse, France*	In season from November to July.
Mostoffait *France*	A little-known product of Champagne.

Mother's milk

In his book about French varieties, *Les Fromages,* Maurice des Ombiaux sums up the many exotic milks made into cheese and recounts the story of Paul Bert, who served a cheese "white as snow" that was so delicately appetizing it was partaken of in "religious silence." All the guests guessed, but none was right. So the host announced it was made of "*lait de femme*" and an astounded turophile exclaimed, "Then all of us are cannibals."

Mountain
Bavaria

Soft; yellow; sharp.

Mountain, Azuldoch

see Azuldoch.

Mount Hope
U.S.A.

Yellow; mellow; mild and porous California Cheddar.

Mouse or Mouse Trap
U.S.A.

Common name for young, green, cracked, leathery or rubbery low-grade store cheese fit only to bait traps. When it's aged and sharp, however, the same cheese can be bait for caseophiles.

Mozzarella
Italy

Soft; water-buffalo milk; moistly fresh and unripened; bland, white cooking cheese put up in balls or big bowl-like cups weighing about a half pound and protected with wax paper. The genuine is made at Cardito, Aversa, Salernitano and in the Mazzoni di Capua. Like Ricotta, this is such a popular cheese all over America that it is imitated widely, and often badly, with a bitter taste.

Mozzarella-Affumicata, also called Scamozza
Italy

Semisoft; smooth; white; bland; unsalted. Put up in pear shapes of about one pound, with tan rind, from smoking.

Eaten chiefly sliced, but prized, both fresh and smoked, in true Italian one-dish meals such as Lasagne and Pizza.

Mozzarinelli
Italy

A pet name for a diminutive edition of Mozzarella.

Mrsav

see Sir Posny.

Münster
Germany

German originally, now made from Colmar, Strassburg and Copenhagen to Milwaukee in all sorts of imitations, both good and bad. Semihard; whole milk; yellow inside, brick-red outside; flavor from mild to strong, depending on age and amount of caraway or anise seed added. Best in winter season, from November to April.

Münster is a world-wide classic that doubles for both German and French. Géromé is a standard French type of it, with a little longer season, beginning in April, and a somewhat different flavor from anise seed. Often, instead of putting the seeds inside, a dish of caraway is served with the cheese for those who like to flavor to taste.

In Alsace, Münster is made plain and also under the name of Münster au Cumin because of the caraway.

American imitations are much milder and marketed much younger. They are supposed to blend the taste of Brick and Limburger; maybe they do.

Mustard
U.S.A.

A processed domestic, Gruyère type.

Myjithra	Imitated with goat's milk in Southern Colorado.
Mysost, Mytost *Scandinavia*	Made in all Scandinavian countries and imitated in the U.S.A. A whey cheese, buttery, mild and sweetish with a caramel color all through, instead of the heavy chocolate or dark tobacco shade of Gjetost. Primost is a local name for it. The American imitations are cylindrical and wrapped in tin foil.

N

Nagelkassa (Fresh), Fresh Clove Cheese, called Nägeles in Holland *Austria*	Skim milk; curd mixed with caraway and cloves called nails, *nagel*, in Germany and Austria. The large flat rounds resemble English Derby.
Nantais, or Fromage du Curé, Cheese of the Curate *Brittany, France*	A special variety dedicated to some curate of Nantes.
Nessel *England*	Soft; whole milk; round and very thin.
Neufchâtel, or Petit Suisse *Normandy, France*	Soft; whole milk; small loaf. See Ancien Impérial, Bondon, and Chapter 9.
New Forest *England*	Cream cheese from the New Forest district.
Nieheimer *Westphalia, Germany*	Sour milk; with salt and caraway seed added, sometimes beer or milk. Covered lightly with straw and packed in kegs with hops to ripen. Both beer and hops in one cheese is unique.

Niolo
Corsica

In season from October to May.

Noekkelost or Nögelost
Norway

Similar to spiced Leyden or Edam with caraway, and shaped like a Gouda.

Nordlands-Ost "Kalas"
U.S.A.

Trade name for an American imitation of a Scandinavian variety, perhaps suggested by Swedish Nordost.

Nordost
Sweden

Semisoft; white; baked; salty and smoky.

North Wilts
Wiltshire, England

Cheddar type; smooth; hard rind; rich but delicate in flavor. Small size, ten to twelve pounds; named for its locale.

Nostrale
Northwest Italy

An ancient-of-days variety of which there are two kinds:

I. *Formaggio Duro:* hard, as its name says, made in the spring when the cows are in the valley.

II. *Formaggio Tenero:* soft and richer, summer-made with milk from lush mountain-grazing.

Notruschki (cheese bread)
Russia

Made with Tworog cheese and widely popular.

Nova Scotia Smoked
U.S.A.

The name must mean that the cheese was smoked in the Nova Scotia manner, for it is smoked mostly in New York City, like sturgeon, to give the luxurious flavor.

Nuworld
U.S.A.

This semisoft newcomer arrived about 1954 and is advertised as a brand-new variety. It is made in the Midwest and packed in small, heavily waxed portions to preserve all of its fine, full aroma and flavor.

A cheese all America can be proud of, whether it is an entirely new species or not.

O

Oaxaca

see Asadero.

Oka, or La Trappe
Canada

Medium soft; aromatic; the Port-Salut made by Trappist monks in Canada after the secret method of the order that originated in France. *See* Trappe.

Old English Club
U.S.A.

Not old, not English, and representing no club we know of.

Old Heidelberg
U.S.A.

Soft, piquant rival of Liederkranz.

Oléron Isle, Fromage d'Ile d'Oléron
France

A celebrated sheep cheese from this island of Oléron.

Olive Cream
U.S.A.

Ground olives mixed to taste with cream cheese. Olives rival pimientos for such mildly piquant blends that just suit the bland American taste. A more exciting olive cream may be made with Greek Calatma olives and Feta sheep cheese.

Olivet
Orléans, France

Soft sheep cheese sold in three forms:

I. Fresh; summer. white; cream cheese.

II. Olivet-Bleu—mold inoculated; half-ripened.

III. Olivet-Cendré, ripened in the ashes. Season, October to June.

Olmützer Quargel, also Olmützer Bierkäse
Austria

Soft; skim milk-soured; salty. The smallest of hand cheeses, only ⅛ of an inch thick by 1½ inches in diameter. Packed in kegs to ripen into beer cheese and keep the liquid contents of other kegs company. A dozen of these little ones are packed together in a box ready to drop into wine or beer drinks at home or at the bar.

Oloron, or Fromage de la Vallée d'ossour
Béarn, France

In season from October to May.

Onion with garlic links
U.S.A.

Processed and put up like frankfurters, in links.

Oporto
Portugal

Hard; sharp; tangy. From the home town of port wine.

Orkney
Scotland

A country cheese of the Orkney Islands where it is buried in the oat bin to ripen, and kept there between meals as well. Oatmeal and Scotch country cheese are natural affinities. Southey, Johnson and Boswell have all remarked the fine savor of such cheese with oatcakes.

Orléans
France

Named after the Orléans district. Soft; creamy; tangy.

Ossetin, Tuschninsk, or Kasach
Caucasus

Comes in two forms:

I. Soft and mild sheep or cow cheese ripened in brine for two months.

II. Hard, after ripening a year and more in brine. The type made of sheep milk is the better.

Ostiepek, Oschtjepek, Oschtjpeka
Czechoslovakia

Sheep in the Carpathian Mountains supply the herb-rich milk for this type, similar to Italian Caciocavallo.

Oswego
U.S.A.

New York State Cheddar of distinction.

Oude Kaas
Belgium

Popular in France as Boule de Lille.

Oust, Fromage de
Roussillon, France

Of the Camembert family.

Óvár
Hungarian

Semisoft to semihard, reddish-brown rind, reddish-yellow inside. Mild but pleasantly piquant. It has been called Hungarian Tilsit.

Ovcji Sir
Yugoslavian Alpine

Hard, mountain-sheep cheese of quality. Cellar-ripened three months. Weight six to ten pounds.

Oxfordshire
England

An obsolescent type, now only of literary interest because of Jonathan Swift's little story around it, in the eighteenth century:

"An odd kind of fellow, who when the cheese came upon the table, pretended to faint; so somebody said, 'Pray take away the cheese.'

" 'No,' said I, 'pray take away the fool. Said I well?'

"To this Colonel Arwit rejoins: 'Faith, my lord, you served the coxcomb right enough; and therefore I wish we had a bit of your lordship's Oxfordshire cheese.' "

P

Pabstett
U.S.A.

The Pabst beer people got this out during Prohibition, and although beer and cheese are brothers under their ferment, and Prohibition has long since been done away with, the relation of the processed paste to a natural cheese is still as distant as near beer from regular beer.

Packet cheese
England

This corresponds to our process cheese and is named from the package or packet it comes in.

Paglia
Switzerland

Italian-influenced Canton of Ticino. Soft. A copy of Gorgonzola. A Blue with a pleasant, aromatic flavor, and of further interest because in Switzerland, the motherland of cheese, it is an imitation of a foreign type.

Pago
Dalmatia, Yugoslavia

A sheep-milk specialty made on the island of Pago in Dalmatia, in weights from ½ to eight pounds.

Paladru
Savoy, France

In season from November to May.

Palpuszta
Hungary

Fairly strong Limburger type.

Pannarone
Italy

Gorgonzola type with white curd but without blue veining.

Parenica
Hungary

Sheep. Caciocavallo type.

Parmesan, Parmigiano
Italy

The grand mogul of all graters. Called "The hardest cheese in the world." It enlivens every course from onion soup to cheese straws with the demitasse, and puts spirit into the sparse Lenten menu as *Pasta al Pesto,* powdered Parmesan, garlic, olive oil and basil, pounded in a mortar with a pestle.

Passauer Rahmkäse, Crème de Passau *German*	Noted Bavarian cream cheese, known in France as Crème de Passau.
Pasta Cotta *Italy*	The ball or *grana* of curd used in making Parmesan.
Pasta Filata *Italy*	A "drawn" curd, the opposite of the little balls or grains into which Grana is chopped. (*See* Formaggi di Pasta Filata.)
Pasteurized Process Cheese Food *U.S.A.*	This is the ultimate desecration of natural fermented cheese. Had Pasteur but known what eventual harm his discovery would do to a world of cheese, he might have stayed his hand.
Pastorella *Italy*	Soft, rich table cheese.
Patagras *Cuba*	Similar to Gouda.
Pecorino *Italy*	Italian cheese made from ewe's milk. Salted in brine. Granular.
Pelardon de Rioms *Languedoc, France*	A goat cheese in season from May to November.
Peneteleu *Rumania*	One of the international Caciocavallo family.
Penicillium Glaucum and Penicillium Album	Tiny mushroom spores of *Penicillium Glaucum* sprinkled in the curd destined to become Roquefort, sprout and grow into "blue" veins that impart the characteristic flavor. In twelve to fifteen days a second spore develops on the surface, snow-white *Penicillium Album.*
Pennich *Turkey*	Mellow sheep cheese packed in the skin of sheep or lamb.

Pennsylvania Hand Cheese
U.S.A.

This German original has been made by the Pennsylvania Dutch ever since they arrived from the old country. Also Pennsylvania pot, or cooked.

Penroque
Pennsylvania, U.S.A.

Cow milk imitation Roquefort, inoculated with *Penicillium Roqueforti* and ripened in "caverns where nature has duplicated the ideal condition of the cheese-curing caverns of France." So any failure of Penroque to rival real Roquefort is more likely to be the fault of mother cow than mother nature.

Pepato
Italy

Hard; stinging, with whole black peppers that make the lips burn. Fine for fire-eaters.

An American imitation is made in Northern Michigan.

Persillé de Savoie
Savoie, France

In season from May to January, flavored with parsley in a manner similar to that of sage in Vermont Cheddar.

Petafina, La
Dauphiné, France

Goat or cow milk mixed together, with yeast of dried cheese added, plus salt and pepper, olive oil, brandy and absinthe.

Petit Carré
France

Fresh, unripened Ancien Impérial.

Petit Gruyère
Denmark

Imitation Gruyère, pasteurized, processed and made almost unrecognizable and inedible. Six tin-foil wedges to a box; also packaged with a couple of crackers for bars, one wedge for fifteen cents, where free lunch is forbidden. This is a fair sample of one of several foreign imitations that are actually worse than we can do at home.

Petit Moule
Ile-de-France, France

A pet name for Coulommiers.

Petit Suisse
France

Fresh, unsalted cream cheese. The same as Neufchâtel and similar to Coulommiers. It comes in two sizes:
Gros—a largest cylinder
Demi—a small one
Keats called this "the creamy curd," and another writer has praised its "La Fontaine-like simplicity." Whether made in Normandy, Switzerland, or Petropolis, Brazil, by early Swiss settlers, it is ideal with honey.

Petit Vacher
France

"Little Cowboy," an appropriate name for a small cow's-milk cheese.

Petits Bourgognes
Lower Burgundy, France

Soft; sheep; white, small, tangy. Other notable Petits also beginning with B are Banons and Bressans.

Petits Fromages de Chasteaux, les
France

Small, sheep cream cheeses from Lower Limousin.

Petits Fromages de Chèvre
France

Little cheeses from little goats grazing on the little mountains of Provence.

Petits Pots de Caillé de Poitiers
Poitou, France

Clotted milk in small pots.

Pfister
Cham, Switzerland

Emmentaler type, although differing in its method of making with fresh skim milk. It is named for Pfister Huber who was the first to manufacture it, in Cham.

Philadelphia Cream
U.S.A.

An excellent cream cheese that has been standard for seventy years. Made in New York State in spite of its name.

Picnic
U.S.A.

Handy-size picnic packing of mild American Cheddar. Swiss has long been called picnic cheese in America, its home away from home.

Picodon de Dieule Fit
Dauphiné, France

In season from May to December.

Pie, Fromage à la
France

Another name for Fromage Blanc or Farm; soft, creamy cottage-cheese type.

Pie Cheese
U.S.A.

An apt American name for any round store cheese that can be cut in wedges like a pie. Perfect with apple or mince or any other pie. And by the way, in these days when natural cheese is getting harder to find, any piece of American Cheddar cut in pie wedges before being wrapped in cellophane is apt to be the real thing—if it has the rind on. The wedge shape is used, however, *without any rind,* to make processed pastes pass for "natural" even without that identifying word, and with misleading labels such as old, sharp Cheddar and "aged nine months." That's long enough to make a baby, but not a "natural" out of a processed "Cheddar."

Pimiento
U.S.A.

Because pimiento is the blandest of peppers, it just suits our bland national taste, especially when mixed with Neufchâtel, cream, club or cottage. The best is homemade, of course, with honest, snappy old Cheddar mashed and mixed to taste, with the mild Spanish pepper that equals the Spanish olive as a partner in such spreads.

Pimp

see Mainzer Hand Cheese.

Pineapple

see Chapter 4.

Piora *Tessin, Switzerland*	Hard cheese with small eyes. Whole milk, either cow's or a mixture of goat's and cow's.
Pippen *U.S.A.*	Borden brand of Cheddar. Also Pippen Roll.
Pithiviers au Foin *France*	Orléans variety ripened on hay from October to May.
Poitiers *France*	Goat's milker named from its Poitou district.
Pommel *France*	All year. Double cream; unsalted.
Ponta Delgada *Azores*	Semifirm; delicate; piquant.
Pontgibaud *France*	Similar to Roquefort. Ripened at a very low temperature.
Pont l'Evêque	Characterized as a classic French *fromage* "with Huge-like Romanticism." (*See* Chapter 3.) An imported brand is called "The Inquisitive Cow."
Poona *U.S.A.*	Semisoft; mellow; New York Stater of distinctive flavor. Sold in two-pound packs, to be kept four or five hours at room temperature before serving.
Port-Salut, Port du Salut	*see* Chapter 3.
Port, Blue Links *U.S.A.*	"Blue" flavored with red port and put up in pseudo-sausage links.
Pot cheese *U.S.A.*	Cottage cheese with a dry curd, not creamed. An old English favorite for fruited cheese cakes with perfumed plums, lemons, almonds and macaroons.

In Ireland it was used in connection with the sheep-shearing ceremonies, although itself a common cow curd. Pennsylvania pot cheese is cooked.

Potato
Germany and U.S.A.

Made in Thuringia from sour cow milk with sheep or goat sometimes added. "The potatoes are boiled and grated or mashed. One part of the potato is thoroughly mixed or kneaded with two or three parts of the curd. In the better cheese three parts of potatoes are mixed with two of curd. During the mixing, salt and sometimes caraway seed are added. The cheese is allowed to stand for from two to four days while a fermentation takes place. After this the curd is sometimes covered with beer or cream and is finally placed in tubs and allowed to ripen for fourteen days. A variety of this cheese is made in the U.S. It is probable, however, that it is not allowed to ripen for quite so long a period as the potato cheese of Europe. In all other essentials it appears to be the same." From U.S. Department of Agriculture *Bulletin* No. 608.

Potato Pepper
Italy

Italian Potato cheese is enlivened with black pepper, like Pepato, only not so stony hard.

Pots de Crème St. Gervais
St. Gervais-sur-mer, France

The celebrated cream that rivals English Devonshire and is eaten both as a sweet and as a fresh cheese.

Pouligny–St. Pierre
Touraine, France

A celebrated cylindrical cheese made in Indre. Season from May to December.

Poustagnax, le
France

A fresh cow-milk cheese of Gascony.

Prato
Brazil

Semihard, very yellow imitation of the Argentine imitation of Holland Dutch. Standard Brazilian dessert with guava or quince paste. Named not from "dish" but the River Plate district of the Argentine from whence it was borrowed long ago.

Prattigau
Switzerland

Aromatic and sharp, Limburger type, from skim milk. Named for its home valley.

Prestost or Saaland Pfarr
Sweden

Similar to Gouda, but unique—the curd being mixed with whiskey, packed in a basket, salted and cellared, wrapped in a cloth changed daily; and on the third day finally washed with whiskey.

Primavera, Spring
Minas Geraes, Brazil

Semihard white brand of Minas cheese high quality, with a springlike fragrance.

Primost
Norway

Soft; whey; unripened; light brown; mild flavor.

Primula
Norway

A blend of French Brie and Petit Gruyère, mild table cheese imitated in Norway, sold in small packages. Danish Appetitost is similar, but with caraway added.

Processed
U.S.A.

From here around the world. Natural cheese melted and modified by emulsification with a harmless agent and thus changed into a plastic mass.

Promessi
Italy

Small soft-cream cheese.

Provatura
Italy

A water-buffalo variety. This type of milk makes a good beginning for a fine cheese, no matter how it is made.

Providence
France

Port-Salut from the Trappist monastery at Briquebec.

Provole, Provolone, Provolocine, Provoloncinni, Provoletti, and Provolino
Italy

All are types, shapes and sizes of Italy's most widely known and appreciated cheese. It is almost as widely but badly imitated in the U.S.A., where the final "e" and "i" are interchangeable.

Cured in string nets that stay on permanently to hang decoratively in the home kitchen or dining room. Like straw Chianti bottles, Provolones weigh from *bocconi* (mouthful), about one pound, to two to four pounds. There are three- to five-pound Provoletti, and upward with huge Salamis and Giants. Small ones come ball, pear, apple, and all sorts of decorative shapes, big ones become monumental sculptures that are works of art to compare with butter and soap modeling.

P'teux, le, or Fromage Cuit
Lorraine, France

Cooked cheese worked with white wine instead of milk, and potted.

Puant Macere
Flanders

"The most candidly named cheese in existence." In season from November to June.

Pultost or Knaost
Norway

Sour milk with some buttermilk, farm made in mountains.

Pusztador
Hungary

Semihard, Limburger-Romadur type. Full flavor, high scent.

Pyrenees, Fromage des
France

A fine mountain variety.

Q

Quartiolo *Italy*	Term used to distinguish Parmesan-type cheese made between September and November.
Quacheq *Macedonia, Greece*	Sheep, eaten both fresh and ripened.
Quargel	*see* Olmützer.
Quartirolo *Italy*	Soft, cow's milk.
Queijos—Cheeses of the Azores, Brazil and Portugal	*see* under their local or regional names: Alentejo, Azeitao, Cardiga, Ilha, Prato and Serra da Estrella.
Queso Anejo *Mexico*	White, dry, skim milk.
Queso de Bola *Mexico*	Whole milk, similar to Edam.
Queso de Cavallo *Venezuela*	Pear-shaped cheese.
Quesos Cheeses: Blanco, Cartera and Palma Metida	*see* Venezuela.
Queso de Cincho *Venezuela*	Hard, round orange balls weighing four pounds and wrapped in palm leaves.
Queso de Crema *Costa Rica*	Similar to soft Brick.
Queso de Hoja, Leaf Cheese *Puerto Rico*	Named from its appearance when cut, like leaves piled on top of each other.

Queso de Mano *Venezuela*	Aromatic, sharp, in four-ounce packages.
Queso del Pais, Queso de la Tierra *Puerto Rico*	White; pressed; semisoft. Consumed locally.
Queso de Prensa *Puerto Rico*	The name means pressed cheese. It is eaten either fresh or after ripening two or three months.
Queso de Puna *Puerto Rico*	Like U.S. cottage or Dutch cheese, eaten fresh.
Queso de Tapara *Venezuela*	Made in Carora, near Barqisimeto, called *tapara* from the shape and tough skin of that local gourd. "It is very good fresh, but by the time it arrives in Carora it is often bad and dry." D. K. K. in *Bueno Provecho.*
Queso Fresco *El Salvador*	Cottage-cheese type.
Queville	*see* Chapter 3.
Queyras	*see* Champoléon.

R

Rabaçal *Coimbra, Portugal*	Semisoft; sheep or goat; thick, round, four to five inches in diameter. Pleasantly oily, if made from sheep milk.
Rabbit Cheese *U.S.A.*	A playful name for Cheddar two to three years old.
Radener *Germany*	Hard; skim, similar to Emmentaler; made in Mecklenburg. Sixteen by four inches, weight 32 pounds.

Radolfzeller Cream *Germany, Switzerland, Austria*	Similar to Münster.
Ragnit	*see* Tilsit.
Rahmkäse, Allgäuer *German*	Cream.
Rainbow *Mexico*	Mild; mellow.
Ramadoux *Belgium*	Soft; sweet cream; formed in cubes. Similar to Hervé.
Rammil or Rammel *England*	André Simon calls this "the best cheese made in Dorsetshire." Also called Rammilk, because made from whole or "raw milk." Practically unobtainable today.
Rangiport *France*	A good imitation of Port-Salut made in Seine-et-Oise.
Rarush Durmar *Turkey*	Brittle; mellow; nutty.
Rächerkäse	The name for all smoked cheese in Germanic countries, where it is very popular.
Raviggiolo *Tuscany, Italy*	Ewe's milk. Uncooked; soft; sweet; creamy.
Rayon or Raper *Switzerland*	A blind Emmentaler called Rayon is shipped young to Italy, where it is hardened by aging and then sold as Raper, for grating and seasoning.
Reblochon or Roblochon *Savoy*	Sheep; soft; whole milk; in season from October to June. Weight one to two pounds. A cooked cheese imitated as Brizecon in the same section.

Récollet de Gérardmer
Vosges, France

A harvest variety similar to Gerome, made from October to April.

Red
Russia

see Livlander.

Red Balls
Dutch

see Edam.

Reggiano

see Grana.

Regianito
Argentine

Italian Reggiano type with a name of its own, for it is not a mere imitation in this land of rich milk and extra fine cheeses.

Reichkäse
German

Patriotically hailed as cheese of the empire, when Germany had one.

Reindeer
Lapland, Iceland, Sweden, Norway

In all far northern lands a type of Swiss is made from reindeer milk. It is lightly salted, very hard; and the Lapland production is curiously formed, like a dumbbell with angular instead of round ends.

Relish cream cheese
U.S.A.

Mixed with any piquant relish and eaten fresh.

Remoudon, or Fromage Piquant
Belgium

The two names combine in re-ground piquant cheese, and that's what it is. The season is winter, from November to June.

Requeijão
Portugal and Brazil

Recooked.

Resurrection

see Welsh.

Rhubarbe
France

A type of Roquefort which, in spite of its name, is no relation to our pie plant.

Riceys — *see* Champenois.

Ricotta Romano
Italy
Soft and fresh. The best is made from sheep buttermilk. Creamy, piquant, with subtle fragrance. Eaten with sugar and cinnamon, sometimes with a dusting of powdered coffee.

Ricotta
Italy and U.S.A.
Fresh, moist, unsalted cottage cheese for sandwiches, salads, lasagne, blintzes and many Italian dishes. It is also mixed with Marsala and rum and relished for dessert. Ricotta may be had in every Little Italy, some of it very well made and, unfortunately, some of it a poor substitute whey cheese.

Ricotta Salata
Hard; grayish white. Although its flavor is milk it is too hard and too salty for eating as is, and is mostly used for grating.

Riesengebirge
Bohemia
Semisoft; goat or cow; delicate flavor, lightly smoked in Bohemia's northern mountains.

Rinnen
Germany
This traditional Pomeranian sour-milk, caraway-seeded variety is named from the wooden trough in which it is laid to drain.

Riola
Normandy, France
Soft; sheep or goat; sharp; resembles Mont d'Or but takes longer to ripen, two to three months.

Robbiole
Robbiola
Robbiolini
Lombardy
Italian
Very similar to Crescenza (*see.*) Alpine winter cheese of fine quality. The form is circular and flat, weighing from eight ounces to two pounds, while Robbiolini, the baby of the family tips the scale at just under four ounces.

Roblochon, le	Same as Reblochon. A delicious form of it is made of half-dried sheep's milk in Le Grand Bornand.
Rocamadur *Limousin, France*	Tiny sheep milk cheese weighing two ounces. In season November to May.
Rocroi *France*	From the Champagne district.
Rokadur *Yugoslavia*	Imitation Roquefort.
Roll *England*	Hard cylinder, eight by nine inches, weighing twenty pounds.
Rollot or Rigolot *Picardy and Montdidier, France*	Soft; fermented; mold-inoculated; resembles Brie and Camembert, but much smaller. In season October to May. This is Picardy's one and only cheese.
Roma *Italy*	Soft cream.
Romadour, Romadura, and other national spellings *Germany, Austria, Hungary, Switzerland*	A great Limburger. The eating season is from November to April. It is not a summer cheese, especially in lands where refrigeration is scarce. Fine brands are exported to America from several countries.
Romano, Romano Vacchino *Italy*	Strong flavoring cheese like Parmesan and Pecorino.
Romanello *U.S.A.*	Similar to Romano Vacchino and Old Monterey Jack. Small grating cheese, cured one year.
Roquefort *France*	King of cheeses, with its "tingling Rabelaisian pungency." *See* Chapter 3.

Roquefort cheese dressing, bottled
U.S.A.
Made with genuine imported Roquefort, but with cottonseed oil instead of olive, plain instead of wine vinegar, sugar, salt, paprika, mustard, flour and spice oil.

Roquefort de Corse
Corsica, France
This Corsican imitation is blue-colored and correctly made of sheep milk, but lacks the chalk caves of Auvergne for ripening.

Roquefort de Tournemire
France
Another Blue cheese of sheep milk from Languedoc, using the royal Roquefort name.

Rougerets, les
Lyonnais, France
A typical small goat cheese from Forez, in a section where practically every variety is made with goat milk.

Rouennais
France
This specialty, named after its city, Rouen, is a winter cheese, eaten from October to May.

Round Dutch
Holland
An early name for Edam.

Rouy, le
Normandy, France
From the greatest of the cheese provinces, Normandy.

Royal Brabant
Belgium
Whole milk. Small, Limburger type.

Royal Sentry
Denmark
Processed Swiss made in Denmark and shipped to Americans who haven't yet learned that a European imitation can be as bad as an American one. This particular pasteurized process-cheese spread puts its ingredients in finer type than any accident insurance policy: Samsoe (Danish Swiss) cheese, cream, water, non-fat dry milk solids, cheese whey solids and disodium phosphate.

Ruffec, Fromage de
Saintonge, France
Fresh; goat.

Runesten
Denmark and U.S.A.

Similar to Herrgårdsost. Small eyes. "Wheel" weighs about three pounds. Wrapped in red transparent film.

Rush Cream Cheese
England and France

Not named from the rush in which many of our cheeses are made, but from the rush mats and nets some fresh cream cheeses are wrapped and sewed up in to ripen. According to an old English recipe the curds are collected with an ordinary fish-slice and placed in a rush shape, covered with a cloth when filled. Lay a half-pound weight in a saucer and set this on top of the strained curd for a few hours, and then increase the weight by about a half pound. Change the cloths daily until the cheese looks mellow, then put into the rush shape with the fish slice. The formula in use in France, where willow heart-shape baskets are sold for making this cheese, is as follows: Add one cup new warm milk to two cups freshly-skimmed cream. Dissolve in this one teaspoon of fine sugar and one tablespoon common rennet or thirty drops of Hauser's extract of rennet. Let it remain in a warm place until curd sets. Rush and straw mats are easily made by cutting the straw into lengths and stringing them with a needle and thread. The mats or baskets should not be used a second time.

S

Saaland Pfarr, or Prestost
Sweden

Firm; sharp; biting; unique of its kind because it is made with whiskey as an ingredient and the finished product is also washed with whiskey.

Saanen
Switzerland

Semihard and as mellow as all good Swiss cheese. This is the finest cheese in the greatest cheese land; an Emmentaler also known as Hartkäse, Reibkäse and Walliskäse, it came to fame in the sixteenth century and has always fetched an extra price for its quality and age. It is cooked much dryer in the making, so it takes longer to ripen and then keeps longer than any other. It weighs only ten to twenty pounds and the eyes are small and scarce. The average period needed for ripening is six years, but some take nine.

Sage, or Green cheese
England

This is more of a cream cheese, than a Cheddar, as Sage is in the U.S.A. It is made by adding sage leaves and a greening to milk by the method described in Chapter 4.

Saint-Affrique
Guyenne, France

This gourmetic center, hard by the celebrated town of Roquefort, lives up to its reputation by turning out a toothsome goat cheese of local renown.

We will not attempt to describe it further, since like most of the host of cheeses honored with the names of Saints, it is seldom shipped abroad.

Saint-Agathon
Brittany, France

Season, October to July.

Saint-Amand–Montrond
Berry, France

Made from goat's milk.

Saint-Benoit
Loiret, France

Soft Olivet type distinguished by charcoal being added to the salt rubbed on the outside of the finished cheese. It ripens in twelve to fifteen days in summer, and eighteen to twenty in winter. It is about six inches in diameter.

Saint-Claude *Franche-Comté, France*	Semihard; blue; goat; mellow; small; square; a quarter to a half pound. The curd is kept five to six hours only before salting and is then eaten fresh or put away to ripen.
Saint-Cyr	*see* Mont d'Or.
Saint-Didier au Mont d'Or	*see* Mont d'Or.
Saint-Florentine *Burgundy, France*	A lusty cheese, soft but salty, in season from November to July.
Saint-Flour *Auvergne, France*	Another seasonal specialty from this province of many cheeses.
Saint-Gelay *Poitou, France*	Made from goat's milk.
Saint-Gervais, Pots de Crème, or Le Saint Gervais	*see* Pots de Crème.
Saint-Heray	*see* La Mothe.
Saint-Honoré *Nivernais, France*	A small goat cheese.
Saint-Hubert *France*	Similar to Brie.
Saint-Ivel *England*	Fresh dairy cream cheese containing *Lactobacillus acidophilus*. Similar to the yogurt cheese of the U.S.A., which is made with *Bacillus Bulgaricus*.
Saint-Laurent *Roussillon, France*	Mountain sheep cheese.
Saint-Lizier *Béarn, France*	A white, curd cheese.

Saint-Loup, Fromage de
Poitou and Vendée, France
Half-goat, half-cow milk, in season February to September.

Saint-Marcellin
Dauphiné, France
One of the very best of all goat cheeses. Three by ¾ inches, weighing a quarter of a pound. In season from March to December. Sometimes sheep milk may be added, even cow's, but this is essentially a goat cheese.

Saint-Moritz
Switzerland
Soft and tangy.

Saint-Nectaire, or Senecterre
Auvergne, France
Noted as one of the greatest of all French goat cheeses.

Saint-Olivet
see Chapter 3.

Saint-Pierre–Pouligny
see Pouligny–Saint-Pierre.

Saint-Reine
see Alise.

Saint-Rémy, Fromage de
Haute-Saône, France
Soft. Pont l'Evêque type.

Saint-Stefano
German
Bel Paese type.

Saint-Winx
Flanders, France
The fromage of Saint-Winx is a traditional leader in this Belgian border province noted for its strong, spiced dairy products.

Sainte-Anne d'Auray
Brittany, France
A notable Port-Salut made by Trappist monks.

Sainte-Marie
Franche-Comté, France
A creamy concoction worthy of its saintly name.

Sainte-Maure, le, or Fromage de Sainte-Maure-de-Touraine
France
Made in Touraine from May to November. Similar to Valençay.

Salamana
Southern Europe
Soft sheep's milk cheese stuffed into bladderlike sausage, to ripen. It has authority and flavor when ready to spread on bread, or to mix with cornmeal and cook into a highly cheese-flavored porridge.

Salame
France
Soft cream cheese stuffed into skins like salami sausages. Salami-sausage style of packing cheese has always been common in Italy, from Provolone down, and now—both as salami and links—it has became extremely popular for processed and cheese foods throughout America.

Salers, Bleu de
France
One of the very good French Blues.

Saligny
Champagne, France
White cheese made from sheep's milk.

Saloio
Lisbon, Portugal
An aromatic farm-made hand cheese of skim milk. Short cylinder, 1½ to two inches in diameter, weighing a quarter of a pound. Made near the capital, Lisbon, on many small farms.

Salonite
Italy
Favorite of Emperor Augustus a couple of thousand years ago.

Saltee
Ireland
Firm; highly colored; tangy; boxed in half-pound slabs. The same as Whitethorn except for the added color. Whitethorn is as white as its name implies.

Salt-free cheese, for diets
U.S. cottage; French fresh goat cheese; and Luxembourg Kochenkäse.

Samsö *Denmark*	Hard; white; sharp; slightly powdery and sweetish. This is the pet cheese of Erik Blegvad who illustrated this book.
Sandwich Nut	An American mixture of chopped nuts with Cream cheese or Neufchâtel.
Sapsago	*see* Chapter 3.
Sardegna *Sardinia*	A Romano type made in Sardinia.
Sardinian *Sardinia, Italy*	The typical hard grating cheese of this section of Italy.
Sardo *Sardinia, Italy*	Hard; sharp; for table and for seasoning. Imitated in the Argentine. There is also a Pecorino named Sardo.
Sarraz or Sarrazin *Vaud, Switzerland*	Roquefort type.
Sassenage *Dauphiny, France*	Semihard; bluer and stronger than Stilton. This makes a French trio of Blues with Septmoncel and Gex, all three of which are made with the three usual milks mixed: cow, goat and sheep. A succulent fermented variety for which both Grenoble and Sassenage are celebrated.
Satz *Germany*	Hard cheese made in Saxony.
Savoy, Savoie *France*	Semisoft; mellow; tangy Port-Salut made by Trappist monks in Savoy.
Sbrinz *Argentine*	Hard; dry; nutty; Parmesan grating type.

Scanno *Abruzzi, Italy*	Soft as butter; sheep; burnt taste, delicious with fruits. Blackened rind, deep-yellow interior.
Scarmorze or Scamorze *Italy*	Hard; buffalo milk; mild Provolone type. Also called Pear from being made in that shape, oddly enough also in pairs, tied together to hang from rafters on strings in ripening rooms or in the home kitchen. Fine when sliced thick and fried in olive oil. A specialty around Naples. Light-tan oiled rind, about 3½ by five inches in size. Imitated in Wisconsin and sold as Pear cheese.
Schabziger	*see* Chapter 3.
Schafkäse (Sheep Cheese) *Germany*	Soft; part sheep milk; smooth and delightful.
Schamser, or Rheinwald *Canton Graubünden, Switzerland*	Large skim-milker eighteen by five inches, weighing forty to forty-six pounds.
Schlickermilch	This might be translated "milk mud." It's another name for Bloder, sour milk "waddle" cheese.
Schlesische Sauermilchkäse *Silesia, Poland*	Hard; sour-milker; made like hand cheese. Laid on straw-covered shelves, dried by a stove in winter and in open latticed sheds in summer. When very dry and hard, it is put to ripen in a cellar three to eight weeks and washed with warm water two or three times a week.
Schlesischer Weichquarg *Silesia, Poland*	Soft, fresh skim, sour curd, broken up and cooked at 100° for a short time. Lightly pressed in a cloth sack twenty-

four hours, then kneaded and shaped by hand, as all hand cheeses are. Sometimes sharply flavored with onions or caraway. Eaten fresh, before the strong hand cheese odor develops.

Schloss, Schlosskäse, or Bismarck
German
This Castle cheese, also named for Bismarck and probably a favorite of his, together with Bismarck jelly doughnuts, is an aristocratic Limburger that served as a model for Liederkranz.

Schmierkäse
German cottage cheese that becomes smearcase in America.

Schnitzelbank Pot
see Liederkranz, Chapter 4.

Schoenland
German
Imitation of Italian Bel Paese, also translated "beautiful land."

Schützenkäse
Austria
Romadur-type. Small rectangular blocks weighing less than four ounces and wrapped in tin foil.

Shottengsied
Alpine
A whey cheese made and consumed locally in the Alps.

Schwarzenberger
Hungary and Bohemia
One part skim to two parts fresh milk. It takes two to three months to ripen.

Schweizerkäse
Switzerland
German for Swiss cheese. (*See* Emmentaler.)

Schweizerost Dansk, Danish Swiss cheese
Denmark
A popular Danish imitation of Swiss that is nothing wonderful.

Select Brick
see Chapter 12.

Selles-sur Cher
Berry, France
A goat cheese, eaten from February to September.

Sénecterre
Puy-de-Dôme, France

Soft, whole-milk; cylindrical, weighing about 1½ pounds.

Septmoncel
France

Semihard; skim; blue-veined; made of all three milks: cow, goat and sheep. An excellent "Blue" ranked above Roquefort by some, and next to Stilton. Also called Jura Bleu, and a member of the triple milk triplets with Gex and Sassenage.

Serbian
Serbia

Made most primitively by dropping heated stones into a kettle of milk over an open fire. After the rennet is added, the curd stands for an hour and is separated from the whey by being lifted in a cheesecloth and strained. It is finally put in a wooden vessel to ripen. First it is salted, then covered each day with whey for eight days and finally with fresh milk for six.

Syria also makes a cheese called Serbian from goat's milk. It is semisoft.

Serbian Butter

see Kajmar.

Serra da Estrella, Queijo da (Cheese of the Star Mountain Range)
Portugal

The finest of several superb mountain-sheep cheeses in Portugal. Other milk is sometimes added, but sheep is standard. The milk is coagulated by an extract of thistle or cardoon flowers in two to six hours. It is ripened in circular forms for several weeks and marketed in rounds averaging five pounds, about ten by two inches. The soft paste inside is pleasantly oily and delightfully acid.

Sharp-flavored cheese

U.S. aged Cheddars, including Monterey Jack; Italian Romano Pecorino, Old

Asiago, Gorgonzola, Incanestrato and Caciocavallo; Spanish de Fontine; Aged Roumanian Kaskaval.

Shefford — *see* Chapter 2.

Silesian
Poland and Germany — White; mellow; caraway-seeded. Imitated in U.S.A. (see Schlesischer.)

Sir cheeses — In Yugoslavia, Montenegro and adjacent lands Sir or Cyr means cheese. Mostly this type is made of skimmed sheep milk and has small eyes or holes, a sharp taste and resemblance to both American Brick and Limburger. They are much fewer than the Saint cheeses in France.

Sir Iz Mjesine
Dalmatia, Yugoslavia — Primitively made by heating skim sheep milk in a bottle over an open fire, coagulating it quickly with pig or calf rennet, breaking up the curd with a wooden spoon and stirring it by hand over the fire. Pressed into forms eight inches square and two inches thick, it is dried for a day and either eaten fresh or cut into cubes, salted, packed in green sheep or goat hides, and put away to ripen.

Sir Mastny
Montenegro — Fresh sheep milk.

Sir Posny
Montenegro — Hard; skim sheep milk; white, with many small holes. Also answers to the names of Tord and Mrsav.

Sir, Twdr — *see* Twdr Sir.

Sir, Warshawski — *see* Warshawski Syr.

Siraz
Serbia

Semisoft; whole milk. Mellow.

Skyr
Iceland

The one standard cheese of the country. A cross between Devonshire cream and cream cheese, eaten with sugar and cream. It is very well liked and filling, so people are apt to take too much. A writer on the subject gives this bit of useful information for travelers: "It is not advisable, however, to take coffee and Skyr together just before riding, as it gives you diarrhea."

Slipcote, or Colwick
England

Soft; unripened; small; white; rich as butter. The curd is put in forms six by two inches for the whey to drain away. When firm it is placed between cabbage leaves to ripen for a week or two, and when it is taken from the leaves the skin or coat becomes loose and easily slips off—hence the name. In the middle of the eighteenth century it was considered the best cream cheese in England and was made then, as today, in Wissenden, Rutlandshire.

Smältost
Sweden

Soft and melting.

Smearcase

Old English corruption of German Schmierkäse, long used in America for cottage cheese.

Smoked Block
Austria

A well-smoked cheese in block form.

Smoked Mozzarella

see Mozzarella Affumicata.

Smoked Szekely
Hungary

Soft; sheep; packed like sausage in skins or bladders and smoked.

Smokelet
Norway
A small smoked cheese.

Soaked-curd cheese
see Washed-curd cheese.

Sorbais
Champagne, France
Semihard; whole milk; fermented; yellow, with reddish brown rind. Full flavor, high smell. Similar to Maroilles in taste and square shape, but smaller.

Sorte Maggenga and Sorte Vermenga
Two "sorts" of Italian Parmesan.

Soumaintrain, Fromage de
France
Soft; fine; strong variety from Upper Burgundy.

Soybean
China
Because this cheese is made of vegetable milk and often developed with a vegetable rennet, it is rated by many as a regular cheese. But our occidental kind with animal milk and rennet is never eaten by Chinese and the mere mention of it has been known to make them shiver.

Spalen or Stringer
Switzerland
A small Emmentaler of fine reputation made in the Canton of Unterwalden from whole and partly skimmed milk and named from the vessel in which five or six are packed and transported together.

Sperrkäse
see Dry.

Spiced
International
Many a bland cheese is saved from oblivion by the addition of spice, to give it zest. One or more spices are added in the making and thoroughly mixed with the finished product, so the cheese often takes the name of the spice: Kuminost

or Kommenost for cumin; Caraway in English and several other languages, among them Kümmel, Nokkelost and Leyden; Friesan Clove and Nagelkass; Sage; Thyme, cloverleaf Sapsago; whole black pepper Pepato, etc.

Spiced and Spiced Spreads
U.S.A.

Government standards for spiced cheeses and spreads specify not less than 1½ ounces of spice to 100 pounds of cheese.

Spiced Fondue
France

see Vacherin Fondu.

Spitz Spitzkäse
Germany

Small cylinder, four by one and a half inches. Caraway spiced, Limburger-like. *see* Backsteiner.

Sposi
Italy

Soft; small; cream.

Spra
Greek

Sharp and pleasantly salty, packed fresh from the brine bath in one-pound jars. As tasty as all Greek cheeses because they are made principally from sheep milk.

Stangenkäse
Germany

Limburger type.

Stein Käse
U.S.A.

Aromatic, piquant "stone." A beer stein accompaniment well made after the old German original.

Steinbuscher-Käse
German

Semihard; firm; full cream; mildly sour and pungent. Brick forms, reddish and buttery. Originated in Frankfurt. Highly thought of at home but little known abroad.

Steppe
Russia, Germany, Austria, Denmark

German colonists made and named this in Russia. Rich and mellow, it tastes like Tilsiter and is now made in Denmark for export, as well as in Germany and Austria for home consumption.

Stilton

see Chapter 3.

Stirred curd cheese
U.S.A.

Similar to Cheddar, but more granular, softer in texture and marketed younger.

Stracchino
Italy

Soft; goat; fresh cream; winter; light yellow; very sharp, rich and pungent. Made in many parts of Italy and eaten sliced, never grated. A fine cheese of which Taleggio is the leading variety. See in Chapter 3. Also see Certoso Stracchino.

Stracchino Crescenza is an extremely soft and highly colored member of this distinguished family.

Stravecchio
Italy

Well-aged, according to the name. Creamy and mellow.

Stringer

see Spalen.

Styria
Austria

Whole milk. Cylindrical form.

Suffolk
England

An old-timer, seldom seen today. Stony-hard, horny "flet milk" cartwheels locally nicknamed "bang." Never popular anywhere, it has stood more abuse than Limburger, not for its smell but for its flinty hardness.

"Hunger will break through stone walls and anything except a Suffolk cheese."

"Those that made me were uncivil
For they made me harder than the devil.
Knives won't cut me; fire won't sweat
  me;
Dogs bark at me, but can't eat me."

Surati, Panir
India

Buffalo milk. Uncolored.

Suraz
Serbia

Semihard and semisoft.

Sveciaost
Sweden

A national pride, named for its country, Swedish cheese, to match Swiss cheese and Dutch cheese. It comes in three qualities: full cream, ¾ cream, and half cream. Soft; rich; ready to eat at six weeks and won't keep past six months. A whole-hearted, whole-milk, wholesome cheese named after the country rather than a part of it as most *osts* are.

Sweet-curd
U.S.A.

Hard Cheddar, differing in that the milk is set sweet and the curd cooked firmer and faster, salted and pressed at once. When ripe, however, it is hardly distinguishable from the usual Cheddar made by the granular process.

Swiss
U.S.A.

In 1845 emigrants from Galrus, Switzerland, founded New Galrus, Wisconsin and, after failing at farming due to cinch bugs gobbling their crops, they turned to cheesemaking and have been at it ever since. American Swiss, known long ago as picnic cheese, has been their standby, and only in recent years these Wisconsin Schweizers have had competition from Ohio and other states who turn out the typical cartwheels, which still look like the genuine imported Emmentaler.

Szekely
Transylvania, Hungary

Soft; sheep; packed in links of bladders and sometimes smoked. This is the type of foreign cheese that set the popular style for American processed links, with wine flavors and everything.

T

Taffel, Table, Taffelost
Denmark

A Danish brand name for an ordinary slicing cheese.

Tafi
Argentina

Made in the rich province of Tucuman.

Taiviers, les Petits Fromages de,
Perigord, France

Very small and tasty goat cheese.

Taleggio
Lombardy, Italy

Soft, whole-milk, Stracchino type.

Tallance
France

Goat.

Tamie
France

Port-Salut made by Trappist monks at Savoy from their method that is more or less a trade secret. Tome de Beaumont is an imitation produced not far away.

Tanzenberger
Carinthia, Austria

Limburger type.

Tao-foo or Tofu
China, Japan, the Orient

Soybean curd or cheese made from the "milk" of soybeans. The beans are ground and steeped, made into a paste that's boiled so the starch dissolves with the casein. After being strained off, the "milk" is coagulated with a solution of gypsum. This is then handled in the same way as animal milk in making ordinary cow-milk cheeses. After being salted and pressed in molds it is ready to be warmed up and added to soups and cooked dishes, as well as being eaten as is.

Teleme
Rumania

Similar to Brinza and sometimes called Branza de Braila. Made of sheep's milk and rapidly ripened, so it is ready to eat in ten days.

Terzolo
Italy

Term used to designate Parmesan-type cheese made in winter.

Tête à Tête, Tête de Maure, Moor's Head
France

Round in shape.
French name for Dutch Edam.

Tête de Moine, Monk's Head
France

A soft "head" weighing ten to twenty pounds. Creamy, tasty, summer Swiss, imitated in Jura, France, and also called Bellelay.

Tête de Mort

see Fromage Gras for this death's head.

"The Tempting cheese of Fyvie"
Scotland

Something on the order of Eve's apple, according to the Scottish rhyme that exposes it:

The first love token ye gae me
Was the tempting cheese of Fyvie.
O wae be to the tempting cheese,
The tempting cheese of Fyvie,
Gat me forsake my ain gude man
And follow a fottman laddie.

Texel

Sheep's milk cheese of three or four pounds made on the island of Texel, off the coast of the Netherlands.

Thenay *Vendôme, France*	Resembles Camembert and Vendôme.
Thion *Switzerland*	A fine Emmentaler.
Three Counties *Ireland*	An undistinguished Cheddar named for the three counties that make most of the Irish cheese.
Thuringia Caraway *Germany*	A hand cheese spiked with caraway.
Thyme *Syria*	Soft and mellow, with the contrasting pungence of thyme. Two other herbal cheeses are flavored with thyme—both French: Fromage Fort II, Hazebrook II.
Tibet *Tibet*	The small, hard, grating cheeses named after the country Tibet, are of sheep's milk, in cubes about two inches on all sides, with holes to string them through the middle, fifty to a hundred on each string. They suggest Chinese strings of cash and doubtless served as currency, in the same way as Chinese cheese money. (*See under* Money.)
Tignard *Savoy, France*	Hard; sheep or goat; blue-veined; sharp; tangy; from Tigne Valley in Savoy. Similar to Gex, Sassenage and Septmoncel.
Tijuana *Mexico*	Hard; sharp; biting; named from the border race-track town.
Tillamook	*see* Chapter 4.
Tilsit, or Tilsiter Käse, also called Ragnit *Germany*	This classical variety of East Prussia is similar to American Brick. Made of whole milk, with many small holes that give it an open texture, as in Port-Salut, which it also resembles, although it is stronger and coarser.

Old Tilsiter is something special in aromatic tang, and attempts to imitate it are made around the world. One of them, Ovar, is such a good copy it is called Hungarian Tilsit. There are American, Danish, and Canadian—even Swiss—imitations.

The genuine Tilsit has been well described as "forthright in flavor; a good snack cheese, but not suitable for elegant post-prandial dallying."

Tilziski
Yugoslavia

A Montenegrin imitation Tilsiter.

Tome de Beaumont
France

Whole cow's milk.

Tome, la
Auvergne, France

Also called Fourme, Cantal, or Fromage de Cantal. A kind of Cheddar that comes from Ambert, Aubrac, Aurillac, Grand-Murol, Roche, Salers, etc.

Tome de Chèvre
Savoy, France

Soft goat cheese.

Tome de Savoie
France

Soft paste; goat or cow. Others in the same category are: Tome des Beagues, Tome au Fenouil, Tome Doudane.

Tomelitan Gruyère
Norway

Imitation of French Gruyère in 2½ ounce packages.

Topf or Topfkäse
Germany

A cooked cheese to which Pennsylvania pot is similar. Sour skim milk cheese, eaten fresh and sold in packages of one ounce. When cured it is flaky.

Toscano, or Pecorino Toscano
Tuscany, Italy

Sheep's milk cheese like Romano but softer, and therefore used as a table cheese.

Toscanello *Tuscany, Italy*	A smaller edition of Toscano.
Touareg *Berber, Africa*	Skim milk often curdled with Korourou leaves. The soft curd is then dipped out onto mats like pancake batter and sun dried for ten days or placed by a fire for six, with frequent turning. Very hard and dry and never salted. Made from Lake Tchad to the Barbary States by Berber tribes.
Tour Eiffel *Berry, France*	Besides naming this Berry cheese, Tour Eiffel serves as a picturesque label and trademark for a brand of Camembert.
Touloumisio *Greece*	Similar to Feta.
Tournette *France*	Small goat cheese.
Tourne de chèvre *Dauphiné, France*	Goat cheese.
Trappe, la, or Oka *Canada*	Truly fine Port-Salut named for the Trappist order and its Canadian monastery.
Trappist	*see* Chapter 3.
Trappist *Yugoslavia*	Trappist Port-Salut imitation.
Trauben (Grape) *Switzerland*	Swiss or Gruyère aged in Swiss Neuchâtel wine and so named for the grape.
Travnik, Travnicki *Albania, Russia, Yugoslavia*	Soft, sheep whole milk with a little goat sometimes and occasionally skim milk. More than a century of success in Europe, Turkey and adjacent lands where it is also known as Arnauten, Arnautski Sir and Vlasic.

When fresh it is almost white and has a mild, pleasing taste. It ripens to a stronger flavor in from two weeks to several months, and is not so good if holes should develop in it. The pure sheep-milk type when aged is characteristically oily and sharp.

Traz os Montes
Portugal

Soft; sheep; oily; rich; sapid. For city turophiles nostalgically named "From the Mountains." All sheep cheese is oily, some of it a bit muttony, but none of it at all tallowy.

Trecce
Italy

Small, braided cheese, eaten fresh.

Triple Aurore
France

Normandy cheese in season all the year around.

Troo
France

Made and consumed in Touraine from May to January.

Trouville
France

Soft, fresh, whole milk. Pont l'Evêque type of superior quality.

Troyes, Fromage de

see Barberey and Ervy.

Truckles
England

No. I: Wiltshire, England. Skimmed milk; blue-veined variety like Blue Vinny. The quaint word is the same as used in truckle or trundle bed.

On Shrove Monday Wiltshire kids went from door to door singing for a handout:

> Pray, dame, something,
> An apple or a dumpling,
> Or a piece of Truckle cheese
> Of your own making.

No. II: Local name in the West of England for a full cream Cheddar put up in loaves.

Tschil
Armenia

Also known as Leaf, Telpanir and Zwirn. Skim milk of either sheep or cows. Made into cakes and packed in skins in a land where wine is drunk from skin canteens, often with Tschil.

Tuile de Flandre
France

A type of Marolles.

Tullum Penney
Turkey

Salty from being soaked in brine.

Tuna, Prickly Pear
Mexico

Not an animal milk cheese, but a vegetable one, made by boiling and straining the pulp of the cactuslike prickly pear fruit to cheeselike consistency. It is chocolate-color and sharp, piquantly pleasant when hard and dry. It is sometimes enriched with nuts, spices and/or flowers. It will keep for a very long time and has been a dessert or confection in Mexico for centuries.

Tuscano
Italy

Semihard; cream color; a sort of Tuscany Parmesan.

Twdr Sir
Serbia

Semisoft sheep skim-milk cheese with small holes and a sharp taste. Pressed in forms two by ten to twelve inches in diameter. Similar to Brick or Limburger.

Twin Cheese
U.S.A.

Outstanding American Cheddar marketed by Joannes Brothers, Green Bay, Wisconsin.

Tworog
Russia

Semihard sour milk farm (not factory) made. It is used in the cheese bread called Notruschki.

Tybo
Denmark
Made in Copenhagen from pasteurized skim milk.

Tyrol Sour
German
A typical Tyrolean hand cheese.

Tzgone
Dalmatia
The opposite number of Tzigen, just below.

Tzigenkäse
Austria
Semisoft; skimmed sheep, goat or cow milk. White; sharp and salty; originated in Dalmatia.

U

Urda
Rumania
Creamy; sweet; mild.

Uri
Switzerland
Hard; brittle; white; tangy. Made in the Canton of Uri. Eight by eight to twelve inches, weight twenty to forty pounds.

Urseren
Switzerland
Mild flavored. Cooked curd.

Urt, Fromage d'
Soft Port-Salut type of the Basque country.

V

Vacherin
France and Switzerland
I. Vacherin à la Main. Savoy, France. Firm, leathery rind, soft interior like Brie or Camembert; round, five to six by twelve inches in diameter. Made in summer to eat in winter. When fully ripe it is almost a cold version of the great dish called Fondue. Inside the hard-rind container is a velvety, spicy, aromatic cream, more runny than Brie, so it can be eaten with a spoon, dunked in, or spread on bread. The local name is Tome de Montague.

II. Vacherin Fondu, or Spiced Fondu. Switzerland. Although called Fondu from being melted, the No. I Vacherin comes much closer to our conception of the dish Fondue, which we spell with an "e."

Vacherin No. II might be called a re-cooked and spiced Emmentaler, for the original cheese is made and ripened about the same as the Swiss classic and is afterward melted, spiced and re-formed into Vacherin.

Val-d'Andorre, Fromage du
Andorra, France
Sheep milk.

Valdeblore, le
Nice, France
Hard, dried, small Alpine goat cheese.

Valençay, or Fromage de Valençay
Touraine, France
Soft; cream; goat milk; similar to Saint-Maure. In season from May to December. This was a favorite with Francis I.

Valio
Finland
One-ounce wedges, six to a box, labeled pasteurized process Swiss cheese, made by the Cooperative Butter Export Association, Helsinki, Finland, to sell to North Americans to help them forget what real cheese is.

Valsic
Albania
Crumbly and sharp.

Varalpenland
Germany
Alpine. Piquant, strong in flavor and smell.

Varennes, Fromage de
France
Soft, fine, strong variety from Upper Burgundy.

Västerbottenost *West Bothnia*	Slow-maturing. One to one-and-a-half years in ripening to a pungent, almost bitter taste.
Västgötaost *West Gothland, Sweden*	Semihard; sweet and nutty. Takes a half year to mature. Weight twenty to thirty pounds.
Vendôme, Fromage de *France*	Hard; sheep; round and flat; like la Cendrée in being ripened under ashes. There is also a soft Vendôme sold mostly in Paris.
Veneto, Venezza *Italy*	Parmesan type, similar to Asiago. Usually sharp.
Vic-en-Bigorre *France*	Winter cheese of Béarn in season October to May.
Victoria *England*	The brand name of a cream cheese made in Guilford.
Ville Saint-Jacques *France*	Ile-de-France winter specialty in season from November to May.
Villiers *France*	Soft, one-pound squares made in Haute-Marne.
Viry-vory, or Vary *France*	Fresh cream cheese.
Viterbo *Italy*	Sheep milk usually curdled with wild artichoke, *Cynara Scolymus*. Strong grating and seasoning type of the Parmesan-Romano-Pecorino family.
Vize *Greece*	Ewe's milk; suitable for grating.
Void *Meuse, France*	Soft associate of Pont l'Evêque and Limburger.

Volvet Kaas
Holland

The name means "full cream" cheese and that—according to law—has 45% fat in the dry product. (*See* Gras.)

Vorarlberg Sour-milk
Germany

Hard; greasy; semicircular form of different sizes, with extra-strong flavor and odor. The name indicates that it is made of sour milk.

Vory, le
France

Fresh cream variety like Neufchâtel and Petit Suisse.

W

Warshawski Syr
Poland

Semihard; fine nutty flavor; named for the capital city of Poland.

Warwickshire
England

Derbyshire type.

Washed-curd cheese
U.S.A.

Similar to Cheddar. The curd is washed to remove acidity and any abnormal flavors.

Wedesslborg
Denmark

A mild, full cream loaf of Danish blue that can be very good if fully ripened.

Weisschmiere
Bavaria, Germany

Similar to Weisslacker, a slow-ripening variety that takes four months.

Weisslacker, White Lacquer
Bavaria

Soft; piquant; semisharp; Allgäuer-type put up in cylinders and rectangles, 4½ by 4 by 3½, weighing 2½ pounds. One of Germany's finest soft cheeses.

Welsh cheeses

The words Welsh and cheese have become synonyms down the ages. Welsh "cheeses can be attractive: the pale, mild Caerphilly was famous at one time, and nowadays has usually a factory flavor. A soft cream cheese can be obtained at some farms, and sometimes holds the same delicate melting sensuousness that is found in the poems of John Keats.

"The 'Resurrection Cheese' of Llanfihangel Abercowyn is no longer available, at least under that name. This cheese was so called because it was pressed by gravestones taken from an old church that had fallen into ruins. Often enough the cheeses would be inscribed with such wording as 'Here lies Blodwen Evans, aged 72.'" (From *My Wales* by Rhys Davies.)

Wensleydale
England

I. England, Yorkshire. Hard; blue-veined; double cream; similar to Stilton. This production of the medieval town of Wensleydale in the Ure Valley is also called Yorkshire-Stilton and is in season from June to September. It is put up in the same cylindrical form as Stilton, but smaller. The rind is corrugated from the way the wrapping is put on.

II. White; flat-shaped; eaten fresh; made mostly from January through the Spring, skipping the season when the greater No. I is made (throughout the summer) and beginning to be made again in the fall and winter.

Werder, Elbinger and Niederungskäse
West Prussia

Semisoft cow's-milker, mildly acid, shaped like Gouda.

West Friesian
Netherlands

Skim-milk cheese eaten when only a week old. The honored antiquity of it is preserved in the anonymous English couplet:

> Good bread, good butter and good
> cheese
> Is good English and good Friese.

Westphalia Sour Milk, or Brioler
Germany

Sour-milk hand cheese, kneaded by hand. Butter and/or egg yolk is mixed in with salt, and either pepper or caraway seeds. Then the richly colored curd is shaped by hand into small balls or rolls of about one pound. It is dried for a couple of hours before being put down cellar to ripen. The peculiar flavor is due partly to the seasonings and partly to the curd being allowed to putrify a little, like Limburger, before pressing.

This sour-milker is as celebrated as Westphalian raw ham. It is so soft and fat it makes a sumptuous spread, similar to Tilsit and Brinza. It was named Brioler from the "Gute Brioler" inn where it was perfected by the owner, Frau Westphal, well over a century ago.

The English sometimes miscall it Bristol from a Hobson-Jobson of the name Briol.

Whale Cheese
U.S.A.

In *The Cheddar Box,* Dean Collins tells of an ancient legend in which the whales came into Tillamook Bay to be milked; and he poses the possible origin of some waxy fossilized deposits along the shore as petrified whale-milk cheese made by the aboriginal Indians after milking the whales.

White, Fromage Blanc
France

Skim-milk summer cheese made in many parts of the country and eaten fresh, with or without salt.

White Cheddar
U.S.A.

Any Cheddar that isn't colored with anatto is known as White Cheddar. Green Bay brand is a fine example of it.

White Gorgonzola

This type without the distinguishing blue veins is little known outside of Italy where it is highly esteemed. (*See* Gorgonzola.)

White Stilton
England

This white form of England's royal blue cheese lacks the aristocratic veins that are really as green as Ireland's flag.

Whitethorn
Ireland

Firm; white; tangy; half-pound slabs boxed. Saltee is the same, except that it is colored.

Wilstermarsch-Käse Holsteiner Marsch
Schleswig-Holstein, Germany

Semihard; full cream; rapidly cured; Tilsit type; very fine; made at Itzehoe.

Wiltshire or Wilts
England

A Derbyshire type of sharp Cheddar popular in Wiltshire. (*See* North Wilts.)

Wisconsin Factory Cheeses
U.S.A.

Have the date of manufacture stamped on the rind, indicating by the age whether the flavor is "mild, mellow, nippy, or sharp." American Cheddar requires from eight months to a year to ripen properly, but most of it is sold green when far too young.

Notable Wisconsiners are Loaf, Limburger, Redskin and Swiss.

Withania
India

Cow taboos affect the cheesemaking in India, and in place of rennet from calves a vegetable rennet is made from withania berries. This names a cheese of agreeable flavor when ripened, but, unfortunately, it becomes acrid with age.

Y

Yoghurt, or Yogurt
U.S.A.

Made with *Bacillus bulgaricus,* that develops the acidity of the milk. It is similar to the English Saint Ivel.

York, York Curd and Cambridge York
England

A high-grade cream cheese similar to Slipcote, both of which are becoming almost extinct since World War II. Also, this type is too rich to keep any length of time and is sold on the straw mat on which it is cured, for local consumption.

Yorkshire-Stilton
Cotherstone, England

This Stilton, made chiefly at Cotherstone, develops with age a fine internal fat which makes it so extra-juicy that it's a general favorite with English epicures who like their game well hung.

York State
U.S.A.

Short for New York State, the most venerable of our Cheddars.

Young America
U.S.A.

A mild, young, yellow Cheddar.

Yo-yo
U.S.A.

Copying pear- and apple-shaped balls of Italian Provolone hanging on strings, a New York cheesemonger put out a Cheddar on a string, shaped like a yo-yo.

Z

Ziegel
Austria

Whole milk, or whole milk with cream added. Aged only two months.

Ziegenkäse
Germany

A general name in Germanic lands for cheeses made of goat's milk. Altenburger is a leader among Ziegenkäse.

Ziger

I. This whey product is not a true cheese, but a cheap form of food made in all countries of central Europe and called albumin cheese, Recuit, Ricotta, Broccio, Brocotte, Serac, Ceracee, etc. Some are flavored with cider and others with vinegar. There is also a whey bread.

II. Similar to Corsican Broccio and made of sour sheep milk instead of whey. Sometimes mixed with sugar into small cakes.

Zips

see Brinza.

Zomma
Turkey

Similar to Caciocavallo.

Zwirn

see Tschil.

Index of Recipes

ABOUT THE AUTHOR

BOB BROWN, after living thirty years in as many foreign lands and enjoying countless national cheeses at the source, returned to New York and summed them all up in this book.

Born in Chicago, he was graduated from Oak Park High School and entered the University of Wisconsin at the exact moment when a number of imported Swiss professors in this great dairy state began teaching their students how to hole an Emmentaler.

After majoring in beer and free lunch from Milwaukee to Munich, Bob celebrated the end of Prohibition with a book called *Let There Be Beer!* and then decided to write another about Beer's best friend, Cheese. But first he collaborated with his mother Cora and wife Rose on *The Wine Cookbook,* still in print after nearly twenty-five years. This first manual on the subject in America paced a baker's dozen food-and-drink books, including: *America Cooks, 10,000 Snacks, Fish and Seafood* and *The South American Cookbook.*

For ten years he published his own weekly magazines in Rio de Janeiro, Mexico City and London. In the decade before that, from 1907 to 1917, he wrote more than a thousand short stories and serials under his full name, Robert Carlton Brown. One of his first books, *What Happened to Mary,* became a best seller and was the first five-reel movie. This put him in *Who's Who* in his early twenties.

In 1928 he retired to write and travel. After a couple of years spent in collecting books and bibelots throughout the Orient, he settled down in Paris with the expatriate group of Americans and invented the Reading Machine for their delectation. Nancy Cunard published his *Words* and Harry Crosby printed *1450–1950* at the Black Sun Press, while in Cagnes-sur-Mer Bob had his own imprint Roving Eye Press, that turned out *Demonics; Gems, a Censored Anthology; Globe-gliding* and *Readies for Bob Brown's Machine* with contributions by Gertrude Stein, Ezra Pound, Kay Boyle, James T. Farrell *et al.*

The depression drove him back to New York, but a decade later he returned to Brazil that had long been his home away from home. There he wrote *The Amazing Amazon,* with his wife Rose, making a total of thirty books bearing his name.

After the death of his wife and mother, Bob Brown closed their mountain home in Petropolis, Brazil, and returned to New York where he remarried and now lives, in the Greenwich Village of his free-lancing youth. With him came the family's working library in a score of trunks and boxes, that formed the basis of a mail-order book business in which he specializes today in food, drink and other out-of-the-way items.